DEATH, BURIAL AND THE INDIVIDUAL IN EARLY MODERN ENGLAND

DEATH, BURIAL AND THE INDIVIDUAL IN EARLY MODERN ENGLAND

CLARE GITTINGS

CROOM HELM
London & Sydney

© 1984 Clare Gittings
Croom Helm Ltd, Provident House, Burrell Row,
Beckenham, Kent BR3 1AT
Croom Helm Australia Pty Ltd,
First Floor, 139 King Street, Sydney, NSW 2001

British Library Cataloguing in Publication Data

Gittings, Clare
   Death, burial and the individual in early modern
   England.
   I. Title
   306.9'0942   HQ1073.5.G7

   ISBN 0-7099-1167-X

Printed and bound in Great Britain

CONTENTS

PLATES

LIST OF TABLES AND GRAPH

Tables

Graph

TO MALCOLM

What a piece of work is a man!
How noble in reason, how infinite in
faculty, in form, in moving, how express
and admirable, in action how like an
angel, in apprehension how like a god,
the beauty of the world, the paragon
of animals! And yet, to me, what is
this quintessence of dust?

Hamlet, Act II, Scene 2

SYSTEM OF REFERENCES

In order to avoid burdening both book and reader with constant, repetitious and unwieldy footnotes, a more succinct form of referencing has been adopted, outlined below. The academic reader may have to turn a few more pages than customarily required with full conventional footnotes, and for this inconvenience I apologise.

(1) Probate Accounts

Where no indication of the source for a funeral is given in the text, the example is taken from a probate account. References for the probate accounts used are given in the manuscript section of the bibliography, together with a select list of 20 accounts particularly rich in funeral details. In the majority of instances, accounts drawn upon in the text are accompanied by sufficient information to identify the document in the appropriate record office with relative ease; accounts in Kent and Lincolnshire are catalogued by date, those in Berkshire and Somerset by the deceased's surname. However, probate accounts used have also been fully referenced in my unpublished Oxford M.Litt. thesis, 'Funerals in England 1580-1640: The Evidence of Probate Accounts', to which the reader should refer in any cases of doubt. All dates relating to probate accounts are in old style, as shown on the documents themselves; the account had to be presented within one year of decease.

(2) Wills

a. The printed medieval wills quoted in the introduction and Chapter 1 are listed in the first note for Chapter 1; these volumes are indexed and/or chronologically arranged; sufficient information is given in the text to trace each quotation.
b. Individual printed wills are listed under 'Will of . . . ', in the printed sources section of the bibliography.
c. Manuscript wills are given in the manuscript section of the bibliography, together with a select list of the principal wills cited.

d. Several wills quoted from secondary sources appear in the notes to Chapter 9. Additional wills taken from secondary sources are those of Charles Dickens and John Wesley, quoted in Wilson and Levy, *Burial Reform*, pp. 102-3.

(3) Literary Sources

Wherever feasible, the author's name is given in the text so that the reader can consult the bibliography. Individual page numbers have been given in the bibliography, as far as possible, to indicate the precise source of the information or the quotation used in the text. In those instances where more than one quotation is taken from a particular work, the reader may have to consult a few other specified pages before finding the particular passage quoted. In the half dozen or so cases where frequent quotation is made from one particular work, the reader is advised to consult its index, and/or make use of its chronological layout, to obtain the precise page reference.

(4) Parish Registers

All extracts from parish registers are from Cox, *Parish Registers*, indexed by place name, except those for certain London churches, which are listed under 'Registers' in the printed sources section of the bibliography, or else as specifically noted.

(5) Epitaphs

All epitaphs are from Ravenshaw, *Antiente Epitaphes*, chronologically arranged, unless otherwise stated.

(6) Bishops' Injunctions

Bishops' injunctions after 1570 are quoted from the *Report of the Ritual Commission*, and pre-1570 injunctions from Frere and Kennedy, ed., *Visitation Articles and Injunctions*, both chronologically arranged.

(7) Aristocratic and Royal Funerals

The sources for the principal funerals discussed in Chapters 8, 9 and 10 are listed in the first note for each chapter.

(8) Scottish Funerals

Details of Scottish burial customs are from Andrews, *Bygone Church Life in Scotland*, pp. 240-53, unless otherwise stated.

ACKNOWLEDGEMENTS

Death is a comparatively new subject for British historians, and its very newness has meant that I have sought, and received, help from a large group of people and encouragement from an even greater number. Although I cannot possibly hope to list all of them here, none the less they have all contributed towards this study and I am most appreciative of their interest.

My research began at Oxford in 1975; I am extremely grateful to Robert Ashton and the faculty of the School of English and American Studies at the University of East Anglia for encouraging me to undertake postgraduate work. I am indebted to the Social Science Research Council for a grant and for a generous extension when I needed more time to complete my M.Litt. thesis. Many people assisted me at Oxford. Keith Thomas first suggested the subject of death, while David Vaisey drew my attention to the probate accounts which form the backbone of my research. My greatest debt is to my supervisor, Paul Slack, whose patience, kindness and good humour were unfailing and whose detailed criticisms of my thesis, chapter by chapter, resulted in immeasurable improvement. I trust that none of those who were concerned with this work during its more academic stage feel that too great a travesty has been committed in turning the thesis into a book. The statistical evidence was checked by Roger Keyes and John Colville, with a speed and precision which I could not hope to have emulated. I would also like to thank the many friends at Oxford whose endless encouragement helped me to see the thesis through to its end.

During the writing of both thesis and book I visited, and was assisted at, many different archives and libraries around the country. I am most grateful to the staff of all these institutions, particularly the Bodleian Library, Oxford; the Kent Archives Office, Maidstone; the Lincolnshire Record Office, Lincoln; the Somerset County Record Office, Taunton; the Berkshire County Record Office, Reading; the Dorset County Record Office and Dorset County Museum, Dorchester; the British Library, the Public Record Office, Lambeth Palace Library and the Greater London Record Office at County Hall, London; Register House and the National Library of Scotland, Edinburgh; the archives of Chatsworth House, Derbyshire; the library of Chichester Theological College and the University Library at Cambridge. I was especially helped by the staff at the West Sussex County Record Office, Chichester, whose detailed knowledge of possible documentary sources was invaluable to me.

To turn a thesis into a book is a somewhat daunting task, made less formidable by the interest shown by so many people, especially Neal Burton, Peter Janson-Smith, Andrew MacLennan and David Way. Advice on sixteenth- and seventeenth-century drama was given by Corinne Richards and Brian Glickman. Throughout the four years that it has taken to write this book, my days have been spent extremely happily, teaching at Sumners County Primary School, Harlow, Essex, and I am most grateful to Ian Sutton, the teachers, pupils and, above all, the children in my own class, who have inspired me with their constant cheerfulness.

In collecting together the illustrations for this book I have received help from many quarters. Diana Foley most generously allowed me to borrow mourning jewellery, which was then skilfully photographed by Cyril Nicholson, who also drew the graph. The British Library and the Bodleian Library, Oxford, gave me permission to reproduce items from their collections. Olive Cook was kind enough to let me use photographs by her late husband, Edwin Smith, and took a personal interest in the whole venture.

The unenviable task of typing the manuscript was most effectively performed by Margaret Mullen and Vivien Gladman, while Caroline Careless did much of the photocopying. In its final form, the book was read by Paula Tate and John Blair, who made many valuable criticisms and saved me from several mistakes. It is a pleasure to thank them for their hard work on my behalf; for those errors that still remain, I am responsible.

My parents, Robert Gittings and Jo Manton, have read both thesis and book at many different stages and have given me constant support throughout. It is difficult to sum up their help, as it has taken so many forms; making valuable suggestions, noting points of style, checking references, proofreading and generally dealing with a whole range of obscure queries, with a speed and breadth of knowledge which never ceases to amaze me. For this and much more, I am extremely grateful.

Only someone who has lived under the same roof as an author can know what a trial this involves and what a multitude of tasks, often of a tedious and time-consuming nature, fall to their lot. To manage to maintain a close interest in someone else's work over many years is no mean feat in itself, without all the other dreadful impositions with which authors burden their companions. Having proofread my first book, 14 years ago, and now being so involved in this work, both as thesis and book, is more than can reasonably be expected of anyone; I am truly grateful to Malcolm Ramsay, for everything.

Clare Gittings
Hertford

SCOPE AND SOURCES: AN INTRODUCTORY SURVEY

Men fear death, as children fear to go in the
dark . . . It is as natural to die as to be born;
and to a little infant, perhaps, the one is as
painful as the other.

Francis Bacon, *Essay II – Of Death*, 1625

The natural processes of corruption and decay
have become disgusting . . . natural death and
physical decomposition have become too horrible
to contemplate or to discuss.

Geoffrey Gorer,
Death, Grief, and Mourning in Contemporary Britain, 1965

'Death comes to every man', in the words of the Bible, but it is remarkable how greatly the reactions of men vary. Some welcome it, others shrink even from any reference to the subject. Today we tend to take the latter course; death is hidden away in hospitals, not openly discussed for fear of acute embarrassment and, in general, forgotten as far as possible. Sociologists and anthropologists alike have labelled death the great taboo subject of Britain and, indeed, the western world in the late twentieth century. However, this taboo has by no means always prevailed; Francis Bacon in early seventeenth-century England could write in his essay *Of Death*: 'but above all, believe it, the sweetest canticle is *Nunc dimittis*'. This book sets out, therefore, to trace how and why the modern reaction has come about, by examining English attitudes towards death since the Middle Ages.

Certain major changes have occurred in the 'facts of death' since the late medieval and early modern period. Natural death is now closely associated with old age; modern men and women can reasonably expect to live into their seventies. By contrast, in 1640 the expectation of life at birth was only 32 years. Between a quarter and a third of all children born would be dead before they reached their fifteenth birthdays, many failing to survive their first year. It was common practice to name a newborn child after a living older brother or sister on the assumption that only one of them would reach adulthood; as late as the mid-eighteenth century, the father of the historian Edward Gibbon was still

7

naming his children in this way. Only a minority of adolescents had both their parents alive and no more than 5 per cent of the population achieved the age of 60.[1]

It would have been impossible to forget about death in the way that has so largely happened today; in pre-industrial England, death was ever-present and could strike at any time. In words which echoed the Bible, a Hull merchant, John Dalton, writing his will in 1487, declared that 'there is no thing more certain than death, and nothing more uncertain than the hour of death'. Unexpected deaths, like this example recorded in one of the Paston letters in 1453, were a frequent occurrence:

> On Tuesday Sir John Heveningham went to his church and heard three masses, and came home again, never merrier, and said to his wife that he would go say a little devotion in his garden, and then he would dine; and forthwith he felt a fainting in his leg and sat down; this was at nine of the clock, and he was dead ere noon.

The great majority of deaths took place at home rather than, as today, in an institution; there was therefore much greater acquaintance with the process of dying. The same letter also describes the death of Sir John Heveningham's grandson who, according to Agnes Paston, 'passed to God on Monday last past with the greatest pain that I ever saw man'; the agony of death was neither concealed in hospitals nor eased with painkillers, as it is now. Death was a popular subject for sermons, unlike today's reticence. Whether congregations understood or believed all they heard is impossible to tell, but many people would regularly have listened to their minister expounding the terrors of the grave and the torments awaiting the damned, since church attendance was, at least in theory, compulsory. Communities were generally more stable and close-knit than in post-industrial society and a man would, walking to his local church each Sunday, pass the graves of many of his relatives, young and old, knowing that he was himself likely to lie among them, quite possibly within a very short space of time.

One particularly horrific form of sudden death in medieval and early modern England was the plague, whose visitations were frequent and severe. The destruction and misery which it caused is hard to appreciate when viewed from the safe, hygienic world of later twentieth-century Britain. The sufferings, recorded in a probate account, of the family of William Dickinson of Claypool, Lincolnshire, in 1605 are typical of plague victims of the period. Plague struck the entire household;

Dickinson, his wife, his son and daughter and his four servants, two male, two female, all caught it. The infected house was padlocked by order of the Justices of the Peace and no provision was made for feeding those incarcerated within. In fact, William's brother John came to their aid, but if he 'had not relieved them they had starved'. The house, locked at Christmas, was not reopened until May; of the entire household, only three of the servants remained alive. This was by no means an exceptional case; there is evidence that some plague sufferers experienced even more unpleasant situations. An entry in the parish register of Malpas, Cheshire, for 1625 reads:

> Richard Dawson being sick of the plague and perceiving he must die at that time, arose out of his bed and made his grave, and caused his nephew John Dawson to cast some straw into the grave which was not far from the house, and went and laid down in the said grave, and caused clothes to be laid upon and so departed out of this world; this he did because he was a strong man and heavier than his said nephew and another wench were able to bury.

The eradication of this ferocious disease in the western world has removed perhaps the most dramatic and terrifying form of sudden death that our ancestors had to face; arguably, however, we have now replaced it with a threat of even greater magnitude, although one more under the control of man–nuclear annihilation.

These changing physical circumstances of death make possible the modern tendency to separate life from death; no longer is it so true that, in the words of the burial service, 'in the midst of life is death'. However, factors such as the increase in life expectancy, the development of hospitals or the abolition of plague cannot, in themselves, explain the positive taboo that now surrounds the process of dying. To account for this revulsion it is necessary to examine one of the basic tenets of western thought during the last five centuries, the uniqueness and importance of the individual. Such individualism emphasises the distinctness and separateness of each person, rather than the common and shared aspects of their humanity; the liberty of the individual has become the cornerstone of western political thought and practice. In cultural terms, individualism results in originality, itself a form of distinctiveness, being more highly prized than skilful imitation, and it gives rise to certain prevalent western art forms such as the character drama or novel, the portrait and the biography or autobiography. However, it seems reasonable to suggest that the more stress is laid on the uniqueness of each individual, the harder it becomes to contemplate the exit of a particular person from this world, since one who is unique can, by definition, never truly be replaced. While the western tradition of individualism may have many commendable aspects, it also raises certain fundamental difficulties, as Lawrence Stone found in his survey of historical attitudes to love and marriage.[2] The crisis of death is possibly the most severe of all the problems resulting from an individualistic philosophy.

So deeply rooted is the cult of the individual in our society that it becomes easy to forget that our viewpoint is merely a result of our social and cultural inheritance rather than being, in any sense, an objective attitude. It is perhaps sobering to remember that while individualism is for the western world a given truth, in global terms it is very much a minority outlook, regarded with derision and hostility by most of the earth's population, for whom it is most commonly associated with narcissism. It is also, historically speaking, a relatively recent development; early medieval man would find our current values puzzling, alien to his way of thought and quite possibly repugnant. Although it seems at present completely embedded in our culture, there is no absolute guarantee that the worship of individuality will continue to reign supreme for ever in western thought; indeed, it is possible that the problems to which it gives rise, such as the crisis of death, may eventually help to undermine it. In examining Western attitudes towards death, one is looking at perhaps the most vulnerable point in a comparatively new philosophical development, which affects only a small proportion of the world's inhabitants, and the continuing existence of which should not be taken completely for granted.

Until recently, death as a subject for research was largely ignored by Western historians, an effect, no doubt, of the general taboo. It is ironic that there have been many more studies of death in so-called primitive societies than of death in our own; the example set by anthropologists needs to be followed by more historians. Much of the pioneering work on western attitudes towards death has taken place in France. This interest is now spreading to the United States but, as yet, little has been written concerning the British way of death; those historians who have considered death in Britain have mainly concentrated on the Victorian period.[3]

Not all historians of western attitudes to death have interpreted their researches in terms of individualism. There have been a number of theologians who have examined the subject in primarily doctrinal terms, producing an essentially Christian interpretation, with its emphasis on concepts of the afterlife. Some historians, particularly in France, have concentrated on the demography of death and the advancement of medicine. However, the development of attitudes traced in this present study seems to bear surprisingly little relationship to mortality rates, particularly among adults, the sense of individual loss seems to have increased through periods of lower and higher mortality alike.

Lawrence Stone's stimulating book, *The Family, Sex and Marriage in England 1500-1800*, traces in great detail the development of the concept of individualism and its effects on personal relationships. As Stone has shown, it is an enormous field of research in its own right and this present study cannot hope to chart the changing perception of the self, except in specific relationship to changes in funeral rituals and attitudes to death.[4] Much initial work on the connections between death and individualism has been carried out by the historian Philippe Ariès, writing principally about his native France. The present work adds an English dimension and, like the research by David Stannard on death in Puritan New England, is indebted to the work of Ariès.[5]

Unlike Ariès's study, this book concentrates primarily on the experiences of the survivors and their reactions to bereavement, rather than attempting to analyse the somewhat more elusive subject of people's feelings about their own deaths. In these pages, the main protagonist in the drama, the person in whose honour the funeral is held, appears only when already a corpse. The same pressures, broadly speaking, were influential in moulding both forms of response — to the death of oneself and to the deaths of others — but the nature of the available evidence suggests that the latter is a more consistently fruitful line of pursuit. Any study of the way people felt about their own deaths would have to rely heavily on diaries, letters and other personal writings. For example, in his diary, Samuel Sewall of Boston records how one day his daughter Betty 'burst out into an amazing cry', because 'she was afraid she should go to Hell, her sins were not pardoned'. She had apparently come to this conclusion from reading the Bible and the religious writings of Cotton Mather. For some time, she could not read her Bible without weeping, saying she was 'a reprobate, loves not God's people as she should'.[6] Such material, moving and graphic though it is, has its drawbacks for the historian. To begin with, it would be hard to decide whether Betty's fear of death is the root cause of her unhappiness or rather a symptom of, say, adolescent depression. As with all diaries, there is the problem of whether the writer's own perceptions are, in fact, accurate; for example, could the printed word really bring on such melancholia? One is also left wondering if Betty would have felt the same way if she were actually on her death bed, which raises the additional problem that no eyewitness account of a deathbed scene, however vivid, can fully reveal the final thoughts of the all-important central character. In historical terms, could one be justified in using the passage about Betty Sewall to say that all children in Puritan New England feared death so profoundly? There is too little of this highly individual, literary material to substantiate wide generalisation and what there is, of course, relates only to the small section of society which has left personal written records.

The same difficulties would beset the tracing of reactions to the death of other people, if diaries, letters and other literary sources such as sermons were all the evidence available. However, there also exist many thousands of documents giving details of funerals of the early modern period; the vast majority of them have never before been examined. Since the funeral marks the ritual separation of the living and the dead, these would seem to be a valuable and sensitive source for revealing attitudes towards death. This is especially true after the Reformation, when the official burial service was considerably shortened, and so accorded the secular elements, determined by custom and traditional usage, a far more prominent role. This material concerning funerals from the mid-sixteenth to the mid-eighteenth centuries is far larger in quantity and far more systematic than occasional remarks in diaries and letters. A study of funerals shows the community or group, rather than just an individual, responding to death, and therefore provides a firmer basis from which to generalise about the attitudes of society as a whole. Perhaps most important of all, these funeral details exist for a much wider social range than is covered by literary material. Much of the evidence occurs in documents produced by ecclesiastical courts in probate cases and concerns people who have left no personal written records behind them; all that is now known of them is when they came into contact with officialdom. In all historical studies of attitudes, it is extremely difficult to find information which relates to ordinary people and historians are often forced to confine their attentions to the upper echelons of society. It is therefore fortunate to have these insights into the funeral practices of 'middling people, among whom', according to Misson, an observer of post-Restoration funeral practices, 'the customs of a nation are most truly to be learned'.

There are, inevitably, certain problems with this type of evidence. The major class of records used, probate accounts, relates only to those people who would have made wills; funerals of married women and children therefore appear very rarely.[7] Probate accounts have only survived for a few counties of England; luckily, however, these are relatively well distributed geographically — Kent, Lincolnshire, Berkshire and Somerset having the largest numbers — although unfortunately no London ones exist, to give a more urban perspective. Because the document was an account of money spent, both on the funeral and other expenses, the details are all financial, and little explanation is given for the purchases, while, naturally, anything that did not involve a monetary transaction is entirely omitted. However, these gaps can, in part, be filled by theological works concerning burial and, subsequently, by descriptions of funeral practices like the one already quoted, written by a Swiss visitor to Britain. Details of the funerals of the poorest and least significant members of society were recorded by the overseers of the poor, as well as by various literate observers. The funerals of the rich were well documented by the College of Arms when heralds were involved in the ceremonies, as were the burials of royalty. For descriptions of non-heraldic burials of the aristocracy more reliance has to be placed on the rather haphazard references in wills, letters and diaries. From all these various sources, a comprehensive picture can be drawn of burial practices in early modern England, encompassing all gradations of society, from paupers to princes.

There is, of course, no direct evidence that alterations in funeral practices were seen by contemporaries as being related to a growing sense of individualism; indeed, it is hard to tell how far people were actually conscious that such changes were taking place at all. The connection is one made by historians with the advantages, and possible disadvantages, of hindsight. It is, however, a connection which seems to accord with the known facts, rather than to be disproved by them, and one which appears interesting and worthwhile to pursue.

The early modern period was characterised by an increasing anxiety over death which showed itself in a variety of ways. One was a growing desire to separate the living from the dead, for example, by prohibiting burials in churches and by reserving graveyards for interments. This was coupled with an intellectual stance which tended to emphasise the difference, rather than tne continuum, between the soul and the body and between the two states of life and death. An unease at the prospect of physical decomposition led to the widespread coffining of bodies, and encouraged the craft of the embalmer. A mounting desire for worldly remembrance stimulated such practices as the preaching of funeral sermons and the erection of tombs, in large numbers. All these

factors combined with a more compartmentalised and materialistic outlook to assist in the establishment of the undertaking profession, the
commercialisation inherent in which, in turn, further modified funeral
rites. At the same time, a strong Puritanical attack on ritual, as a waste
of time and money, influenced people's thinking about burial ceremonies, particularly those accorded to the poor through public charity.
Another element which added to the pain of bereavement was the
gradual breaking down of the older communal solidarity which had previously assisted survivors. The loosening of the traditional group ties
put a stop to the holding of wakes round the corpse and to the games
involving role-reversal which had served as a harmless outlet for destructive impulses aroused by death. The whole process was assisted, particularly in London, by the pressures of urban life itself. In place of the
wider communal links, a new emphasis was placed on the close family
as the social unit designated to carry the burden of death, which was
marked in the distribution of mourning costume and in changing
customs for watching with the dead.

All these different signs of anxiety about death, which are traced in
the course of this book, can be interpreted as arising from a changing
conception of the self and a heightened sense of individuality. This
development is most clearly visible when examining the funeral ceremonies of the aristocracy in the early modern period. The heraldic
funeral, a ritual which emphasised continuity for the purpose of
ensuring political stability, was replaced in the seventeenth century by
night burials, which stressed irreplaceable loss and individual sorrow.
Even royal and state funerals were not immune from the effects of
changing sensibilities, reflected in the emergence of a distinction, by the
eighteenth century, between the public and private person of the
monarch and extolling the individualism of the hero.

Many of our own present-day attitudes towards death originated in
the early modern period. Our segregation of the dying and dead in
hospitals and mortuaries, our total isolation from corpses, our condemnation of lavish expenditure on funeral rituals and the way we shun the
bereaved, can all be traced back to developments in this period, as can
the birth of the undertaking profession itself. Indeed, it could be argued
that individualism has now reached such a peak that nobody can face
with equanimity the idea of their own annihilation, or that of someone
close to them. Death has been hidden and forgotten as far as possible
for much of the twentieth century; it is only recently that the taboo
has begun to be broken down, for example by the hospice movement.
A less inhibited attitude has now started to emerge; the new interest in

the history of death is part of this process.

Because death has been such a taboo subject in the modern era, it is very tempting to see past centuries, in which it appears that people faced death far more easily, as a kind of 'golden age' in which the whole problem was less acute. While to a certain extent this might be so, it must be remembered that although death may genuinely have been less anxiety-provoking, the basic tenets of individualism, which are accepted with little or no question today, were far less fully established; it is not possible, it would seem, to hold both the philosophy of individualism and to have an easy acceptance of death. Certain rituals, when they are first introduced in a particular era, may well at that time reflect a more individualistic approach to death. However, in a later period, the same ritual might inhibit, rather than promote, individualism; the heraldic funeral is just such a case in point. This also applies to the way death is faced in the twentieth century. Modern hospitalised death, depersonalised in the extreme, is actually the product of a highly individualised approach to death.[8]

The onset of industrialisation in the mid-eighteenth century forms a very approximate boundary for this study. However, all such divisions are extremely arbitrary; changes in funeral customs vary greatly according to the different social classes involved, the geographical area, and also between urban and rural communities. Funeral practices that would characteristically be thought of as Victorian, such as the domination of the professional undertaker, began to appear in London well before the end of the eighteenth century, while in rural areas traditional customs persisted long into the nineteenth century.

There are two, on the face of it, antithetical reasons why this book stops short of an analysis of death in the late eighteenth and the nineteenth centuries. It omits the period loosely characterised as 'Romantic' which preceded, and in many ways shaped, the Victorian era, and which was itself a reaction against the rationalism of the eighteenth century. First, as Lawrence Stone has observed, history is not a one-way street.[9] In certain important areas, including familial relationships and, it could be argued, attitudes towards death, much of the nineteenth century represents a turning back of the general trends established during the early modern era. It is these earlier patterns, partly and temporarily disrupted by the Victorians, which eventually shaped the outlook of the twentieth century, rather than the somewhat aberrant stance adopted in the nineteenth century.

In funeral practices, the nineteenth century stand against the prevailing forces of secularisation can be interpreted as one such temporary reversal in the general historical drift. The Victorian attempt to turn back the clock, by investing death with a religious fervour, rested on an unsound theological base, trying as it did to combine aspects of the perceived golden age of medieval England with a strong Puritanical streak. Like the attempts at architectural revival, it inevitably involved uneasy compromises. The result was, in the main, cloying sentimentality about death, which seems so nauseating and repugnant to twentieth-century ways of thinking. One reason for the failure to rekindle 'medieval' religious fervour in the nineteenth century lay in the accelerated growth of the sense of individualism which had occurred during the intervening time span. This ensured that the Victorian attitude towards death and bereavement, as was shown by the Queen herself, could never truly mirror the more reconciled acceptance of death in early medieval society, an ease which was, indeed, already beginning to evaporate during the later Middle Ages. The Victorian trappings of death, despite all protestations of religion, remained a testament to a solidly materialistic and worldly society.

A study of nineteenth-century funeral rituals, fascinating as it may be in its own right, is far more revealing about the Victorians themselves, their beliefs and fears, than of the way twentieth-century funeral practices, and underlying attitudes towards death, have developed. Perhaps only in the field of medical science and hygiene can a clear line of development be traced from nineteenth- to twentieth-century attitudes towards death, a continuation of the process of separating the living from the dead begun in the early modern era. Even in this sphere the influence of the religious revival was apparent, religious enthusiasm combining with hygienic considerations in the widespread creation of new cemeteries.

The second reason for not discussing in this book the Romantic and Victorian approach to death is that, when one delves beneath the surface, nineteenth-century attitudes are far closer to our own beliefs than all the funeral paraphernalia would at first suggest. In many respects, the Victorians can be seen as denying the reality of death, although adopting a very different mode from the denial of death in the twentieth century. Whereas twentieth-century death is essentially hidden, the nineteenth century wallowed in death to such an extent that it ceased to have any true meaning; the graveyard euphemisms 'sleeping', 'passed on', 'resting' and 'gone before', began to take over from the reality. Similarly, the frequently found sentiment in literature for children that death is something to be wished for, and that those who die young are fortunate, blindly ignores the unpleasant facts of bodily decay. Adults, too, were encouraged in this belief, as this verse from a memorial card for a baby shows, echoing a hymn by Wesley:

A lovely flower soon snatched away
To bloom in realms divine
Thousands will wish at judgement day
Their lives were short as mine.[10]

A further manifestation of the Victorian denial of death was the great development of interest in spiritualism, diminishing the finality of death through belief in contacts with the 'other world'.

The whole edifice of Romantic and Victorian responses to death began to crumble during the last quarter of the nineteenth century; its fate was finally sealed by the impact of the First World War.[11] If, however, as it has been suggested, nineteenth-century funerary rituals reflect a situation in which death was already being denied, then it becomes all the more important to turn to earlier centuries, to pre-industrial England, to understand how present-day anxieties have developed.

It is hoped that this small but pioneering study will play some part in the rediscovery of the changing pattern of attitudes towards death during the last six centuries. If any further justification need be given for death to be considered a relevant subject for historical, and indeed human, inquiry it may be found in the words of John Weever, writing his famous book of epitaphs in 1631:

So many burials, reader, in one book
Warn thee, that one day, thou for death must look.

Notes

1. Stone, *Family, Sex and Marriage*, pp. 58, 66-73 and 409.
2. Ibid., esp. Chapter 6, pp. 221-69.
3. Principal works in English on the subject are Ariès, *Western Attitudes towards Death*; Ariès, *The Hour of Our Death*; Stannard, *The Puritan Way of Death*; McManners, *Death and the Enlightenment*; Whaley, *Mirrors of Mortality*; Boaze, *Death in the Middle Ages*; Morley, *Death, Heaven and the Victorians*; Curl, *The Victorian Celebration of Death*.
4. For a discussion of individualism before the early modern period, see Macfarlane, *The Origins of English Individualism*, in which he argues that indivi-

dualism was already a well-established phenomenon in the later Middle Ages; its effects on medieval attitudes towards death are touched on in Chapter 1 of this book.

5. The central theme developed by Ariès (*The Hour of Our Death*, p. 602), the 'relationship between man's attitude towards death and his awareness of self, of his degree of existence, or simply of his individuality' is also pursued in this book. Ariès's three other themes (ibid., p. 603), 'the defence of society against untamed nature, belief in an afterlife, and the belief in the existence of evil', are touched upon, but only in passing. Many of the individual strands of his argument, for example the desire to separate the living and the dead, are supported by the English evidence examined here. However, Ariès's division of attitudes towards death into five named periods (ibid., p.603), 'the tame death, the death of the self, remote and imminent death, the death of the other, and the invisible death', has not been adopted. Instead, attention is focused on the simultaneous existence of a variety of attitudes which changed and developed at differing rates in separate geographical areas of the country. This study also differs from Ariès's work in its methodology (ibid., p. xvii), in its time scale (ibid., pp. xvi-xvii) and, indeed, in its main objective (ibid., p. xiv). The twin aims of this book are to document, as dispassionately as possible, both the changes and continuities in English funeral practices and to suggest an interpretative framework within which these alterations might usefully be explained.

6. Quoted in Stannard, *The Puritan Way of Death*, pp. 68-70 and 149.

7. The term probate accounts has been used throughout to cover both executors' and administrators' accounts. These accounts were presented to the probate court by the executor or administrator as a record of how the deceased's estate had been handled, the funeral being among the necessary and allowable expenses. The accounts for Berkshire, Oxfordshire, Somerset and Lincolnshire, and most of those for Kent, are administrators' accounts, while those for Sussex, Dorset and Oxford University are executors' accounts. In several instances in Kent, executors' accounts have been matched with the relevant wills.

8. Illich, *Medical Nemesis*, p. 204.

9. Stone, *Family, Sex and Marriage*, p. 666. The interpretation, suggested here, that the nineteenth century represents a reverse, or at least a hiatus, in the general development of attitudes towards death is also noted by Ariès, *The Hour of Our Death*, p. 609.

10. From the author's collection of ephemera.

11. Similar conclusions about Victorian attitudes towards death are reached by Cannadine in Whaley, ed., *Mirrors of Mortality*. Cannadine discusses death in the nineteenth century more fully than is possible here and describes in detail the social and psychological impact of the carnage of the First World War. It is, however, unfortunate that in his zeal to overturn accepted interpretations, he so greatly underplays the problem of death in the late twentieth century, dismissing all too readily the work of 'those many historians, sociologists and doctors who have analysed the subject in the present' (ibid., p. 240).

1 THE LEGACY OF THE MIDDLE AGES

When examining burial rituals of the past it is important to realise that the present-day usage of the words 'death' and 'funeral' is itself heavily influenced by our own culture and time. Nor are the meanings of these terms irrevocably fixed, even by ourselves; developments in medical technology are constantly necessitating the establishment of new and more physiologically exact definitions of death. Through twentieth-century eyes, both death and burial are seen as reasonably clear-cut events, pinpointed at a precise instant in time, but this view is by no means shared by all nations of the world, nor by our own ancestors. The anthropologist Robert Hertz has noted the existence, among various far-flung tribes and peoples, of a double burial ceremony where the body is temporarily interred for some months until decomposition is complete and then buried again, with further and more elaborate funeral rituals. Although not actually accompanied by a reburial, the medieval observance of a 'month's mind', four weeks after the interment, involved repetition of the funeral service and of other burial rituals such as feasting, bell-ringing and the distribution of a dole to the poor. Lady Margaret Beaufort, the mother of Henry VII, when drawing up directions for her 'funerals', embraced within that term a whole series of services and prayers, at many different churches, involving dozens of clergy and taking place over several weeks.[1] In these cases the sense in which 'funeral' is used differs considerably from our accepted meaning of the word.

We, in the modern, western world, have invested the moment of physical death with an intense emotional and social significance, holding it to mark the occurrence of a major and irreversible change. However, in various primitive societies, it is not the point of death which is of supreme importance, but a later event, often when the body has decomposed and is reburied. Death merely marks the beginning of a waiting or 'liminal' period, culminating in a more decisive change. A further element in the primitive view of death is that the living are duty-bound to behave in a certain manner during this liminal period, until the final burial rites have taken place; the distinction between the living and the dead, so strong in our society, is seen more as two aspects of one continuum by these peoples.

These three concepts concerning the dead in certain less advanced societies, that burial is not a contemporaneous event, that a physical death is not the moment of supreme significance and that the behaviour of the living is linked to the state of the dead, are demonstrated in the words, recorded by Hertz, which a dying Maori chief addressed to his son:

> For three years . . . you must remain apart from the tribe . . . for during all that time my hands will gather earth and my mouth will feed constantly on worms and vile food, the only kind that is offered to spirits in the underworld. Then when my head falls upon my body [i.e. the flesh has decomposed] and when the fourth year has come, waken me from my sleep, show my face to the light of day. When I arise, you will be free.

These same three ideas are to be found in medieval attitudes towards the dead, which continued to hold sway until the Reformation. One way of charting the development of our own notions about death is to trace where and why these particular concepts, which could be characterised as 'primitive', disappeared in England. It could also be suggested that the loss of these three beliefs marks an increase in anxiety aroused by death. Without these three, death becomes a moment of far more dramatic significance, burial is a far sharper point of separation and comfort can no longer be obtained from the ritual ties uniting the living with the dead. However, none of these three traditional concepts is readily compatible with a fully developed, individualistic and worldly philosophy of the kind that now dominates western society.

In early medieval eschatology, or scheme of beliefs about the after-life, bodily death played a subsidiary role; indeed, throughout the Middle Ages there was a far greater perception of continuity between the states of being alive and being dead than we feel today, both living and dead being included within the one framework of the Universal Church. In the early Middle Ages, the event of supreme importance was the Second Coming of Christ, when the general resurrection of the dead would occur. At death, the soul entered a time of waiting until the day of the Second Coming; early medieval statues show such souls resting in Abraham's bosom. Initially there was no mention of judgement being passed on the individual; the resurrection was seen as a collective and corporate event at which the whole company of the faithful would arise and enter paradise. Gradually, however, the Second Coming became associated with the Last Judgement at which each soul would be weighed in the balance and, if found wanting, be dispatched to hell.[2]

It is, perhaps, no coincidence that it is far easier to describe early medieval views of the Last Judgement, frequently blazoned across the walls of churches, than to discover much about the burial practices of the time. Some scant glimpses of early medieval funerals may be gleaned from manuscripts and other visual sources. The Bayeux Tapestry shows the corpse of Edward the Confessor being carried to burial in the newly built Westminster Abbey. The shrouded body is carried to the grave on a bier borne by eight men wearing ordinary coloured clothing; it was not until later that black became the general colour of mourning. Over the bier lies a multi-coloured pall surmounted by two crosses. Two attendants carry hand-bells and the corpse is followed by priests with open books. A manuscript in the Bodleian Library, of about 1150, shows a very similar procession, while a further contemporary illustration shows a shrouded body, tied with bands, being lowered into a stone sarcophagus.

As individualistic elements became stronger, during the twelfth century, so the balance of medieval eschatology altered. The historian Colin Morris sums up these changes:

> In this new scheme the decisive moment is the death of the individual . . . Earlier eschatology had kept a balance, or alternatively a tension, between an individual and a corporate expectation . . . Imaginatively, the whole strength of eschatology now became attached to the individual . . . attention was concentrated upon one's personal answer and personal hope of heaven — if necessary, after a stay in purgatory . . . The destiny of the individual was becoming the centre of attention, and the theme of the renewal of all things was slipping into a secondary place.

It is, perhaps, helpful to analyse these developments in terms of the three 'primitive' beliefs concerning the dead. This new scheme clearly focuses more attention and anxiety than before on the actual moment of death, for it is then that the soul is initially judged. The majority of people, having led neither totally blameless nor completely evil lives, could expect their souls to be confined to purgatory for a period of time, till they had been exculpated for their misdeeds. However, although greater importance was attached to death in this new eschatology, the judgement made then was not usually for eternity since souls, having spent their allotted time in the torments of purgatory, would later be admitted to heaven, purged of their sins. The doctrine of death adopted in the later Middle Ages therefore forms a halfway stage between the 'primitive' belief that death is an event of lesser importance and the modern view which accords to physical death supreme significance.

Various types of evidence remain of the increase in anxiety aroused by death in later medieval England. By the end of the fifteenth century a whole series of books had appeared on 'the art of dying well'. Often they were illustrated with woodcuts showing angels and devils fighting in the dying man's bedchamber for possession of his soul, and the tradition grew up that the whole of his life flashed before the dying person's eyes, an early precursor of the genre of biography. Further evidence of intensified attention being paid to the moment of death is found in the frequent instructions in wills of the period for masses to be said 'in all possible haste' after the testator died. Robert Preston, a York glazier, who died in 1503, specified that masses should begin in the hour of his death, while Thomas, Duke of Exeter, in 1426, required that no less than one thousand were to be performed on the day following his decease, 'if possible'.

Late medieval eschatology, through the doctrine of purgatory, ensured that the living and the dead were closely bound by ritual ties, as in more primitive societies today. Through their prayers and intercessions, the living were able to shorten the period which the dead person's soul was required to spend in purgatory and so reduce the soul's agonies and hasten its passage to paradise. Late medieval testators were obviously keen to provide for as many prayers and masses as possible to assist their souls in purgatory. Lord Bergavenny ordered 10,000 masses to begin as soon as he was dead, while in 1459 Sir Robert Hungerford, not content with a sequence of masses, required a thousand priests to be found, to say the 'exequies of the dead, commendations, seven penitential psalms with the litanies accustomed', each receiving 12d for their pains.

The comfort provided for the dying person by this doctrine is well attested in wills, but of its benefits for the survivors no direct historical evidence remains. However, it seems reasonable to conjecture that the ability to assist the deceased in the afterlife would have reduced the survivors' feelings of helplessness in the face of death, which modern researchers frequently report. Late medieval eschatology led to the establishment of a pattern of ritual which the survivors went through, circumventing, it could be argued, the alarming feelings of inertia experienced by the bereaved today. This ritual sequence marked a liminal period for the bereaved, the cathartic effects of which are suggested by the anthropologists van Gennep and Turner. The late medieval doctrine of purgatory, and the rituals which developed around it, seem therefore to have acted as a powerful force, mitigating the growing anxiety over death, attendant upon the nascent individualism of the period.

Although there was no direct medieval equivalent of the twofold interments practised by the primitive peoples described in Hertz's work, the late medieval burial services and ceremonies themselves would often be repeated for many years after a person's actual decease. While interment was obviously an event clearly pinpointed in time, the general burial rituals which accompanied it would stretch over a much longer time-span. It is not uncommon to find wills ordering 'obits' to be held for ten or 20 years or even longer, 99 years being another popular length of time. From the early fourteenth century, the founding of chantries became prevalent among rich testators, who would have expected these funeral rites to be continued for ever in their memory. As has been shown, 'funeral' had a much less specific meaning in the late Middle Ages than it does nowadays; it could be suggested that this long-drawn-out process reduced the emotional intensity for the bereaved which today is channelled into a few short minutes of ritual.

St Augustine said, and has often been paraphrased by writers down the centuries, that funerals are rather for the living than for the dead. At first sight, the funerals of late medieval England would seem to be the exception to this rule. The picture obtained from wills of the period is of testators attending closely to the organisation of burial rituals which will assist their souls in the hereafter. On one level this is clearly true; it is no coincidence that with the advent of the doctrine of purgatory the historian is presented with large quantities of evidence, in the form of wills, concerning the burial of the dead. However, these rituals, although described in eschatological terms, have psychological implications, some of which have already been discussed, together with an unstated social significance and a more worldly purpose. A dual function may be traced in the funeral rites of late medieval England. In terms of a more individualistic outlook on the world, the same rites which commended the deceased person's soul to its maker also served to keep that person's memory alive on earth, a source of comfort both to the dying person and to those who were bereaved. Similarly, the large funeral gatherings, ostensibly arranged to provide a multitude of intercessions for the testator's soul, also enabled the bereaved to share the burden of their sorrow, in the words of the anthropologist Malinowski, creating 'a social event out of a natural fact'.

The various social functions of funerals will be further discussed in later chapters of this book. However, it is important to realise that, although the available information about late medieval funeral practices is couched very much in eschatological terms, being drawn almost entirely from wills, there is nevertheless this strong element of social and psychological solace running through the rituals. In the late Middle Ages the twofold function of funerals, the eschatological and the social, harmonised so as to provide considerable comfort both for the dying individual and for the bereaved.

It is hoped that this analysis of the purposes, both manifest and latent, lying behind late medieval funeral rituals, will enable the reader to view them in a slightly more sympathetic light than the nineteenth-century editor of a volume of wills, F.J. Furnivall, who wrote in his introduction:

> But the most surprising and regrettable thing in these wills is the amount of money shown to have been wasted in vain prayers, or orders for them . . . I only hope some sensible executors handed over the money to the testators' wives and children, or the poor.

It is clearly difficult to view such lavish expenditure on the seemingly useless with complete impartiality although, interestingly, two anthropologists, Huntingdon and Metcalf, have recently published a defence, couched in very much the same terms as this chapter, of contemporary American expenditure on the death industry, so savagely exposed by Evelyn Waugh and Jessica Mitford. Tempting as it is to criticise the folly of others, it is important to look beyond the expense and see the attempts to mitigate the fear of death which lie behind these rituals, a fear which we, too, have failed to conquer.

It is not easy to assess exactly how much money was devoted by men and women in the late Middle Ages to 'the health of their souls', as it is often described in wills. However, a few examples will give some idea of the range of expenditure. The most helpful wills in this context are those which dictate the proportion of the estate to be devoted to the testator's soul, rather than stating a specific sum. Robert Corn, citizen of London, making his will in 1387, wrote: 'I bequeath my goods in two parts, that is for to say half to me [for his soul] and the other . . . to Watkin my son and to Katherine my daughter.' William Stark of Frome, Somerset, in 1417 willed: 'My debts and funeral expenses being paid, one part of my goods which remain to be distributed for my soul, the second part to William, my son, and Dionisia, his sister. The third part to Lucy, my wife.' This division of the estate into three with one third earmarked for the testator's soul is quite commonly found in late medieval wills. Even more frequent is the request that the residue of the estate, after particular legacies had been paid, should be devoted to this purpose.

However, more extreme cases are also to be found. Richard Gray of St Bartholomew's, London, making his will in 1432, left his entire estate 'to [the] health and salvation of my soul'; his wife and two sons who witnessed the will were left nothing at all. William Beny of Somerset clearly expected some opposition from his son, to whom he did not bequeath anything, and tried, in the wording of his will, to add an extra element of moral coercion: 'The residue of my goods, after the payment of my debts and deduction of my funeral expenses, I give to my son John . . . to dispose for the good of my soul and the souls of my ancestors, as he will answer therein before the Supreme Judge.'

A reasonable number of late medieval wills state the exact sum to be spent on the funeral and, although an extensive survey of such burial costs falls outside the scope of this book, it is possible to draw certain conclusions from this evidence. Even a cursory examination is sufficient to show that the cost of funerals was very much an individual matter in the late Middle Ages. It would be impossible to talk about the usual cost of, say, a knight's funeral in the early fifteenth century, since the variation was so extreme. For example, in 1411, Sir John Wadham left £10 to pay for his burial, but another Somerset knight, Sir Robert Allere, left only 13s 4d in 1421 to cover his funeral costs, while Sir Robert Hungerford, of Hungerford in Berkshire, left £100 for his interment in 1459. Another characteristic aspect of late medieval funeral costs is that, while the clergy customarily requested funerals without worldly affectation, the actual sums they left to be expended often belie their protestations about simplicity. John Forest, Dean of Wells Cathedral, wrote in 1443, 'my funeral expenses shall be made in all things without worldly pomp', but left £20 to cover the cost. Another cleric, John Hertylpole, rector of both Sandy in Bedfordshire and Brigham in Cumberland, left '£40 or more' to pay for his burial 'without pomp'.

Perhaps the most striking feature of all the details concerning the cost of burial in late medieval England is the level to which expenditure on the funerals of the aristocracy had risen by the late fifteenth and early sixteenth centuries. Nor is this simply based on sums dictated in wills, as proposed expenditure on burials; actual accounts exist which show that certain members of the aristocracy had funeral ceremonies costing over £1,000. In 1489, £1,038 was spent on the burial of Henry, Fourth Earl of Northumberland, who was murdered near Thirsk, Yorkshire and interred in Beverley Minster; the funeral of Thomas, Second Duke of Norfolk, in 1524, cost £1,340. As Lawrence Stone has shown, this period marks the zenith of expenditure on funerals among the aristocracy, who never again reached this level of extravagance.[3]

On what, precisely, was all the money, devoted to the burial of the dead in late medieval England, expended? The following survey is based largely on the evidence of wills and therefore reveals projected, rather than actual expenditure; however, there seems little reason to suppose that the two differed greatly. No systematic attempt has been made to analyse the rituals on the basis of social class or of geographical locality; such a task would require a far longer and more detailed study than this. This account is written very much in the language of the testators themselves and therefore tends to stress the eschatological role of funeral rituals of the period. As in many of the wills, items of more material funeral expenditure are discussed first, followed by an examination of the various forms of burial service and prayers for the dead which characterised late medieval funerary rituals.

A considerable amount of money was spent to secure a large attendance at a late medieval funeral. One particular group, whom many testators wished to attract to their burials, was the clergy; five hundred priests were paid 12d each to be present at the Earl of Northumberland's interment in 1489, while a further one thousand clerks each received 4d. At more modest burials the same principle was applied, if on a less lavish scale. Robert Benn of Frieston, Lincolnshire, willed that the Prior of Frieston 'and his brethren thereof of their charity do meet my body at the church door after my decease and there to give me absolution, and so bring me into the kirk with prayer and devotion, and to have for their labour 3s 4d'. Many late medieval wills record a small sum of money to be paid to every priest who attends the burial, since, presumably, their prayers were held to be particularly efficacious and their presence at the funeral had a status-enhancing quality.

Another group whom the testator would encourage to attend was his friends, neighbours, kinsmen and the like. Their most usual reward consisted of food and drink after the funeral; Thomas, Earl of Warwick, in 1400 willed 'that all my friends attending my funeral shall have good entertainment, viz. a supper overnight and a dinner on the next day'. Henry Machyn, a keen attender of funerals in the mid-sixteenth century, sometimes recorded particularly sumptuous meals, such as, on one occasion in August 1558, 'venison, fresh salmon and fresh sturgeon and with many dishes of fish', and on another, two weeks later, 'a noble dinner as has been seen, for there lacked no good meat both flesh and fish and 20 marchepanes'. At the funeral feast for Thomas Howard, Second Duke of Norfolk, in 1524, four hundred different dishes were served at a 'magnificent entertainment'. At grander funerals the guests might also receive gifts of black cloth to make mourning gowns; at the funeral of the Earl of Northumberland, twelve gowns for lords cost £21, 20 gowns for gentlewomen cost £15 and 24 gowns with hoods for lords and knights, £60. However, not everyone approved of these great acts of conspicuous expenditure; as Thomas de Bekynton, Bishop of Wells, put it in 1464: 'I will that my funeral expenses shall be moderate, that they shall be rather in the recreation and relief of the poor than in the solace of the rich and powerful'.

A rather different perspective is shown by Robert Lascelles of Brakenburgh in Yorkshire, who, in 1508, wished that: 'All other honest and worshipful folks, friends and kinsmen that comes to do my body worship . . . have meat and drink honestly to God's pleasure and according to their degrees.'

If the deceased had been a member of a guild or company then its members would be present at the funeral. The company would also provide the necessary funds to bury an impoverished member, as this extract from the charter, transcribed in 1389, of the guild of carpenters of London, makes clear:

It is ordained when any brother or sister of this fraternity dieth within the city of London or in the suburbs that all the brethren and sisteren shall them gather together at the house where the dead body is and bring the body to church . . . and abide there till the corpse be buried . . . Also [it] is ordained that, if any brother or sister dieth and have nowt of his own for to be buried, he shall be honestly buried at the costage of the brotherhood.[4]

A third group of people who were enticed to come to a burial in late medieval England were the poor. Poor people flocked in droves to attend the funerals of their social superiors; many wills record the distribution of doles to a hundred poor folk, and it is not uncommon to find mention of an even bigger crowd. Thomas Brooke of Thorncombe, Dorset, in 1415 left meat, drink and 3d to each of three hundred poor adults at his funeral, with 1d to three hundred poor children, 'if there be so many children'. Elizabeth, Countess of Salisbury, buried at Montacute in 1414, willed that a thousand poor people should receive alms at her burial. When Henry Percy, Fourth Earl of of Northumberland, left 2d to each poor person who attended his funeral, 13,340 arrived to claim this dole. Given the large numbers of poor people at a late medieval burial it is not surprising to find Margaret, Countess of Devon, in 1391, dictating that, although she did not want a hearse over her corpse, there should be provided 'plain bars to keep off the press of people'.

The dole would be distributed in money or food, or in both; a Somerset testator, William Felawe, specified that each poor person at his burial should receive 'one loaf worth ½d of good dough'. One testator, Henry Carnbull, Archdeacon of York, was concerned about the customary treatment of the poor at funerals and willed that:'Every poor man, woman and child asking alms be given for God's sake a penny, without any excessive challenge or objection made against any of them.' However, it is more usual to find testators specifying that only 'honest poorfolk' should be given the dole. One Yorkshire testator, Robert Lascelles, singled out 'pure creatures' to receive 1d at his burial.

The poor were not summoned to medieval funerals just to swell the numbers. Often a selected group of poor people was used in the actual pageantry and display of the funeral itself. Most commonly, a chosen number, dressed in specially made gowns, held tapers at the burial or processed behind the body on its way to church. Hugh, Earl of Stafford in 1385 was borne to his grave followed by a hundred poor men clothed in white, 'with a cross behind and before on their garments, each of them to carry a torch'. The corpse of Henry Percy was carried from Wresill to Leckinfield, a distance of 18 miles, accompanied by 40 poor men on horseback bearing torches, and then on to Beverley with 100 men on foot; altogether, 160 poor folk were given gowns of 'coarse black' for this funeral.

The number of poor singled out to play a special part in the funeral was usually rather smaller than this. Sometimes one poor person would be chosen for each year of the testator's age. Another popular number was 13, being the number of people present at the Last Supper, although sometimes this was reduced to twelve with the omission from the reckoning of Judas Iscariot. However, it was very much a matter for the testator's own preference and considerable variety is found. Nor was there any set colour for the clothing of this group; black was perhaps the most popular, but there are many instances of white, or a combination of the two, as well as frequent directions for 'russet broadcloth' to be used. Some testators also willed 'hoods, hose and shoes', to complete the effect. A few people used the poor to display their coats of arms; in 1520, one Yorkshire knight, Sir Henry Thwaites, ordered that 13 poor children should hold tapers at his burial 'having on rochets with mine arms thereupon'. All this attention to the precise details of the display illustrates the intense involvement of the dying in their own funeral preparations in late medieval England.

There were also various other items of expenditure which added to the solemnity and grandeur of the occasion. One was the provision of numerous tapers and candles to burn round the corpse, the burning of a candle being a form of intercession in late medieval England. Testators were often most specific about the provision of lights at their funerals, even down to directing the weight of wax to be burned. A Yorkshire woman, Alice Thwaites, in 1485 ordered 15 lb of wax to be used, while William Stourton, buried in London, requested five wax lights each weighing 1 lb. William Wright of Bishopthorpe, Yorkshire, left to his local church 'an old stock of bees with a swarm' to provide wax for his burial and obits. Frequently, poor people would be required to hold wax candles at the funeral; an interesting variant on this theme is to be found at the burial of the Second Duke of Norfolk in 1524 where 'there was in wax an hundred bedesmen in mourning, with beads in their hand'.

The burning of candles took place at the funerals of members of most social classes in late medieval England, but there were also other items of expenditure mainly confined to the upper social ranks. One of these was the embalming of the corpse. An entry in the account for the burial of the Fourth Earl of Northumberland reads 'for the embalming, fencing and scouring of the corpse, with the web of lead and chest £13 6s 8d'. Embalming was a necessity if the corpse had to be kept for a long time while a lavish burial was being organised. However, there seem in general to have been two opposing viewpoints as to how soon after death the body should be buried. Some testators requested that this should be done as quickly as possible. Dame Joan Boynton of Yarm, Yorkshire, wished in 1486 to be 'buried in all goodly haste as may be', while Agnes, Countess of Pembroke, in 1367 wanted to be buried 'within two days after my death' and Elizabeth, Lady Despencer, in 1409 asked to be interred three days after she died. Dame Maud de Say seems to have expected some opposition to her wish for a speedy and simple burial, for she wrote in her will in 1369: 'I desire that no feast be made on my funeral day, but that immediately after my decease my corpse shall be carried to burial, covered only with a linen cloth . . . and I charge my son, William de Say, that he do nothing contrary thereto.'

On the other hand, various testators specifically requested that they should not be interred too soon after death, presumably for fear of being mistakenly buried alive; in the days before the development of medical science this must have been a very real danger, possibly accounting for the origin of stories about vampires. Elizabeth de Burgh, the founder of Clare Hall, Cambridge, in 1355 wrote, 'I will that my body be not buried for fifteen days after my decease', and Henry, Duke of Lancaster, requested five years later 'that our body be not buried for three weeks after the departure of our soul'. In 1397 John, Duke of Lancaster willed that his body 'not be buried for forty days, during which I charge my executors that there be no searing or embalming my corpse'; his funeral, when it finally occurred, cannot have been a pleasant occasion for those present.

Another item of expenditure that occurred frequently at grander funerals was the provision of a hearse, under which the corpse would lie. This was a large wooden or metal structure, usually set with candles. At the Second Duke of Norfolk's funeral in 1524 the hearse bore seven hundred lights and was surrounded by a valance of black sarsenet fringed with black silk and Venice gold. In the funeral charges for the Fourth Earl of Northumberland's burial, the timber for the hearse and painting it are recorded as costing £5, while 'the wax of the hearse' cost a further £26 13s 4d. In addition to candles, the hearse was decorated with the deceased's coat of arms, usually painted on buckram, and more of these were hung about the church. In 1397, William, Earl of Salisbury willed that to each pillar of the church where he was buried should be attached a great banner displaying his arms, while for the Second Duke of Norfolk's burial the entire priory church at Thetford was hung with black cloth emblazoned with his arms.

A further addition to a really grand funeral was for the dead man's charger to attend the corpse to the burial. William de Beauchamp in 1268 willed 'that a horse, completely harnessed with all military caparisons, precede my corpse', and in 1296 the Earl of Warwick requested two great horses 'which shall carry my armour at my funeral'. However, the horse was not absolutely obligatory at the funerals of the aristocracy; Sir Otho de Grandison wrote, in 1358, 'I entreat that no armed horse or armed man be allowed to go before my body on my burial day', a sentiment also expressed by Roger, Lord La Warre in 1368, who wished to be buried 'according to the custom of mean people'. Perhaps they felt that these extravagant trappings with their display of worldly pomp detracted from the more sacred aspects of the funeral ritual.

By the late Middle Ages an extremely complex sequence of religious rituals had grown up around the process of burial.[5] The actual burial services would begin the evening before the interment itself with the Vespers of the Office of the Dead, commonly called the *placebo* after the opening words of the antiphon with which the service started. At any time from midnight onwards Mattins of the Office of the Dead would be celebrated, again commonly referred to by its opening word *dirige*, from which is derived the modern term 'dirge'. Usually these services would take place in the church with the corpse already lying there, though Edward Browne, a Lincoln jeweller, specifically asked in 1505 that these ceremonies should be conducted in his house. Extra psalms and antiphons were sometimes added to the *placebo* and *dirige*, in particular the *Commendatio animarum*, which was requested in many wills. The interment followed the Mass for the Dead or Requiem Mass, which began with the words, '*requiem aeternam dona eis domine et lux perpetua luceat eis*' (Oh Lord, grant them eternal peace and let the everlasting light shine upon them). This sequence of services is shown in the will of a canon of Wells who, in 1400, bequeathed: 'To each of my brother canons and vicars of the said church of Wells, present by night at my obsequies 4d, and to each of them being present at mass during the day 4d, and to each of them present at the closing of my tomb 1d.'

It is interesting that the moment of interment was accorded less significance than the three burial services which preceded it; indeed, at really grand funerals it seems that the majority of mourners had actually left the church before the body was placed in its grave. This would confirm the suggestion of a greater perceived continuity existing between the states of being alive and being dead in the later Middle Ages, rendering the disposal of the physical body a less traumatic event than it is now, with the ceremonial lowering of the body into the grave as the focal point of the modern ritual. Death was seen then not so much as a break or rupture but more as a passing from one form of being to another, again causing it to appear less fearsome both to the dying and to the bereaved.

The funeral services already described were often repeated seven days later, and again on the thirtieth day or 'month's mind'. They occurred again after a year, at an occasion called the anniversary, twelve month's mind, year-day or obit. These services, as has been shown, could continue for many years or even, at least in theory, in perpetuity. As well as repeating the funeral offices, wills of the period often order a 'trental' to be sung or said. This consisted of 30 masses, celebrated either on one day or on 30 consecutive days.

Although these were the most common commemorative services, wills also provide examples of testators dictating their own form of ritual to be observed. Miles Metcalf, a York gentleman, specified in 1486 that his eighteenth day was to be celebrated. Robert Johnson, alderman of the same city, willed in 1497 that when the priest each day 'hath said mass, that he shall stand afore my grave in his alb, and there to say the psalm of *De Profundis*, with the collects, and then cast holy water upon my grave'. In 1392, Thomas Aliston, Canon of Wells, worked out a whole weekly sequence of masses to be said for his soul: on Sunday '*de Trinitate*', on Monday '*de angelis*', on Tuesday '*de sancto Thoma Martyre*', and so on.

As well as specifying the rites to be carried out, several testators were also concerned as to what kind of priest should perform them; as Chaucer has shown, not all medieval clerics lived up to their priestly vows. One frequent concern among testators was that the priest should be honest; many unscrupulous priests must have taken money for masses that were never celebrated. The Yorkshire knight, Sir Ralph Bigod, requested in his will 'a well disposed priest and virtuous', while Steven Ellis, a rector in the same county, asked for 'well disposed priests of the most honest and clean conversation'.

Very occasionally a testator shows that he realises his requests will place a considerable load on the clergy concerned. John Sperhauke in 1472 left 4s to each priest at Hitchin church to pray for 30 days for his soul, adding 'but I call God to witness that I do not wish to burden them too heavily'. Joan Kay of Stixwold, Lincolnshire, having dictated her desire for a priest to pray daily for her, added realistically, 'if he be in health that he so may conveniently do'. Certainly all these prayers, although they may have been a burden to conscientious priests, brought in considerable revenue to the clergy; in one will seven priests were left £46 13s 6d to pray for one year, while another testator paid 20 marks for 3,000 masses.

Church services were not, however, the only form of commemoration of the dead in late medieval England. Sometimes testators would pay a particularly holy person to pray for them. John Stone, Rector of Tintinhull in Somerset, left: 'To the Bedeman of Tintinhull that he may pray for my soul whenever he passes, praying through the town 6s. 8d.' One Buckinghamshire testator, John Olney, left money in 1420 to the Anchoress of Northampton to pray for him, while Alice, Lady West of Hampshire, in 1395 willed a similar payment to a 'recluse friar'.

Charitable bequests, another form of commemoration in late medieval England, had the dual advantage both of being worthy acts in themselves and at the same time encouraging the recipients to pray for the donor's soul. Often testators would exhort their executors to search out the cases of most need. When John Carre of York died in 1487 his generosity extended to the leper house, to prisoners and to buying new bedding for poor men and women in the city and suburbs. This was in addition to the £7 which he ordered to be given to the poor 'as soon as I am dead without any tarrying, for my soul and my friends' souls'. These bequests underline the mutual benefit expected of almsgiving in late medieval England.

There were also more ostentatious ways of obtaining prayers for the deceased's soul. In 1485, Stephen Forster, citizen and fishmonger of London, directed that his executors 'shall give 20d to each person delivering a public sermon of God before men thronging together as the custom is at the cross of St Pauls, London and at the cross of the hospital of the Blessed Mary outside Bishopsgate, London . . . to the intent that each person delivering such a sermon shall declare my soul to be recommended in the devout prayers of the people standing by'. As he left £10 to pay for these sermons, he obviously expected his message to reach a large number of people.

More wealthy testators sometimes financed a pilgrimage on behalf of their souls. William Baret, a gentleman of Bury St Edmunds, paid for a priest to go 'to the court of Rome' to pray for his soul and that of his father, 'as other priests do that go to Rome'. In 1268 William de Beauchamp ordered his son Walter to go on a pilgrimage to the Holy Land on behalf of him and his wife. The Crusades offered the opportunity for a further form of commemorative gesture; in 1296 the Earl of Warwick left £100 'to the maintenance of two soldiers in the Holy Land'.

A rather different form of commemoration was provided by the erection of a memorial to the deceased. From the early fourteenth century these increased in number, as is reflected in the spread of monumental brasses. Unlike earlier tombs which were often anonymous, the name of the person commemorated was now displayed on the monument. Both developments are symptomatic of a growing emphasis on the individual. It is in figurative monuments that, *par excellence*, can be seen the two parallel themes of intercession for the soul of the deceased coupled with worldly remembrance of the dead. The dead man, or woman, lies with hands held in an attitude of perpetual prayer, at the same time displaying to future generations their earthly status, through coats of arms, inscriptions and the sumptuousness of the monument itself. Art historians have commented that the developing naturalism of tomb sculpture towards the latter years of the Middle Ages is a reflection of the increasing sense of individualism of the period.[6] The evidence of wills suggests the growing desire of testators to leave a durable record of their physical appearance through monuments; in 1409, Elizabeth, Lady Despencer, requested a marble stone to be placed on her grave with her 'portraiture thereon', while Isabel, Countess of Warwick, in 1439 wrote: 'I will that my statue be made, all naked, with my hair cast backwards . . . with Mary Magdalen . . . and St. John the Evangelist . . . and St Anthony.'

This outline of late medieval burial practice has inevitably looked at the rituals very much from the point of view of a dying person writing his or her will. Indeed, perhaps the most striking feature of all this evidence is the amount of personal control which the testator desired to exercise over the funerary arrangements. An extreme example was the will of Robert Fabyan, a London merchant and author of a famous chronicle, who died in 1512. Amid a mass of funerary details, he directed his executor to purchase 24 treen (wooden) platters and 24 treen spoons on which to serve 24 pieces of beef and mutton at his month's mind, though if it were to fall during Lent or on a fast day then fish was to be substituted, each piece being at least to the value of 1d. He then proceeded to design his own monumental brass, costing '53s 4d at the most', in elaborate detail, giving the precise wording of the inscription. Sometimes such detailed requests could result in directions verging on the humorous, as in the will of the organ-maker, William Biront of York, who appears to have been extremely particular about the musical qualifications of the priest chosen to bury him, demanding that he should be able to 'sing both plain song and prick song'. At other times these personalised details can be most moving; Richard, Earl of Arundel, in 1375 ordered that his burial should be as similar as possible to that of his dead wife, Eleanor: 'I desire that my tomb be no higher than her's; that no men at arms, horses, hearse or other pomp, be used at my funeral, but only 5 torches . . . as was about the corpse of my wife.'

It has often been suggested that people in the late Middle Ages seem to have been obsessed with death; this is the period when the dance of death emerges as a popular theme and when worm-infested corpses, or *transi*, appear in tomb sculpture. A particularly striking example is the brass to Ralph Hamsterley, engraved about 1510, at Oddington, Oxfordshire; the shrouded skeleton is being eaten by enormous worms which weave between the bones and slither through the eyesockets and jaws. A three-dimensional representation, dating from 1477, occurs at Ewelme in the same county, where the dignified alabaster figure of Alice, Duchess of Suffolk, reposing on a table tomb, contrasts starkly with the repulsive cadaver glimpsed through the arches beneath. Certainly these artistic manifestations suggest a growing concern with death. A Freudian interpretation might link the somewhat erotic images of the dance of death with the struggle for individualism, while the horrific decomposing bodies shown on tombs are further evidence of the newfound naturalism in sculpture.[7] However, when the demographic realities of life in late medieval England are considered, in particular the savage scourges of the Black Death, it is perhaps surprising that there was not even greater anxiety and despair aroused by death, crushing all glimmerings of emergent individualism. That this did not occur is in part attributable, it could be argued, to the doctrine of death and the associated burial rituals, in some respects not dissimilar to those of certain primitive tribes today, developed in this period. The perceived continuity of life and death and the mitigating aspects of the doctrine of purgatory meant that death for most people did not bring an irrevocable judgement; indeed, the living could assist their condition in the hereafter. At the same time, the doctrine was sensitive to growing individualism; although there was a collective approach to death, the individual stood very much in the centre of the ritual, as is emphasised by testators' involvement in their own funeral arrangements. Lastly, there is the close parallel between eschatological requirements and the performance of those rituals most beneficial, psychologically and socially, to both the dying person and to the bereaved.

The funeral rituals so far described continued to be practised unchanged, with only minor variations, throughout the later Middle Ages. However, towards the end of the period, two new and important developments took place. One was the request for simple burial by the Lollards, the precursors of English Protestantism, and the other, the rise of the elaborate heraldic funeral ritual. K.B. McFarlane, in his study of the Lollards, has identified a particular type of will, written, he argues, by Lollards, which stresses the testator's unworthiness, his contempt for his physical body and his desire for a simple funeral, without worldly pomp. Certainly the wills McFarlane cites are most striking in their language; for example, Thomas Brooke of Thorncombe, Dorset, a 'wretched sinner', wished to be buried 'at the church at the south side right as they may step on me', not in a coffin, but in a 'great cloth', to cover his 'foul carrion'. However, McFarlane tends to lay rather too much emphasis on the exceptional nature of these wills; as this chapter has shown, many medieval wills in fact request simple funeral rites. There appears to have been a rather wider range of acceptable burial rituals from which the medieval testator might choose than is generally appreciated. This fact would also seem to weaken the argument of certain anthropologists that funereal grandeur is directly proportional to the extent of the loss a society will feel at the death of that particular member.

Returning to McFarlane's main assertion, it does seem reasonable to suggest that, in the later Middle Ages, there were a number of people, many, no doubt, deserving the title 'Lollard', who rejected the full-blown funeral ritual in favour of a more simple form of burial. These people still ordered prayers for their souls; they certainly were not directly challenging the doctrine of purgatory. However, their emphasis on personal unworthiness and their strict injunctions against funeral pomp suggests a lack of enthusiasm for the accepted notion that the sins of a lifetime could be eliminated by the intercessions of others. They are, therefore, in one sense, pointing the way to the changes wrought at the Reformation. Indeed, it would have been an impossible task to eradicate the doctrine of purgatory, if the seeds of doubt were not already present in some form, however slight and vague.

It is, however, perhaps worth questioning McFarlane's crucial assumption that funeral rituals mirror religious beliefs so closely. As this chapter has shown, religion can exercise a powerful influence over burial rites, but it is not the only factor involved. The other principal determinants were rather more obscure in the Middle Ages, since psychological and social benefits were derived from the rituals necessitated by religious belief. However, when these two paths divided, it is apparent that the religious forces carried rather less weight than might perhaps have been expected; the next chapter, *Funerals and Faith*, takes up this theme in greater detail.

The other major development in burial practices in the later years of the Middle Ages was the introduction of the heraldic funeral. The first recorded funeral attended by heralds and other members of the College of Arms was that of the Earl of Salisbury at Bisham in 1463.[8] The heralds accompanied the corpse to the church, and there, wearing the arms of the dead man, presented his coat of arms, sword, shield, helm and crest at the altar. These they then handed to the Bishop of Worcester, who officiated at the ceremony. In turn, he delivered them to the heir, the Earl of Warwick, in recognition that they were now rightfully his, and then they were given back to their heralds. For their services at this burial the two Kings of Arms received £3, and 10s a day, the heralds 40s each, and the pursuivants 20s, with 5s as their daily allowance.

Members of the College of Arms attended various other aristocratic and royal funerals during the last years of the fifteenth century; in the early sixteenth century, they began to be present at lesser people's burials too. In 1489, for the funeral of the Fourth Earl of Northumberland, two of the 'officers of arms' each received £10 'for their help and pain in ordering the burial . . . for coming from London, their costs and reward'. At the funeral of the Second Duke of Norfolk in 1524, the heralds were responsible for marshalling the guests and accompanying each of the mourners as they brought their offerings to the altar. As well as presenting the dead man's arms and weapons, the Carlisle herald, just before the actual interment, was asked to 'declare the deeds of this noble prince'.

The heraldic funeral, with its display of worldly status, could be seen initially as further evidence of the desire to express greater individuality in late medieval England. However, by delivering substantial responsibility for the funeral rites of the aristocracy into the hands of the heralds, themselves agents of the Crown, the heraldic funeral eventually brought about a stifling of individuality, from which the nobility only broke out with some difficulty, as Chapters 8 and 9 show.

In terms both of the rituals practised and of the problems posed by nascent individualism, the funerals of the late Middle Ages already contained several of the elements which were to characterise burial rites after the Reformation. The theological changes made during the reign of Henry VIII encapsulated beliefs concerning burial that were already fermenting during the last decades of the fifteenth century, shaping them into a new doctrinal orthodoxy, which all subsequent funeral rites within the Church of England have reflected to this present day.

Notes

1. Wills in this chapter are quoted from Foster, ed., *Lincoln Wills*; Weaver, ed., *Somerset Medieval Wills* (including those of Robert Hungerford, John Hertylpole, Thomas Brooke, Steven Forster and John Sperhauke); Raine, ed., *Testamenta Eboracensia*; Tymms, ed., *Wills of Bury St Edmunds*; Furnivall, ed., *Fifty Earliest English Wills in London* (including those of John Olney and Alice, Lady West). Aristocratic wills, and that of Robert Fabyan, are quoted from Nicolas, ed., *Testamenta Vetusta*. Funeral of Henry, Earl of Northumberland is from Peck, *Desiderata Curiosa*, ii, pp. 246-7; funeral of Thomas, Duke of Norfolk from Blomefield, *History of Thetford*, Appendix VIII.

2. For an illustrated account, see Boaze, *Death in the Middle Ages*.

3. Stone, *Crisis of the Aristocracy*, pp. 576 and 784-6, gives extensive details of funeral costs.

4. Quoted in Wilson and Levy, *Burial Reform*, p. vi.

5. Described in Foster, ed., *Lincoln Wills*, i, pp. 245-7.

6. Stone, *Sculpture in Britain: The Middle Ages*, Part 5, pp. 177-233.

7. Brown, *Life Against Death*, p. 107.

8. Wagner, *Heralds of England*, pp. 106-7; the involvement of members of the College of Arms at funerals is fully described in his book.

2   FUNERALS AND FAITH

All these things, furniture of funerals, order of burying, and the pomp of exequies, are rather comforts to the living than helps to the dead.

> (St Augustine, paraphrased by Archbishop Sandys in a sermon preached at St Pauls on the death of Charles IX of France in 1574)

Late medieval funerals presented a delicate balance between an increasingly individualistic philosophy and a collective approach to the problem of death, with all the psychological comforts that this entailed. However, in the funerals of Lollards and the heraldic burials of the late fifteenth century there were signs that this equilibrium could not have been maintained much longer in the face of a developing individualism. The breakdown came at the Reformation.

The French historian Philippe Ariès has devoted much time to investigating why, in the early modern period, the dying individual ceased to be the focal point of the funeral, as he was in the late Middle Ages. He points out that, although this can be attributed to religious changes, these reflect, 'rather than create, the tendencies of their times'.[1] Turning to the English evidence, the apparent or surface change lay in the abolition of the doctrine of purgatory. One sixteenth-century writer, Philip Stubbes, confuted the central notion on which the whole attitude towards death in the later Middle Ages was based, in these words:

> But alas, who seeth not the vanity of this fond opinion of purgatory? If masses, diriges, trentals, *de profundis* . . . and such pelting trash, could redeem us from pain and punishment after this life, and place our souls in joy and bliss, I pray you then what is left to the blood of Christ to do for us? just nothing at all. And why died Christ, if we might have been redeemed by corruptible money, lands or possessions . . . ?

With the abolition of the doctrine of purgatory, there was no longer any need for the dying person to be involved with his own funeral preparations, since the ritual had ceased to benefit his soul in any way. In this new scheme, death became the decisive moment at which the soul's fate was sealed for ever; there was no longer the halfway house of purgatory, offering a lifeline to the dying and a sense of purpose to the bereaved. The burial service was used solely at the interment, as no further benefit would be gained from repeating it. The ritual ties connecting the living and the dead were severed and the individual alone became responsible for his own fate. It was a more individualistic philosophy which emerged at the Reformation and one in which the dividing line between life and death, the living and the dead, assumed a far greater clarity. As the historian Keith Thomas has written:

> Protestant doctrine meant that each generation could be indifferent to the spiritual fate of its predecessor. Every individual was now to keep his own balance-sheet, and a man could no longer atone for his sins by the prayers of his descendants. This implied an altogether more atomistic conception of the relationship in which members of society stood to each other . . . As a modern French historian puts it, 'Life ceased to look to death for its perspective.'

From the Reformation onwards, the funeral ritual was stripped of any eschatological purposes, but simply served to dispose of the corpse, with no direct theological significance attached. St Augustine's dictum had become unequivocally true. In the words of Hugh Latimer, burnt at the stake by Mary Tudor: 'When one dieth, we must have bells ringing, singing, and much ado: but to what purpose? Those that die in the favour of God are well; those that die out of the favour of God, this can do them no good.'

A further twist to this already more anxiety-provoking attitude towards death was provided by the Calvinist doctrine of predestination. Calvin held that only God could decide who was to be saved; good deeds and a virtuous life were by no means a certain path to paradise. He wrote: 'We must leave to God alone the knowledge of his church, whose foundation is his secret election.'[2] This uncertainty added a further burden to the dying; indeed it was essential for the true Calvinist to be humble and not presume himself to be among 'the elect'. Many doubts and fears and much introspection were the stuff of which a good Calvinist was made. The doctrine of predestination, with all its uncertainties, was a far more individualistic creed than the belief in a general resurrection, with the 'escape clause' of purgatory.

The influence of the Calvinist doctrine of predestination is particularly apparent in the second of the revisions of the prayer book, which took place in 1552, during the reign of Edward VI.[3] The order for

burial, as first revised in 1549, contained remnants of the Roman
Catholic burial service translated into English. The 1549 funeral service
was far shorter than its Catholic predecessor, but still kept the psalms
and an order for the celebration of Holy Communion at the burial.
After the interment, the following prayer was recited:

> We commend into Thy hands of mercy (most merciful Father) the
> soul of this our brother departed, N . And his body we commit to
> the earth, beseeching Thine infinite goodness, to give us grace to live
> in Thy fear and love, and to die in Thy favour: that when the judge-
> ment shall come . . . both this our brother, and we may be found
> acceptable in Thy sight, and receive that blessing which Thy well-
> beloved Son shall then pronounce to all that love and fear Thee,
> saying: 'Come, ye blessed Children of My Father. Receive the King-
> dom prepared for you before the beginning of the world.'

The emphasis of this revision of the service was on a divine judgement
which would not occur for some considerable while; when it does occur
the good will automatically reap their deserved benefits.

By contrast, at the 1552 revision of the *Book of Common Prayer*,
the burial service was drastically shortened, omitting all psalms, prayers
for the dead, and the order for Holy Communion. The tenor of the
substituted prayers was far more Calvinist:

> Almighty God, with Whom do live the spirits of them that depart
> hence in the Lord, and in Whom the souls of them that be elected,
> after they be delivered from the burden of the flesh, be in joy and
> felicity: we give Thee hearty thanks, for that it hath pleased Thee to
> deliver this N, our brother, out of the miseries of this sinful world,
> beseeching Thee . . . shortly to accomplish the number of Thine
> elect, and to haste Thy kingdom; that we with this our brother, and
> all other departed in the true faith of Thy holy Name, may have our
> perfect consummation and bliss, both in body and soul, in Thy
> eternal and everlasting glory.

Even this service did not fully satisfy ardent Calvinists, who felt that
too great an amount of certainty was expressed. In 1661 they were still
trying to get the phrase 'sure and certain' struck out from the words
used at the interment: 'We therefore commit his body to the ground in
sure and certain hope of the resurrection to eternal life.'

While the late medieval burial service had focused on the deceased, the 1552 order for burial avoided mention of the dead person as far as was possible; much more emphasis was laid on the general concept of election. Logically, since the deceased was now either among the elect or the damned, no purpose was served by praying for his soul and so the burial service could be far shorter. This shortening of the service had an important consequence. The late medieval funeral had been dominated by religious activities; the secular aspects of the ritual, in terms of time spent and of significance, took second place. However, with the dramatic curtailment of the sacred portion of the post-Reformation ritual the balance was tipped, bringing the secular burial customs, the eating and drinking both before and after the interment, into far greater prominence than previously. Once again, St Augustine's observation can be seen to take on a renewed significance in the early modern period.

It was the 1552 order for burial which was reintroduced, following the brief return to Catholicism under Mary Tudor, in the Elizabethan prayer book of 1559. However, paradoxically, the Elizabethan Primer contained distinct prayers for the dead, and praying for the dead was never forbidden. As Richard Field, Dean of Gloucester, wrote in the early seventeenth century: 'Prayer for the resurrection, public acquittal in the day of judgement, and perfect consummation, and bliss of them that are fallen asleep in the sleep of death, is an apostolical tradition.'[4] The simultaneous use of the doctrinally Calvinist 1552 burial service with prayers for the dead reveals clearly the compromise nature of the Elizabethan settlement, made, as it was, to placate all parties rather than to establish a firm doctrine for the English Church.

The changes which occurred at the Reformation, both in the doctrines surrounding death and in the orthodox burial service, were extremely deep and far-reaching. This alteration in the theological position and practice of the English Church raises the question how the laity reacted to such a fundamental transformation of belief and ritual. This, for example, was how Henry Machyn described the funeral of a lady on 7 April 1559, shortly after the return to Protestantism following Mary Tudor's death:

There was a great company of people, 2 and 2 together, and neither priest nor clerk, the new preachers in their gowns like laymen neither singing nor saying till they came [to the grave] and before she was put into the grave a [collect] in English, and then put into the grave; and after [took some] earth and cast it on the corpse and read a thing . . . and cast the earth into the [grave] and . . . read the Epistle of St. Paul to the Thessalonians . . . and after they sang *Pater Noster* in English, both preachers and others . . . and after one of them went into the pulpit and made a sermon.

To an educated Londoner like Henry Machyn the change was a matter for note rather than for anxiety. Many other people must have taken it in this manner, having, by 1559, become accustomed to a variety of changes in religious observance during the previous 30 years. However, there were some people who were not so ready to give up the older rituals. The reformed clergy devoted considerable attention to making their wayward laymen conform.

One method used to make sure that the population no longer clung to old beliefs consisted of questions, known as injunctions, which bishops sent to be answered by all their parish clergy. These give some idea of the sort of problems the Reformed Church faced in eradicating medieval Catholic doctrines and rites. Hooper, Bishop of Gloucester and Worcester during the reign of Edward VI, made enquiries about the following points. Was the communion service used like the old trentals of masses, was the burial service repeated more than once for any one corpse or do 'they keep and use any month-ends [or] anniversaries . . . which is the maintenance of the purgatory, and false belief and state and condition of the dead?'

Hooper, who later was burnt by Mary Tudor for his beliefs, also took pains to ensure that the 'service for burial in the King's Majesty's Book for thanksgiving unto God for deliverance of the dead out of this miserable world' was used, rather than 'the dirge, wherein they prayed for the dead'. He was also concerned lest any crosses of wax or wood were 'put secretly upon or about the dead body; or else whether any pardons, cloths, relics, or such other be buried with the dead body'. Finally, he enquired whether All Souls Day was still observed 'after the popish and superstitious order.'

Questions revealing concern over lingering Roman Catholic beliefs continued to appear in bishops' injunctions throughout the reign of Elizabeth I and even beyond. Parker, Archbishop of Canterbury, asked in 1560 whether anyone had left in their wills 'any sums of money, jewels, plate, ornaments or annuities for the erection of any obits, diriges, trentals, or any such like use, now by the laws of this realm not permitted'.

In 1565 Bentham, Bishop of Coventry and Lichfield, wrote in an injunction:

Away with your lights at the burial of the dead, and instead thereof exhort them duly to receive the light of the Gospel, which is the true light . . . [Ensure] that you do not make the communion a Mass of Requiem for lucre and gain, persuading the people to pray for the dead, but rather call upon them daily to live godly here in this life.

In 1571 Archbishop Grindal inveighed against bell-ringing on All Saints Day, and in 1583 Middleton, Bishop of St David's, listed a large collection of popish abuses which he was determined to stamp out, including offerings at burials. As late as 1629, Potter, Bishop of Carlisle, was enquiring about 'praying for the dead at crosses or places where crosses have been in the way to the church, or any other superstitious use of crosses, with towels, palms or metwands or other memories of idolatory at burials'.

Unfortunately, the bishops' injunctions, useful as they may be for their details of forbidden practices, give no clue as to how extensively such deviation was to be found. It is, of course, impossible to estimate just how frequently Roman Catholic rites continued to be carried out after the Reformation, but a small amount of evidence does still remain. One point is clear; the north and west of England were far more 'backward' with regard to lingering Catholic traditions than were the south and east of the country, a point borne out by the bishops' injunctions already quoted. This geographical difference struck Edmund Grindal in 1570 on his translation to the see of York from London. On 29 August, he wrote to William Cecil:

I am informed that the greatest part of our gentlemen are not well affected to godly religion, and that among the people there are many remnants of the old. They keep holy days and fasts abrogated, they offer money, eggs, etc. at the burial of their dead: they pray on beads, etc.: so as this seemeth to be, as it were, another church, rather than a member of the rest.

Eighteen months later, Grindal was writing to Henry Bullinger:

I have laboured to the utmost of my power, and still continue to do . . . in getting rid of those remaining superstitions which have maintained their place more firmly in this part of the country. . . I wish I had found them as well instructed in the true religion, as I left my flock in London and Essex to my successor.[5]

To give only two actual examples of the kind of practices which Grindal and his successors were combating, in 1615 a man was presented at the Archbishop of York's visitation for 'putting the metwand into the winding sheet in a superstitious manner', and in 1623 Thomas Bird of Masham, Yorkshire, was presented for 'having superstitious crossings with towels at the burial of one of his children'.[6]

The same point concerning the backwardness of the north and west in funeral practices is shown by the antiquarian, John Aubrey, in the late seventeenth century. A keen collector of strange burial customs, he found many examples of Catholic rituals and beliefs remaining in the parts of England most distant from the capital. Aubrey recorded that in Shropshire on All Souls Day

> there is set on the board a high heap of soul-cakes, lying one upon another like the picture of the sew-bread in the old Bibles. They are about the bigness of twopenny-cakes, and every visitant that day takes one; and there is an old rhythm or saying,
>
> 'A soul-cake, a soul-cake
> Have mercy on all Christian souls for a soul-cake.'

At Yorkshire funerals 'till about 1624', according to Aubrey, a version of the lykewake dirge was sung, one of the verses of which ran:

> From Brig of Dread that thou may pass
> Every night and all,
> To Purgatory fire thou com'st at last
> And Christ receive thy soul.

Warner, visiting Wales as late as 1800, found that belief in purgatory still lingered among some Anglicans there. Aubrey also noted that the practice of making offerings at funerals continued, in 1686,

> over all the counties of North Wales . . . 'where a small tablet or board is fixed near the altar, upon which the friends of the defunct lay their offerings in money according to their own ability, and the quality of the person deceased. This custom proves a very happy augmentation to some of the very poor vicars, and is often the best part of their maintenance.'

While it was possible to alter the official theology and ritual of the country by publishing revised prayer books, it was less easy to change the beliefs and customs of all lay people, particularly in less accessible areas. As Aubrey shows, it was not altogether in the interests of the clergy to stamp out the older traditions. The comforting nature of the Catholic doctrines regarding death no doubt made them particularly difficult to eradicate. Even in the more forward-looking south and east it was still possible for Catholic beliefs to be viewed with some sympathy. There was sufficient willing suspension of disbelief among the audiences of *Hamlet*, set as it was in a framework of Catholic doctrine, to arouse pity for the ghost of Old Hamlet,

> Doom'd for a certain term to walk the night,
> And for the day confin'd to fast in fires,
> Till the foul crimes done in my days of nature
> Are burnt and purg'd away.

Just as, at the Reformation, there were people who still clung to the beliefs of the late Middle Ages, so there were some who felt that the changes made at the Reformation did not go far enough, and who would have liked a more wholehearted adoption of Calvinist doctrine. These people, often loosely designated by the term Puritans, held a wide variety of beliefs, but a basic difference in attitude towards the dead body existed between these extremists and more moderate members of the English Church. To the more traditionally minded, the physical body was 'the image of God' and 'the tabernacle of the Holy Spirit'. As Veron put it, in 1561: 'We should do great wrong unto our bodies, which have been the temples of the Holy Ghost . . . if we should cast them forth unto the dogs'. The same sentiment was expressed by Bishop Hall in his reply to 'the over-just sect commonly called Brownists':

> We do neither scorn the carcasses of our friends . . . nor . . . respect them more than when they were informed with a living soul . . . using them as remainders of dead men, yet as dead Christians . . . we have learned to honour a reasonable (much more a Christian) soul and to commit the instrument or case of it honourably to the grave.

A very different viewpoint was presented by Robert Bolton, expounding a more logically Calvinist attitude towards the dead corpse:

> Thy body, when the soul is gone, will be an horror to all that behold

it; a most loathsome and abhorred spectacle. Those that loved it most, cannot now find it in their hearts to look on't, by reason of the griefly deformedness which death will put upon it. Down it must into a pit of carrions and confusion, covered with worms . . . and so moulder away into rottenness and dust. 4—

Malinowski, drawing on anthropological studies of widely varying cultures, suggests that these two conflicting attitudes towards the dead body are 'the dominant elements' in the reaction to death in all societies: 'Passionate attachment to the personality still lingering about the body and a shattering fear of the gruesome thing that has been left over, these two elements seem to mingle and play into each other.' He also suggests that the actual burial rituals practised are not

determined by mere accident of belief . . . In these customs is clearly expressed the fundamental attitude of mind of the surviving relative, friend or lover, the longing for all that remains of the dead person and the disgust and fear of the dreadful transformation wrought by death.

The Puritans' insistence on the simple disposal of the corpse, which they viewed with such disgust, could be interpreted as a new development in attitudes towards death. It also marks an increased sense of individualism, the personality of the deceased being seen as completely divorced from the physical body in which it had lived.

Both the Puritans and the more moderate Anglicans held opinions concerning correct burial rituals which reflected their respective theological standpoints on the nature of the dead body. The traditionalists' view was that 'it is a Christian duty' to bury the dead 'honourably and magnificently', for three reasons. First, it served 'to witness our reciprocal love and charity towards another'; secondly, 'to show our assured hope of resurrection in others', and thirdly, 'to be a lesson that as others die so shall we.' Cleland concluded that: 'God's word commands, and commends burial in express terms and practice . . . It is not fit that the image of God should be exposed to beasts, or ravenous fowls.' For Richard Hooker,

the end of funeral duties is first to show that love towards the party deceased that nature requireth . . . but the greatest thing of all other about this duty of Christian burial is an outward testification of the hope we have touching the resurrection of the dead.

A very different purpose and perspective is suggested by the directions for conducting burials given in the Scottish *First Book of Discipline*, written under the auspices of John Knox in 1560:

> For avoiding all inconveniences we judge it best that neither singing nor reading be at the burial . . . yea without all kind of ceremony heretofore used, other than that the dead be committed to the grave with such gravity and sobriety as those that be present may seem to fear the judgement of God, and to hate sin, which is the cause of death.

In 1644 a similar code was prescribed for England, in the *Directory for the Public Worship of God*:

> When any person departeth this life, let the dead body, upon the day of burial, be decently attended from the house to the place appointed for public burial, and there immediately interred, without any ceremony. And because the customs of kneeling down, and praying by, or towards the dead corpse, and other such usages, in the place where it lies, before it be carried to burial, are superstitious: and for that praying, reading, and singing, both in going to, and at the grave, have been grossly abused, are in no way beneficial to the dead, and have proved many ways hurtful to the living, therefore let all such things be laid aside.

The *Directory* also suggests that 'Christian friends which accompany the dead body . . . do apply themselves to meditations, and conferences suitable to the occasion'. No minister need be present at the burial, but if one should happen to be there, he must put those attending 'in remembrance of their duty', with respect to private meditation.

Not surprisingly, a considerable amount of invective arose on both sides of the debate concerning the proper mode of burial. Both Puritans and traditionalists frequently resorted to satire to make their respective points. This, for example, is how the separatist Henry Barrow viewed the orthodox burial service:

> The priest meeting the corpse at the church style in white array . . . with a solemn song or else reading aloud certain of their fragments of scripture, and so carry the corpse either to the grave . . . or else

(if he be a rich man) . . . into the church . . . where his dirge and trental is read over him after they have taken off the holy covering cloth wherewith the corpse is dressed until it come . . . unto that holy ground (lest sprites in the meantime should carry it away) the priest there pronounceth, that almighty God hath taken the soul of that their brother or sister unto him, be he heretic, witch, conjurer, and desiring to meet him with joy in the resurrection, etc., who after he hath cast on the first shovelful of earth in his due time with his due words, committing earth to earth, ashes to ashes, etc., then may they boldly proceed to cover him, while the priest also proceedeth to read over his holy gear, and say his *Pater Noster* (which fitteth all assays) and his other prayers over the corpse.

On the other hand, traditionalists characterised their more Puritan brethren as being fanatical and over-particular or obsessional about the minute details of burial rituals. Of 'Martin Marprelate', a pseudonymous Elizabethan Puritan, it was written that he

should not be buried in any church (especially cathedral which he ever detested) chapel, nor churchyard, for that they had been prophaned with superstition: but in some barn, outhouse, or field (yea, rather than fail, dunghill) where their privy prophesyings had been used, without bell, pomp or any solemnity, save that his friends should mourn for him in gowns, and hoods, of a bright yellow . . . Minister he would have none to bury him, but his son, or someone of his lay bretheren, to tumble him into the pit. He would not be laid East and West (for he ever went against the hair) but North and South.

Some idea of what Puritan burials were actually like during this period can be gleaned from a number of sources, including wills and prosecutions in the church courts. In January 1561, Henry Machyn attended the funeral of Master Flammoke, a grocer, at St Peter, Cornhill, London. 'He was carried to the church without singing or clerks and at the church a psalm sung after Geneva and a sermon.' In his will, dated 1577, Sir John Millicent of Barham, Cambridgeshire, wrote:

I give my wretched body to the earth from whence it came, to feed the seely [lucky] poor worms, so that the burial be done without any manner of pomp, and without the wearing of black gowns or coats, or the jangling or ringing of any bells, or any other ceremonies to be had thereat, for they are but vain, chargeable and superstitious.

Millicent's complaint against the traditional funeral rituals, that they were 'chargeable', is of particular interest. It is a sentiment which adds some further weight to the parallel, drawn by some historians, between Protestantism and the ethos of capitalism. Early Puritans, like Millicent, argued strongly that the performance of rituals was a waste of money, a belief which is still to be found, particularly among certain sections of the British middle class in the twentieth century. However, the work of modern anthropologists and psychologists calls for a reassessment of the role of ritual, indicating that it may be of far greater value to the participants than is commonly allowed.

In 1589, a case of unlawful burial appeared before the ecclesiastical courts in Essex. Mistress Quarles had ordered a maidservant to be interred in the orchard 'without any ceremony and not according to the communion book'. Mistress Quarles was assisted in this act by the local schoolmaster, a well-known Puritan, who 'threw the earth on her and covered her'. Both were punished for this offence.[7] The simple Puritan-style burial was sometimes even requested by clergy of the Church of England. In 1616, Samuel Hurlstone, MA, rector of Ickham, Kent, wrote in his will: 'I will have my body to be buried within the churchyard of Ickham aforesaid, by my wife and faithful lover, and that without any delay after my death, without popish pomp, vain compliments and ringing.'

The Puritan drive to simplify funeral rituals should, on the face of it, have been most effective. As has been shown, the burial service, after the Reformation, served little theological purpose, since it no longer was held to assist souls in purgatory. In many ways, the simple, Puritan-style burial was the logical extension of this development, taking burial totally out of the sphere of religious ceremony. Certain historians have, until now, tended to believe that the movement towards the widespread adoption of Puritan burials was successful, basing their argument on about half a dozen contemporary writers' descriptions of what occurred. However, the details of many thousands of actual funerals recorded in probate accounts present new evidence and require a fresh examination of the question.

The historian Keith Thomas has written: 'In England funerals became so much simpler that by 1649 a contemporary could describe them as "in a manner profane, in many places the dead being thrown into the

ground like dogs, and not a word said".' Another historian, David
Stannard, suggests that

> in England during the seventeenth century there was a powerful,
> successful and largely Puritan-motivated effort to reduce the com-
> plexity and significance of the funeral ritual . . . The words of the
> *Directory* were merely the formal seal of approval for behaviour at
> funerals that had long since been the practice in England.

However, it is necessary to look more closely at the 'evidence' on which
both these statements rest. In fact, the supposedly impartial descriptions, on which both historians base their views, actually relate far more
closely to the writers' own polemical intentions than to any objective
reality. The seventeenth century polemicists were mainly concerned
with religious issues. N. Strange, the 'contemporary', was writing the
introduction to a Catholic propagandist treatise published in France in
1649 and dedicated, somewhat belatedly, to Charles I in an attempt to
persuade him to restore England to Roman Catholicism. Pierre Muret,
another writer whom historians have cited, was himself a French
Catholic, and so described the funeral rituals of Catholic France considerably more favourably and fairly than those of Protestant England,
which appeared under the chapter title 'The Funerals of Heretics'.
David Person, a Scottish Catholic, dwelt at length on the virtues of
Catholic burials with their 'pompous solemnities . . . the sound of bells
and cymbals, tapers, torches, prayers, music, church ornaments, solemn
processions', and the 'kind of pious compassion' induced among those
present, with 'content to their eyes and ears'. It is therefore hardly
surprising that he should then comment unfavourably on 'our dumb
and silent obsequies'.

Historians have also misunderstood some of the polemicists writing
from the extreme Puritan standpoint. John Canne, in *A Necessity of
Separation from the Church of England*, published in 1634, stated:

> The Nonconformists will have the dead to be buried in this sort,
> (holding no other way lawful), namely, that it be conveyed to the
> place of burial, with some honest company of the church, without
> either singing or reading, yea, without all kinds of ceremony hereto-
> fore used, other than that the dead be committed to the grave, with
> such gravity and sobriety as those that be present may seem to fear
> the judgements of God, and to hate sin, which is the cause of
> death; and thus do the best and right reformed churches bury their

dead, without any ceremonies of praying or preaching at them.

Canne is not, as one historian has suggested, referring to contemporary practices in England in this passage. In fact, his choice of words betrays the origin of his statement, being lifted, in some parts verbatim, from the Scottish *First Book of Discipline*.

Lawrence Stone, in his study of the English aristocracy in the early modern period, cites John Weever who, in 1631, lamented the decline of the English funeral from a non-religious standpoint: 'Funerals in any expensive way here with us, are now accounted but as a fruitless vanity, in so much that almost all the ceremonial rites of obsequies heretofore used, are altogether laid aside.'

However, Weever then explained the true object of his concern, which was the loss of fees to the 'Officers of Arms [heralds], whose chiefest support and maintenance hath ever depended on the performance of such funeral rites and exequies'. In fact, it was specifically the decline of the heraldic funeral and 'the slight regard we have of the needful use of heralds' which Weever bewailed, rather than a genuine reduction in all burial ceremonies.

It is now possible to turn to the evidence of probate accounts to provide a rather more impartial picture. The graph (see Appendix) traces the changes in average funeral cost recorded, for four counties, from 1580 through to the Civil War. It is reasonable to suggest that, if the Puritan style of burial were being adopted on a wide scale in the seventeenth century, the sums spent would decline, there being no expenditure on bell ringing, the attendance of the minister and clerk, a pall or any luxuries such as mourning garments. The effect of monetary inflation on funeral expenses was apparent to contemporaries, one accountant in Somerset in 1611 added to the items in her account the phrase 'being in the dear year'. All the figures on which the graph is based have therefore been deflated to make them comparable with prices in the decade 1580 to 1590.

From the graph it is possible to say with confidence that, even allowing for inflation, average funeral costs were not decreasing generally during these decades in any of the four counties for which evidence is available. Indeed, it would seem that the average expenditure on funerals actually increased during the first half of the seventeenth century in Berkshire, Kent and Somerset. Neither the poorest nor the very grandest funerals covered by probate accounts show any decline in cost during this period. It seems that no major reduction in funeral expenditure can be found in these four widely separated counties of

England. It would therefore be reasonable to suppose that the dramatic Puritan success in simplifying burial rituals has little or no basis in reality, but is a distortion fabricated by polemical writers and perpetuated by unwary historians.

This conclusion is supported by the detailed contents of the probate accounts themselves, where all the funeral rituals so hated and despised by Puritans are to be found in plenty, with no diminution as the seventeenth century progressed. Nor do Puritan-style burials seem to have appeared very frequently either in parish registers or in churchwardens' presentments. For example, in 19 parishes in the diocese of Oxford between the late sixteenth century and the Civil War, there was only a total of three cases of illicit burial.[8] When such Puritan burials are recorded in parish registers, it is clear from the wording used that they were considered rare, rather than commonplace, events, and are often accompanied by scathing and opprobrious comments.

In examining the effectiveness, or otherwise, of the Puritan desire to simplify burial rituals, it is particularly interesting to look at what occurred during the period of the Civil War and Interregnum, following the introduction of the *Directory* in 1644. Here, if anywhere, the Puritan order for burial should have come into its own, since it was now officially sanctioned and enforceable. It should initially, however, be noted that the Scots attending the Westminster Assembly of 1643, which led to the publication of the *Directory*, had immense trouble in persuading English ministers to give up the burial service of the *Book of Common Prayer*. As one Scottish participant wrote home from the Assembly: 'We have, with much difficulty, passed a proposition for abolishing their ceremonies at burials, but our difference about funeral sermons seems irreconcilable . . . After three days' debate, we cannot yet find a way of agreeance.'

The breakdown of the system of ecclesiastical records during the Interregnum inevitably hampers attempts to discover what actually was the practice of the time. No doubt traditional rituals were maintained, especially in the more out of the way areas. Even in London, John Evelyn recorded that he managed to have Lady Brown buried in Deptford Church in September 1652 'according to the Church Office . . . after it had not been used in that church of 7 years'. From those few probate accounts which survive from this period, it is impossible to detect that any major changes, as set out in the *Directory*, had actually taken effect. All the rituals previously performed were still being carried out; ringing the bells, burial within the church, the attendance of the minister and clerk, the preaching of sermons, the use of the pall and so on. To give some Lincolnshire examples, William Baker was buried in Cranwell Church in 1650 for a fee of 10s, while a sermon was preached at the funeral of Frances Deighton of Ownby in 1649. At some of these funerals the 'drinking' sounds as though it were any- thing but solemn and sober. After the burial of James Lawes, a Lincoln plumber, in 1649, 16 gallons of ale, 2½ gallons of muscadine, 10 pounds of biscuits, 18 dozen cakes and 48½ dozen loaves of bread and buns were consumed, not to mention 2 pounds of sugar, and an ounce of nutmeg and ginger, costing in all £6 2s 11d. At the funeral of William Gilding of Donnington-in-Holland, Lincolnshire, in 1649, a dole of 10s was distributed to the poor, while at John Tower of Lincoln's funeral in 1648, 32 yards of black ribbon were given to the guests. Even mourning clothes were still worn at these funerals and, on occasion, the church was hung with black cloth. Four Kent probate accounts state that the number attending the funeral was particularly large and cer- tainly the evidence of these accounts suggests that there was no altera- tion in the burial rituals performed.

However, it is perhaps just possible to discern very faintly from these probate accounts that something has changed in the general attitude towards burial itself. After 1644, there appears, in several Kent accounts, an emphasis on the deceased being 'decently buried' or 'decently in- terred'. For example, the account of William Pix in 1645 states that 'his wife and children wanted him decently buried', while that of John Baxley, in the following year, records that he was 'buried decently as a last duty by his friends'. This justification of 'decency', not found in previous accounts, might well reflect conscious resistance to the new, simpler form of burial. One Berkshire account, that for Toby Embrie, dated 1651, reveals a confusion as to the correct terminology now to be used. It initially recorded a payment of £1 10s to the 'minister and clerk'; but these words have been crossed out, and 'preacher' substi- tuted, although from the sum involved this was clearly for more than just a sermon. However, these indications of problems concerning burial rituals after the introduction of the *Directory* are very slight; the detailed evidence of the probate accounts calls into question just how effective the Puritan insistence on simple burial was even during the Civil War and the Interregnum itself.

A further complication is that not all those who actually used the simple form of burial during this period were viewed with favour. In the parish registers of Hackness, Yorkshire, the following entry occurs:

1653 Richard Cockwell died on Wednesday the 14th day of September and was buried the next day being Thursday and there was many of them called Quaker at his burial. And Mr Prowde [the minister] did exhort and argue with them at the grave.

Not surprisingly, when George Watson, 'being of the Quaker sect', died in 1656, 'many of them were at the burial but Mr Prowde was not called to bury him, and after they see him buried they went away'.

A final paradoxical dimension, which could be added to this picture of funerals during the Interregnum, appears on looking at the burials of the architects of the revolution and their kin. These funerals were anything but simple and austere; 'more than regal' was one later comment, by Noble, on the Lord Protector's obsequies. John Evelyn declared it to be 'the joyfulest funeral I ever saw, for there were none that cried but dogs, which the soldiers hooted away with a barbarous noise, drinking and taking tobacco in the streets as they went'. Certainly the leaders of the parliamentary side in the Civil War and Commonwealth periods did little to set an example, through their own burials, of sobriety, simplicity and godliness.

Why do the funeral rituals of this period not respond more clearly to changes in religious beliefs? One reason is to be found in St Augustine's famous maxim. Theological debates and developments concerning burials relate solely to the condition of the dead themselves and the nature of the afterlife. However, as St Augustine has said, it is the needs of the living which principally determine the rituals of burial, not eschatological considerations. Even the stark rubric of the *Directory* acknowledged that funerals had a social function too. The following mitigating clause was added to its stern injunctions concerning simplicity at funerals: 'This shall not extend to deny any civil respects or differences at the burial, suitable to the rank and condition of the party deceased whilst he was living.'

The importance of these social rites cannot be over-estimated; it was this loophole which accounted for the less than austere funerals of the principal political figures of the Interregnum. A similar phenomenon is found in Puritan New England where extremely elaborate and expensive burials were accorded to many fervent Calvinists. No doubt to the majority of ordinary lay people in England, the social rites of funerals, the re-establishing of relationships during the eating and drinking which followed a burial, contained far greater comfort for the bereaved than did the harsh uncertainty of the doctrine of predestination.

Not surprisingly, at the Restoration, the pre-Civil War burial rites were officially re-established with little effort or difficulty. The old fervour about burial rituals had, for the most part, burned itself out. After a few minor adjustments in 1661, the order for burial in the prayer book was left unaltered until the late twentieth century. Revealingly, what concern there was in post-Restoration England over burial mainly took the form of trying to protect the English economy by forcing people to be buried in woollen shrouds or else to forfeit a fine — and, later, an attempt to introduce death duties.

Nonconformists were permitted their own burial grounds and could practise their own ceremonies. For example, the will of John Hopkins of Broad Street, London, proved in 1732, directed that £100 be spent

> in the walling in and enclosing of all that piece of ground in or near the town of Sherborne in the County of Dorset which is now used by dissenters promiscuously as a burying place and in making a proper gateway or portal into the same ground provided that the said piece of ground be preserved and appropriated . . . for the same use to which it is now put.

Dissenters' funerals were often sizeable affairs, and the social display was sometimes quite considerable, even if the actual interment was simply performed; in 1675 Anthony à Wood noted that 3,000 people attended one Nonconformist burial, while in 1691, 5,000 saw a Non-conformist minister to his grave. The freedom of practice at burials could lead to some strange occurrences. One man, enraged that the local vicar would not bury him with his favourite horse, had a private burial ground instituted for himself where his desired ceremony duly took place, occasioning some comment in *The Christian Reformer*.

Anglican funerals of the eighteenth century were often remarkably secular in tone. This was how a man of the cloth, Parson Woodforde, described the funeral of 'an old acquaintance' in 1796:

> It was a very handsome funeral indeed. Two mourning coaches and four, one mourning chariot and pair, two postchaises, besides other carriages . . . The pallbearers [of whom Woodforde was one] each . . . had a rich black silk scarf and hatband, and a pair of beaver gloves . . . A great number of people attended indeed. Chocolate, cold ham, veal, etc. at the side tables in the room we were in, the best parlour. We returned back to the house after the interment, took some little refreshment, and then each went to their respective

homes.

Foreign visitors to England, from Misson in the late seventeenth century onwards, described English funerals solely in terms of their pageantry and show, omitting virtually all reference to the religious aspects of the ritual. La Rochefoucauld, in the late eighteenth century, commented at length on the 'magnificent' funerals of the English gentlemen; his only reference to the sacred element of the ritual was that 'the rector conducts the burial without ceremony'.

The secular tone of burials in the eighteenth century was the logical outcome of the process of whittling down the religious elements of the funeral ritual, a process which had begun at the Reformation. As the religious elements dwindled, so the social aspects of the ritual took on greater importance, to meet the needs of a more secular society. The fundamental association which funerals held for eighteenth-century Englishmen is very nicely revealed in a dream which Parson Woodforde had on 8 January 1795. Having met two corpses on the way to church, he dreamt that he went to bury one and ordered the second

> to be carried into the chancel, till the other was buried. When I returned to the chancel, thought I saw a most elegant dinner served up — particularly fish — whether I waked then or not I cannot tell, but could recollect nothing more of my dream besides.

The growing secularisation of eighteenth-century funeral rituals was paralleled by a more questioning attitude in matters of doctrine. First privately, and later more publicly, the inconsistencies and possible illogicalities of Calvinist theology were exposed to scrutiny and criticism. Perhaps not surprisingly, a religious creed which had encouraged introspection and self-doubt and had indeed fostered individual awareness found its own tenets being exposed to the same type of ruthless search for truth which it had sought to implant in the private lives of its followers.

Two potential weak spots in the Calvinist doctrine concerning death lay in the problems posed by predestination and by the eternal damnation of the wicked. The notion of an omnipotent deity who yet allowed the eternal damnation of some of his creation began to be viewed with distaste; it was felt to be inconsistent with the idea of a loving, merciful God. That He should actually predestine men and women to such a fate became an idea totally repugnant to rational thinkers. By 1743, this rejection of the concept of hell had become sufficiently widespread for a preacher to complain: 'It is but too visible, that since men have learned to wear off the apprehension of eternal punishment, the progress of impiety and immorality among us has been very considerable'.[9]

The decline of belief in rigid predestination meant that people no longer attributed each small occurrence to the will of God. Even deaths were less frequently said to be the result of God's design; a generally more pragmatic concept of man's fate emerged, in many ways not that dissimilar to the common view of causality held in the latter half of the twentieth century.[10] An important exception to the acceptance of this philosophical trend was represented by the Wesleyan Methodists who maintained belief in the actuality of divine intervention. They were later to have a profound effect on the Victorian view of God, in many ways reversing the drift towards pragmatism and reviving elements of English Puritanical doctrine, largely rejected during the eighteenth century.

It might be thought that these changes in perception in the eighteenth century, especially the rejection of the notion of hell, would have eased the problem of death and dying. In fact, the difficulty remained as great as ever, despite the change in its nature. Lady Mary Wortley Montagu in 1749 shrewdly, if cynically, pointed to the shift in concern from the Middle Ages to her own time:

> When I recollect the vast fortunes raised by doctors amongst us, and the eager pursuit after every new piece of quackery that is introduced, I cannot help thinking that there is a fund of credulity in mankind that must be employed somewhere, and the money formerly given to monks for the health of the soul is now thrown to doctors for the health of the body, and generally with as little real prospect of success.

Indeed, far from causing a diminution in anxiety about death, there is evidence to suggest that, towards the end of the eighteenth century, death became an event of even greater trauma for the bereaved. This was particularly true of the death of children, where some improvement in the life expectancy of infants led to much closer familial ties being sundered when a child died. If the child was past infancy, as in the case of Arthur Young's favourite daughter Martha, known affectionately as Bobbin, the suffering which parents experienced could be devastating:

It is beyond my power to describe what is struggling within me! My sorrow has softened me and wrings my very heartstrings! How hard does it appear submissively to bow to that text, 'He that loveth son or daughter more than Me is not worthy of Me.'

The eighteenth-century attitude towards death further supports the general hypothesis put forward in this chapter, that religious and doctrinal changes have little actual effect on people's reaction to death and burial. In an individualistic society, it is, ultimately, the feeling of loss, rather than concepts of the afterlife, which dominate and shape responses to bereavement and death. As John Moore lamented in 1617, in *A Mappe of Man's Mortalitie*: 'Every one feareth the death of the body, but few are afraid of the death of the soul. That which cannot possibly be avoided, men seek to shun; but to avoid sin (that they may live for ever) few or none do care.'

Notes

1. Ariès, *The Hour of Our Death*, p. 314.
2. Quoted in Stannard, *The Puritan Way of Death*, p. 73; Chapters 3 and 4 of his book examine the psychological consequences of Calvinist doctrine. For a contemporary English discussion of the problem, see Boswell, *Life of Johnson*, ii, pp. 554-5.
3. This account is based on Proctor and Frere, *New History of the Book of Common Prayer* and Pullan, *The Book of Common Prayer*.
4. Quoted in Pullan, *The Book of Common Prayer*, p. 237.
5. Robinson, H., ed., *The Zurich Letters*, pp. 259-60.
6. Described in *Folklore*, lxiv, p. 367 and Gutch, *Folklore of the North Riding of Yorkshire*, p.308; a metwand is a measuring rod, its religious significance is unclear, though it might represent the length of Christ's body.
7. Described in Emmison, *Elizabethan Life*, p. 173.
8. Peyton, ed., *Churchwardens' Presentments in Oxfordshire*, pp. 116, 141 and 204.
9. Quoted in Walker, *The Decline of Hell*, p. 3; his book traces changing beliefs concerning damnation.
10. For further discussion, see Stone, *Family, Sex and Marriage*, pp. 246-53.

3 FUNERALS OF THE UNFORTUNATE

> Take some pity on me . . . for my friends is very poor, and my mother is very sick, and I'm to die next Wednesday morning, so I hope you will be so good as to give my friends a small trifle of money to pay for a coffin and a shroud, for to take my body away from the tree in that I am to die on.

These words, written in 1739 by a condemned thief, Richard Tobin, to his former master, reflect the intense preoccupation with 'decent interment in a Christian manner' in pre-industrial England.[1] A variety of reasons underlie this concern. No doubt some people, particularly among the uneducated, held extremely literal interpretations of the resurrection, making the correct burial of dead bodies a matter of vital importance in their eschatological scheme. In popular belief, a Christian funeral was held to assist the passage of the soul to the hereafter. Without these rites, it was felt, the soul might 'walk'; as Dorothy Rowland wrote to Lot Cavenagh, a highwayman awaiting execution in Newgate in 1743: 'I have endeavoured to assist you . . . to do that THING which you requested of me, touching the saving of your body [for Christian burial, yet] you speak threatening words to me, telling me, that if you can, you will trouble me after you are dead.'[2]

At a more fundamental level, this emphasis on proper Christian burial owed much to the great social importance of this ceremony which, in its turn, helped to maintain and uphold the fabric of the social order. Although the actual interment was carried out under the auspices of the Church, the desire for 'Christian burial' included the traditional social rites and far transcended the religious significance of the ritual. It may seem strange to twentieth-century ways of thinking that a man awaiting execution should have been as concerned about the fate of his body as about his impending doom or the possible destiny of his soul. However, it could well be argued that the modern clarity of distinction between mind and body is simply a reflection of the contemporary philosophy of individualism. The personality is now seen solely as the mind, rather than the physical case which it inhabits. In the less individualistic world of pre-industrial England, this distinction was formulated with far less clarity.

To appreciate the extent, nature and strength of the concern over correct rites of funeral in early modern England, it is revealing to look at the burials of those on the fringes of society, the poor, those people at odds with the law, those who died during the crisis of plague outbreaks and those who failed to survive childhood or infancy. The condemned criminal, the most miserable pauper and the victims of fearful epidemics all hoped fervently to be buried in the traditional manner, according to the customary rituals of Church and society. How both Church and society at large reacted to the wishes of these unfortunates highlights the significance of funerals in the mentality of early modern England.

The funerals of paupers were paid for by the parish in which they had lived, from a rate levied on all property owners. However, these burials were not as mean as possibly might be expected from the way they were financed; more than the bare minimum was usually provided. In Kent, for example, from the mid-seventeenth century onwards, a coffin was always used at a pauper burial, though in other areas even quite well-to-do people were not invariably accorded this dignity. Certain parishes throughout the country owned a communal coffin, in which, at least, to carry pauper corpses to the grave; in 1569 the parish of St Alphege, London Wall, spent 5s on purchasing such a coffin.[3]

Usually food and drink would be provided at a pauper's burial, again at the expense of the parish. An entry in the poorbook of Folkingham, Lincolnshire, records that after the burial of John Gibson in 1641, a dozen loaves of bread, costing 1s, and a quart of beer, costing 6s, were consumed. At Algarkirk in the same county, on 7 March 1653, when Thomas Lanies was buried, 2s worth of bread, 2s worth of beer and butter costing 9d were distributed, in addition to the payment of 10d for bellringing and for making his grave. The funerals of the most lowly members of society were still felt to be worthy occasions for a social gathering; indeed, it could be argued that the 'drinking' after the interment was as much an integral part of the ritual as the presence of the vicar or the words of the burial service itself.

Even nameless strangers were accorded the minimum decent burial rites. An unknown poor traveller found dead in the parish of Woodchurch, Kent, in March 1616, received a burial which cost the parish 4s 9d. On discovery, his body was carried into a barn and shrouded in two ells of canvas; the canvas cost 2s 2d and the two men who 'wound' him and then carried him to church received 16d. The use of canvas, rather than a less substantial material, and the high payment to the two men who prepared the body for burial suggest possibly that the body may have lain decomposing for some time before it was found. A further 15d was then spent on making the stranger's grave and ringing his knell.

If an attempt were made to bury a pauper without observing the necessary decencies, the minister might intervene. The parish register of Poyning, Sussex, records the burial of John Skerry, a poor man who had died in a stable 'and being brought half naked with his face bare, the parson would not bury him so, but first he gave a sheet and caused him to be sacked therein, and they buried him more Christian like, being much grieved to see him brought so unto the grave'.

An eye-witness account of a rural pauper burial at the beginning of the nineteenth century is provided by Dorothy Wordsworth. On 3 September 1800, she attended a funeral near her home in the Lake District and was 'affected to tears' by its simple dignity. As with the earlier pauper burials, food and drink were provided, served before, rather than after, the ceremony. On this occasion, it was the parson who detracted from the solemnity of the ritual:

> Went to a funeral at John Dawson's. About 10 men and 4 women. Bread, cheese and ale. They talked sensibly and cheerfully about common things. The dead person, 56 years of age, buried by the parish. The coffin was neatly lettered and painted black, and covered with a decent cloth. They set the corpse down at the door; and . . . the men with their hats off sang with decent and solemn countenances a verse of a funeral psalm. The corpse was then borne down the hill . . . When we came to the bridge, they began to sing again, and stopped during four lines before they entered the churchyard. The priest met us. He did not look as a man ought to do on such an occasion. I had seen him half-drunk the day before in a pot-house. Before we came with the corpse one of the company observed he wondered what sort of cue our parson would be in! NB It was the day after the Fair.

In March 1808 Dorothy Wordsworth was invited to another funeral which, while not actually paid for by the parish, involved a case of extreme poverty and tragedy. It is clear from what she writes that financial considerations were in no way permitted to affect the carrying out of traditional rituals at this burial. Her account is particularly interesting since she attempted to put into words the sense of community feeling and solidarity which the funeral ritual engenders in a traditional society. George Green and his wife, walking to the local market town, had perished in a blizzard on the fells, leaving six young orphaned children. Dorothy wrote:

> Before the bodies were taken up a threepenny loaf of bread was
> dealt out to each of the guests. Mary [Wordsworth] was unwilling
> to take hers, thinking that the orphans were in no condition to give
> away anything; she immediately however perceived that she ought to
> accept it; and a woman who was near us observed it was an ancient
> custom now much disused; but probably as the family had lived long
> in the Vale and had done the like at funerals formerly, they thought
> it proper not to drop the custom on this occasion. The funeral pro-
> cession was very solemn passing through the solitary valley of Ease-
> dale, and altogether I never witnessed a more moving scene. As is
> customary here, there was a pause before the bodies were borne
> through the churchyard gate, while part of a psalm was sung, the
> men standing with their heads uncovered. In the Church the two
> coffins were placed near the altar, and the whole family knelt on the
> floor on each side of the father's coffin, leaning over it . . . Many
> tears were shed by persons who had known little of the deceased;
> and all the people who were gathered together appeared to be united
> in one general feeling of sympathy for the helpless condition of the
> orphans.

It might seem that the social gathering at such a burial in early
modern England, with the sharing of food and drink, was an unneces-
sary luxury among people so poor, or those buried by charity funds.
However, as has been suggested, it was a vital element in the ritual and
part of the whole process whereby a community coped with death, the
emotional aspect of which was so well described by Dorothy
Wordsworth.

Any society which accorded its poorest members this degree of
dignity at their funerals must certainly have held decent burial at a
premium. However, the pressures of urban life, particularly in the metropolis, had begun to erode the traditional decencies of poor people's
funerals as early as the initial decades of the eighteenth century. The
increase in the urban population had serious repercussions; in 1747, the
Rector of St Andrew's, Holborn, London, attributed the 'offensive'
nature of the parish churchyards to the fact that 'the number of inhabitants in the said parish is increased near double in the last forty years'.[4]
The results of such population explosions were graphically described by
a writer in 1721:

It is well known that several out-parishes . . . are very much strait-ened for room to bury their dead; and that to remedy in part that inconvenience, they dig in their church yards or other annexed burial grounds, large holes or pits in which they put many of the bodies of those whose friends are not able to pay for better graves, and then those pits or holes (called the poor's holes) once opened are not covered till filled with dead bodies.

An account, in 1774, of how the poor were buried in one particular churchyard in central London, gave further details of these interments:

The greatest evil is what is called parish or poor's graves: these are pits capable of holding three or four coffins abreast and about seven in depth; are always kept open till they are full, then the tops are covered over with earth; and another pit about the same size is dug on the side of it, leaving the sides of the former coffins always open.[5]

Overcrowding in graveyards was not the sole cause of this alteration in the funeral rites of the urban poor. The social dislocation resulting from rapid urbanisation struck at the roots of the kind of communal solidarity which characterised, and indeed upheld, funeral rites among the rural poor. For example, it was necessary, in 1617, for the Port Moot of Liverpool to add a degree of compulsion to funeral attendance in the town:

We do agree that when it pleaseth God to call any neighbour to His mercy, that every neighbouring dwelling in the street where the party deceased did dwell, that of every house one shall go to accom-pany the corpse to the church, or else pay 6d, to be collected by the Mayor's appointment.[6]

Unfortunately, insufficient documentary evidence remains to be able to trace the effect of urbanisation on funeral rituals in the metropolis during the sixteenth and seventeenth centuries. In the counties where probate accounts have survived, the urban centres are comparatively small and are almost indistinguishable, in terms of burial practices, from the surrounding countryside.

An additional influence on the funerals of urban paupers was pointed out earlier this century by Sir Arnold Wilson and Professor Hermann Levy in their book, *Burial Reform* — the growth of a more

Puritanical attitude towards the poor themselves, from the late seventeenth century onwards. Poor people were blamed increasingly for their own poverty, an outlook which led to the setting up of workhouses. The horror of a pauper burial was a useful stick with which to goad the poor to greater efforts; at any rate, it was argued, public money should not be wasted on needless ritual for mere indigents. One direct consequence of the degradation of urban pauper burials was the enrichment of the undertaking profession, since even the most poverty-stricken would try to put money aside, often through burial clubs, to pay for a 'respectable' funeral.

The burial rites of the poor are symptomatic of general attitudes towards funeral rituals within society. The accepted provisions for the disposal of the bodies of those who have lived on the margins of society are scarcely dignified even today. For the poor of our own society, the inadequate death grant, the alienation of post-industrial life and the emphasis on individual rather than community feeling combine to provide meagre burial rites, as in the Lennon and McCartney song, 'Eleanor Rigby', who 'died . . . and was buried along with her name — nobody came'.

Another group of people in pre-industrial England, who could little afford lavish burials, were those who died in debt. According to the letter of the law, the funeral of a debtor was meant to be paid for without the debts being taken into consideration, which suggests a rather different order of priorities from that of late twentieth-century Britain.[7] This legal ruling seems almost always to have been adhered to, often with catastrophic results for the deceased's estate, leaving the executors with a considerable problem on their hands. One Kent executor, in 1629, having stated the cost of the funeral in his account, which included wine, cakes and the attendance of a group of soldiers, added ruefully, 'his debts not then known to be so great as since they have appeared to be'. Sometimes money was even borrowed to pay for the funeral; in 1574, 38s had to be borrowed to bury Michael Jackson, in Lincolnsire, 6s 8d of which was spent on the avoidable luxury of having him interred inside the church. It appears that, by and large, the dictates of finance were ignored when it came to the burial of those who died in debt.

This point is confirmed when the funerals are examined of those people whose creditors actually administered their estates after they had died. It might be expected that a creditor, being unrelated to the deceased, would have no personal reasons for providing a lavish funeral and, indeed, would have wished to keep the cost as low as possible. A passage in Richard Burn's *Ecclesiastical Law*, quoting a ruling of 1693, reads: 'In general, it is said, that no more than 40s for funeral expenses, shall be allowed against creditors.' While, legally, expenditure was permitted on the shroud and coffin, digging the grave, ringing the bell and paying the parson, the clerk and the bearers, no pall or other 'ornaments' were allowable. However, it appears that the '40 shillings' rule was largely ignored, many people having far more costly funerals with a considerable number of 'ornaments'. In one case in 1638 in Kent, the expenditure for a funeral was the cause of not a little friction between the administrator, a creditor of the deceased, and the surviving 'kindred and friends'. There was some delay in granting the letters of administration, so the relatives and friends of the dead man, Isaac Menton, began to make purchases for the funeral. These included cakes and other food, gloves and mourning cloaks. As the administrator, Jonathan Smith, rather crossly records, these came to £14 16s. However, it is interesting to note that Smith did not try to challenge this bill, but paid it, if somewhat ungraciously, despite the fact that Menton's debts amounted to nearly twice the value of his worldly goods.

Although, for the most part, debtors were readily accorded funerals commensurate with their status rather than their means, there were from time to time extremely unpleasant scenes at their burials. While never strictly legal, the custom of arresting a corpse for debt was still practised in pre-industrial England. In 1598, Thomas Bett appeared before the Church courts in Essex because 'he did go into the grave made for the body of Edward Godfrie and did there arrest the body with very unseemly, unrelevant and intemperate speech, whereby [the] minister would not bury him or read the burial service for him'.[8] The parish register of Sparsholt, Berkshire, describes another such incident in 1689:

The corpse of John Matthews, of Fawley, was stopped on the church way for debt August 27. And having lain there four days was by justices warrant buried in the place to prevent annoyances − but about six weeks after it was by an Order of Sessions taken up and buried in the churchyard by the wife of the deceased.

This peculiar custom suggests a much less strong differentiation between the living and the dead in legal or quasi-legal matters than is prevalent in the twentieth century; it is perhaps analogous with the law of deodands, only abolished in 1846, whereby an inanimate object could actually be found guilty of, rather than just the cause of, someone's death. Our division between the living and the dead, the animate and inanimate, is a concept which was not so finely developed in the pre-industrial era.

If a totally impecunious debtor died in gaol, then the prison would provide for his funeral; during the eighteenth century, debtors dying in Ludgate were buried in Moorfields at the expense of the 'house fund'.[9] Usually, however, when an ordinary prisoner died while incarcerated, the corpse, after it had been viewed by the coroner, would be returned to the relatives for burial; in 1622, when Richard Bigg died in prison at Evelchurch, Somerset, his body was taken back to his native parish of Wellow for burial. Just occasionally, a prisoner's body would be buried in the church nearest to the gaol in which he died. When Philip Howard, First Earl of Arundel, died in the Tower in October 1595, his remains were buried in the chancel of St Katharine's, Tower Hill. In part, this choice of burying place may have been affected by the length of his stay in the Tower, ten years, and the fact that he was a Roman Catholic; also it is possible that he had genuinely been poisoned, as it was rumoured, causing the Crown to be unwilling to return the body to his family. His burial was a simple affair; the clerk dug the grave and then repaved it and the parson received the three yards of black cloth, costing 30s, which had been used to cover the coffin.[10]

The vast majority of people who were actually executed for their crimes were laid to rest in the churchyard of the parish in which the gaol stood; the parish register for St Mary's, Reading, records that on 26 March 1679 four men were 'hanged and buried'. Sometimes malefactors were also baptised in the church before the execution; an entry in the parish register of St Mary-le-Bow, Durham, for 1722 reads: '30 August. Bur[ied] James Graham, a felon, he was hanged the same morning just after Bap[tism] .'

It perhaps seems ironic, but is also most revealing, that a legal code which sanctioned the loss of life for such petty crimes as picking a pocket of more than 1s, the most trivial of robberies and, after the 'Black Act' of 1723, even cutting down trees or sending anonymous letters, only denied the rites of Christian burial to the most serious offenders, those committing high treason and, after 1751, murderers.

The popular attitude towards the bodies of executed criminals in early modern England is itself most fascinating and contradictory. The touch of the hand of someone who had been publicly hanged was thought to cure a variety of such diseases as skin complaints and tumours. Meister, a visitor to England, noted this practice with horror, in a letter published in 1799:

> I observed a number of men and women carried to the scaffold to be stroked by the hands, still quivering in the agony of death, of the suspended criminals, under the notion that such an application will be of efficacy in working a cure for several complaints; amongst the rest I remarked a young woman, with an appearance of beauty, all pale and trembling, in the arms of the executioner, who submitted to have her bosom uncovered, in the presence of thousands of spectators, and the dead man's hand placed upon it. Cruel, incomprehensible superstition! thus to outrage the good sense, the decency, and decorum of an enlightened people.

This strange custom plays a vital role in a macabre short story by Thomas Hardy, *The Withered Arm*, published in 1888. Gertrude Lodge is told by the local 'cunning man' that her deformed arm is caused by witchcraft and can only be cured if she were to

> touch with the limb the neck of a man who's been hanged . . . Before he's cold — just after he's cut down . . . It will turn the blood and change the constitution . . . You must get into jail and wait for him when he's brought off the gallows. Lots have done it . . . I used to send dozens for skin complaints . . . in former times.

The dénouement of this story takes place over the corpse of an executed criminal.

The reasoning behind this peculiar belief is not easy to fathom. A reversal seems to have taken place in the popular imagination at the moment of execution, causing that which had been, while living, harmful and threatening to society, to take on healing and beneficial powers instead, almost as a form of compensation. This transformation in the popular perception of the executed bodies helps to explain why it was felt that they should be given decent Christian burials. Extremes of evil are balanced with those of good, the process of balancing acting as a containing and controlling force on the extremes. This same type of balancing of opposites is to be found in certain aspects of the burial rituals of ordinary people in early modern England, too, for example in the holding of wakes where humour was used to counteract sorrow. This use of opposites in rituals was part of the way that pre-industrial society tackled the forces that were most threatening to its survival, whether these were death or lawbreaking.

A similar kind of reversal appears again in the ritual surrounding the execution itself, through the association of hangings with weddings. Misson, noting that the English make it a 'mighty matter' to be hanged, described the preparations of the victim:

He that is to be hanged, or otherwise executed, first takes care to get himself shaved and handsomely dressed, either in mourning or in the dress of a bridegroom . . . Sometimes the girls [among the spectators] dress in white, with great silk scarves, and carry baskets full of flowers and oranges, scattering these favours all the way they go.

Gemmelli, an Italian visitor to England, who published an account of his travels in 1701, remarked 'with the greatest amazement' that the condemned man approached the gallows 'as if he was going to a wedding'. There was even a custom whereby a criminal could be saved from the gallows if a woman would agree to marry him, as was witnessed by Anthony à Wood. 'The maids of the town had dressed up an ordinary body to beg him to be her husband; and she appeared at the gallows and desired him, but was denied him', because he refused to betray his accomplices. Sentence was duly carried out; afterwards, the body of this 'handsome' youth 'was supported by young men, and being carried with a white sheet, the said sheet was held up by maids in white, with innumerable women, maidens, and children following. After prayers said, he was buried in All Saints churchyard . . . in the north churchyard.'

The parallel between hangings and weddings has similarities with the burials of virgins, where again elements of a wedding appear in the ritual. This, too, may be seen in terms of a balance; the ritual which legitimises procreation, marriage, is used to counterbalance the annihilating force of death. For both groups of people, the criminals and the virgins, death is unnatural; marriage would normally have been a more appropriate ritual for someone of their age to undergo, had death, in one guise or another, not intervened.[11] The deaths of these people, usually in the prime of life, posed a severe threat to society, which was then reduced through the imagery of the ritual.

Those executed for high treason were felt to have committed so dire an offence that they were denied the rites of Christian burial. Their bodies were, in Weever's words, laid to rest 'near or under the gallows', but usually not for some time after the execution. The desire for vengeance on these criminals was such that it extended to punishing their bodies after they were actually dead, as is amply revealed in the *State Trials*. The execution of Christopher Norton, who took part in the Northern Rebellion and died for it in 1570, shows the treatment meted out to a traitor. He had just watched his uncle's execution 'knowing, and being well assured, that he himself must follow the same way'; standing on the executioner's cart, he said the Lord's Prayer and made his confession:

> With that, the hangman executed his office: and being hanged a little while, and then cut down, the butcher opened him, and as he took out his bowels, he cried, and said, 'Oh Lord, Lord, have mercy upon me' and so yielded up the ghost. Then being likewise quartered, as the other [his uncle] was, and their bowels burned, as the manner is, their quarters were put into a basket, provided for the purpose, and so carried to Newgate, where they were parboiled; and afterwards, their heads set on London Bridge, and their quarters set upon sundry gates of the city of London, for an example to all traitors and rebels, for committing high treason against God and their prince.

This gruesome ritual was obviously intended to have a deterrent effect on others, but it also had a symbolic function in terms of punishment, which went far beyond merely taking life and causing pain. This symbolism was spelt out in the sentence passed on John Owen, who in 1615 declared that it was lawful to kill the King since he had been excommunicated by the Pope:

> The judgement upon a traitor is, that he shall be drawn to execution, for as much as he is not worthy to walk upon the earth: 2. His privy members cut off . . . which shows that his issue is disinherited with the corruption of blood . . . 3. His bowels burned because in them he hatched the treason: 4. Beheaded: 5. Dismembered.

The case of William Stayley, a Roman Catholic executed in 1678 on a charge of high treason for wishing to kill the King, shows that the portion of the sentence concerning the disposal of the body still held importance in the late seventeenth century. Stayley was executed at Tyburn in the customary manner and his quarters brought back to Newgate to be set up on the gates of the city of London. His relatives petitioned the King 'that he would be graciously pleased that his quarters might be delivered back to them to be privately buried'. Since Stayley had 'behaved himself very penitently' in his latter days, the King granted this request. However, Stayley's relatives 'caused several masses to be said over his quarters, and used other ceremonies according to the manner of the Church of Rome'. On 29 November 'there was made a pompous and great funeral, many people following the corpse to the church of St. Paul Covent Garden, where he was buried'. Charles II was 'justly displeased' and ordered the coroner of Westminster to return the body to Newgate. The churchwardens had to dig up the newly buried corpse, and Stayley's quarters were then set up in the positions originally intended for them on the gates of London.

The treatment of those executed for high treason reveals again a lack of differentiation between the living and the dead body, which seems strange from the point of view of late twentieth-century Britain. This desire to punish the dead corpse once life had been extinguished, which strikes the modern mind as pointless and barbaric, makes sense only against the background of a society in which the decent interment of the dead was a matter of the utmost concern.

This point is particularly clearly illustrated by events which took place shortly after the Restoration. On 30 January 1661, the anniversary of the beheading of Charles I, both Evelyn and Pepys recorded that the bodies of Cromwell, Ireton and Bradshaw, having been disinterred from Westminster Abbey, were solemnly hanged at Tyburn and then buried beneath the gallows. By contrast, the corpse of the Marquis of Montrose, who had been executed in Edinburgh in 1650, and then dismembered, received very different attentions. On 7 January 1661,

after an exact search of his Lordship's bones from amongst the corrupt matter contained in the coffin they were washed in aqua vitae, afterwards being scraped and made clean they were a second time washed . . . and then being dried bone by bone they were anointed with odoriferous oils and balsams . . . and the coffin filled with aromatic and specific powders.

On 4 February some more of Montrose's bones were discovered and similarly treated and on 10 May 'there was a full dressing *de novo* of his lordship's bones, with powders and oils'. The surgeon's bill for all this work came to £400 Scots and the total cost of Montrose's magnificent, if somewhat belated, funeral amounted to £9624 12s Scots (£1 Scots = 1s 8d sterling).[12] This concern at the Restoration to alter the

state of the corpses of all these men, long dead, underlines the importance attached to the correct mode of interment in the early modern
period, whether it be a traitor's burial for rebels or a stately funeral for
a hero.

A crime rather different to modern eyes from treason for which, also,
a particular form of non-Christian burial was meted out, coupled with
the physical punishment of the dead corpse, was suicide. Lord Dyer,
presiding over a case concerning the estate of Sir James Hales, who had
drowned himself in 1554, described suicide as 'an offence against nature,
against God, and against the King'. The eighteenth-century legal
commentator, Blackstone, defined the crime of suicide in similar terms,
as usurping the prerogative of God and depriving the King of one of
his subjects.[13] The second of these two considerations would carry very
little weight in modern Britain where, conversely, the issue, in secular
terms, revolves mainly around the concept of the freedom of the individual.

In early modern England, suicides customarily were interred 'in or
near to the highways with a stake thrust through their bodies, to terrify
all passengers, by that so infamous and reproachful a burial, not to
make such their final passage out of this present world'. It is interesting
that the writer, John Weever, should think that an 'so infamous and
reproachful a burial' might deter a potential suicide where the traditional argument had failed — the

> . . . dread of something after death,
> The undiscover'd country from whose bourn
> No traveller returns . . .

Parish registers sometimes record this grisly ceremony being carried
out; this example comes from Pleasley, Derbyshire, in 1573: 'Tho[mas]
Maule f[oun] d hung on a tree by the wayside after a drunken fit April
3. Coroner's inquest in church porch April 5. Same night at midnight
buried at the highest crossroads with a stake in him, many people from
Mansfield.'

This continued to be the legally prescribed treatment for the bodies
of suicides until 1821. Thomas Hardy made the following entry in his
notebook, after reading a published account of a suicide's burial:

> Girl who committed suicide — was buried on the hill where two
> roads meet: but few followed her to her unblest grave: no coffin:

one girl threw flowers on her: stake driven through her body. Earth heaped round the stake like an ancient tumulus. (This is like Mother's description to me of a similar burial on Hendford Hill, when she was a child.)

As is the case with high treason, the particular form taken by the burial was by no means haphazard, but was based on particular beliefs. Crossroads were chosen in order to diffuse the evil influence of the body in several different directions, thus rendering it less harmful; the stake was to prevent the ghost from walking.

The suicide's burial which Thomas Hardy's mother witnessed must have been one of the last carried out before the Act was passed allowing suicides to be buried in the churchyard between the hours of nine and twelve at night. However, even before the law was changed, mercy had sometimes been shown to the bodies of suicides, as it was for Ophelia:

> . . . her death was doubtful,
> And, but the great command o'ersways the order,
> She should in ground unsanctified have lodg'd
> Till the last trumpet; for charitable prayers,
> Shards, flints, and pebbles should be thrown on her;
> Yet here she is allow'd her virgin crants,
> Her maiden strewments, and the bringing home
> Of bell and burial.

The gravediggers' observations on Ophelia's case probably reflected the contemporary situation:

> If this had not been a gentlewoman she should have
> been buried out o' Christian burial . . . And the more pity
> that great folk should have countenance in this world to
> drown or hang themselves more than their even Christian.

Sometimes, too, the bodies of lesser people who had committed suicide were accorded burial in sanctified ground, often on the north side of the church, which was generally only used for such occasions, the interment being duly recorded in the parish register. In 1597 at Drypole, Yorkshire, 'Anne Ruter a single woman drowned herself and was buried the 4th day of July on the north side of the church.'

At Thorpe Achurch, Northamptonshire, in 1734, 'William Greenwood, a dissenting teacher of March in the Isle of Ely, cut his throat at a public house in our parish, and after the coroner's inquest was buried behind the church.' It was, no doubt, the extreme brutality of the traditional burial rites for suicides which led some clergy to be lenient towards the bodies of these unfortunates.

In 1752 the so-called 'Murder Act' (25 Geo. II c. 37) was passed, making murder a crime for which the criminal's corpse, after execution, received further punishment. The Act reads:

> Whereas the horrid crime of murder has of late been more frequently perpetrated than formerly . . . it is thereby become necessary, that some further terror and peculiar mark of infamy be added to the punishment of death . . . The body of any such murderer shall, if such conviction and execution be in the county of Middlesex or within the city of London . . . be immediately conveyed by the sheriff . . . to the hall of the Surgeons' Company . . . and the body so delivered . . . shall be dissected and anatomised by the said surgeons . . . in no case whatsoever the body of any murderer shall be suffered to be buried, unless after such body shall have been dissected and anatomised as aforesaid.

The choice of this particular way to create a 'further terror and peculiar mark of infamy' shows that the importance attached to decent burial had by no means waned by the mid-eighteenth century. Indeed, the first victim of the Act, Thomas Wilford, was, according to the *London Magazine*, 'taken from the bar weeping and in great agonies, lamenting his sad fate', though it was normally most unusual for a convicted man to break down in this manner.

While it is clear from the wording of the 'Murder Act' that Parliament's sole concern was to make the punishment for murder more effective as a deterrent, the Act had other, unintentional, consequences. By the eighteenth century it had become generally accepted that a training in medicine should include a detailed study of anatomy. However, in a society which differentiated less between the body and the soul, and which held at a premium the decent burial of the dead, it was not easy for the medical profession to obtain the corpses it so badly needed; leaving one's body to science was an alien concept in eighteenth-century Britain. By an Act of 1540, surgeons were allowed the bodies of four criminals a year for 'anatomies'. Although this number was slightly increased by subsequent royal grants, by the eighteenth century only about ten corpses were provided each year.

These bodies occasionally appear in London parish registers; for example at St Martin's, Ludgate, on 20 February 1615, 'was buried an anatomy from the College of Physicians'. To augment their statutory allowance, the hospitals and surgeons resorted to attempting to carry off the bodies of those executed at Tyburn, to the extreme indignation of the onlookers who crowded to watch the hangings. This resentment in part stemmed from the belief about the magical powers of the executed corpse, but was also derived from the bond between condemned criminals and the spectators, who usually both came from the lower social ranks. Scuffles and sometimes even riots resulted from these attempts, and the various medical institutions were forced to distribute a considerable amount of money in payments and bribes. The 'Murder Act', by guaranteeing a reasonable supply of corpses to the Company of Barber Surgeons, helped reduce this problem; thus the intentionally brutal 'peculiar mark of infamy' had, in practice, some beneficial, if unsought-after, consequences.

The 'Murder Act' did not, however, assist the plight of the private teaching hospitals in their search for corpses to anatomise. The new medical attitude towards the dead body was diametrically opposed to the current popular beliefs on the subject, so the surgeons received little sympathy. Bernard Mandeville in 1725 argued in vain that the 'superstitious reverence of the vulgar for a corpse, even of a malefactor, and the strong aversion they have against dissecting them, are prejudicial to the public'.

Unfortunately for the eighteenth-century medical profession, the public's priorities were far from being those of the modern western world on this issue. The private hospitals had, therefore, until 1832, to rely on illegal practices to acquire the necessary bodies. John Flint South, who was a contemporary of John Keats, studying medicine in London in the early nineteenth century, gave a detailed account of the 'resurrection men' who provided the hospital with corpses.

Their principal source of supply was the London churchyards, and some of the cheap private burial grounds in the poorer parts of London. The sextons of those places which were robbed were generally in the pay of the resurrection men, and they afforded every facility they could for the purpose . . . It was not uncommon to engage a house overlooking the burial-place, through and in which the business could be carried on without suspicion. A light cart into which three or four subjects, in as many coarse sacks, could be crammed was the ordinary means of transport, but hackney coaches were not infrequently used for the same purpose. The delivery . . . was more commonly late at night, as the work was generally performed in the evening, soon after darkness had set in . . . They found it most convenient to dig down at the head of the grave, knock in the end of the coffin, and drag the body out. It was then disrobed from the shroud, which was most carefully put back into the coffin, to avoid committing a felony, the disturbance of the grave and taking the corpse being merely a misdemeanour. The subject was then doubled up into the smallest possible compass, and either thrust into a coarse sack or an orange basket . . . and laid aside till as many graves as were convenient had been despoiled.

The diary kept by an unknown resurrectionist, during the years 1811 and 1812, reveals the frequency of these nocturnal depredations. Most nights, when not quarrelling or 'intoxicated', he would be active. A typical entry, for Saturday 30 November 1811, reads: 'At night went and got 3, Bunhill Row [burial ground], sold to Mr Cline, St Thomas's Hospital.'[14] John Flint South added that: 'On the comparatively few occasions when these night workers were caught . . . they were, as might be expected, very severely mauled by the lower classes'. In this case the law was more lenient than popular feeling would have wished, hence the care taken about returning the shrouds; the penalty for body-snatching alone was merely a short term of imprisonment.

The various types of criminal who have been looked at so far were all tried in the civil courts. Unlike the civil courts, the ecclesiastical courts of early modern England were unable to sentence people to death, but they exercised considerable social control through their most severe form of punishment, excommunication. As with certain death sentences, excommunication also resulted in the offender not receiving Christian burial. Francis Tate, in 1600, wrote that excommunicates were buried 'without the bounds of the churchyard . . . or in the limits and meres of the parish'. This was quite often in practice the case; at Albrighton, Shropshire, as the parish register records, 'Isabel Keames of the Park Side, widow, deceased the 18th day of August and was buried in the hall orchard near unto the church wall upon the west side thereof, the 20th day of August Anno Dom[ini] 1619, being an excommunicated person.'

In some dioceses, if this law were neglected, the parish concerned was made to suffer; at Weedon Beck, Northamptonshire, in 1615, 'William Radhouse the elder dying excommunicate was buried by stealth in the night time in the churchyard 29 January. Wherefore the church was interdicted for a fortnight.'

However, some bishops and their clergy were prepared to tolerate the burial of excommunicates in the churchyard if it were by night; the parish register of Hathersage, Derbyshire, records the night burials of 13 excommunicated Roman Catholics in the churchyard during the years 1629, 1630 and 1631. While allowed to lie in consecrated ground, these excommunicates were not permitted proper Christian burial. In 1604 at Christchurch, Hampshire, 'Christian Steevens, the wife of Thomas Steevens, was buried in childbirth, and buried by women for she was a papist.'

An excommunicated person could receive Christian burial, however, if the bishop was prepared to grant a faculty for the burial. To obtain this was quite expensive; in 1632 the faculty to bury Elizabeth Hide of Cumnor, Berkshire, 'being a person excommunicate at the time of the life and death of the deceased', cost £1 5s. Nor was a faculty always granted, as this entry in the parish register of Leeds in 1604 reveals:

> Richard Lumbye . . . being a papist not coming to the church the space of 12 years . . . excommunicate, died at Chapeltown the third day of December, and was by his kinsfolk and neighbours brought towards the church to be buried, but at the churchyard gate stopped by the curate and churchwardens where his corpse remained till the seventh day of the same month at night, and his friends could not get a licence to bury him; going to York for that purpose, his said corpse was in the night conveyed and buried.

The Puritan sect of Brownists objected strongly to the practice of the 'absolving of men dying excommunicate after they be dead, and before they may have Christian burial', saying that it suggested a belief in purgatory. Bishop Hall, in reply, defended the practice as being 'but a liberty given by the Church . . . of all those external rites of decent funeral'. To men and women in early modern England 'those external rites of decent funeral' held such importance that even those whom, while alive, the church had disowned, were sometimes brought back into the fold for their burials, as an act of mercy.

The same disparity between official policy and popular attitudes, which emerged concerning the burials of executed criminals, is also to be found when considering the funerals of those who died of the plague. The general policy adopted by the authorities is summed up in an injunction made in 1542 by Bonner, Bishop of London, who decreed, 'that in plague time, no dead bodies or corpses be brought into the church, except it be brought straight to the grave, and immediately buried, whereby the people may the rather avoid infection'.

This type of ruling may be seen in practice in the probate account of Leonard Culmer of Sandwich, Kent, who died in 1642. A funeral sermon was commissioned to be preached at his burial, but was 'contradicted by the mayor of Sandwich because of the . . . infection of the plague'. The preacher, however, still received 5s 'for his study'.

To modern ways of thinking, these regulations seem eminently sensible. In time of epidemic, the most important priority is to avoid spreading the disease, and the prevention of people from meeting together to bury an infected corpse appears to be an obvious and necessary step towards achieving this aim. However, this line of argument was by no means as obvious in pre-industrial England. Pepys wrote in the first week of September 1665: 'But Lord! to consider the madness of the people of the town, who will (because they are forbid) come in crowds along with the dead corpses to see them buried . . . at least forty or fifty people going along with every one of them.'

It was not that the danger arising from contact was not appreciated; indeed, the established procedure was to lock up an infected house with all its residents incarcerated within it. Rather, this lack of concern for the risks run by guests at a funeral was the result of the tremendous emphasis placed on decent burial; the desire to perform the correct rituals outweighed all considerations of safety and hygiene. In fact, it might well have been that, in the crisis of plague-time, the customary rituals took on an even greater significance than under normal circumstances.

Plague-time burials still included the sharing of food and drink after the interment. What was, under ordinary conditions, an important healing ritual for the survivors was transformed by the epidemic into a highly possible passport to death. At the burial of one plague victim, Adrian Ledbury of Oxford, in 1644, wine and cakes costing £1 5s were served, and at the funeral of Catherine de Roo of Sandwich, bread, beer and wine to the sum of 30s 2d were provided. Interestingly, in one case where people were unwilling to carry a victim to burial for fear of infection, they still met together to listen to a sermon and to participate in a 'drinking'.

The prevalent attitude towards the burial of plague victims is very clearly shown by the title page of the tract *London's Lamentation . . . wherein is described certain causes of this affliction and visitation of the plague year 1641* (see Plate 1, p. 124). The page is decorated with two scenes. One is labelled 'London's Charity', and depicts a corpse being carried by four pall-bearers to be buried in a churchyard, with over a dozen mourners following, some holding sprigs of rosemary. The other scene, 'The Country's Cruelty', shows the dead being dragged towards a large pit, either on a sledge or simply pulled along the ground at the end of a lengthy pike. Although this second method of disposal may well have been the more hygienic, the first was definitely more acceptable to many men and women in early modern England. Indeed, the evidence of probate accounts would suggest that both in rural and urban areas traditional rites were maintained in plague times, and that 'The Country's Cruelty' was more propaganda than fact.

When a plague outbreak became really severe it was sometimes necessary to bury the dead in unsanctified ground, if only because the churchyards were already filled. At Great Hampden, Buckinghamshire, the vicar, Robert Lenthall, recorded in 1647 in the parish register that he had to bury most of his family 'in the mead called the kitchen mead, by the hedgeside as you go down into it on your left hand, a little below the pond at the entrance into the mead'. On 11 August his daughter Sarah was buried, 'aged 14 years 11 months and 17 days'; sixteen days later her mother, Susanna, was laid beside her, and two days after that, a child who lived at the house was interred there too. On 2 September the vicar records burying 'Adrian Lenthall my son a hopeful young man . . . one and twenty years of age . . . at the head of his sister Sarah's grave'. On 25 September the tragedy was completed with the interment of the vicar's 'cousin John Pickering a lad of about 13 years of age'.

Although in such cases burial in unsanctified ground became a necessity, it was in general avoided as far as possible. A rather embittered inscription on the tombstone of a plague victim, set up in 1646 in a field at Taxal, Cheshire, reads:

Think it not strange my bones lie here
Thine may lie thou knowest not where.[15]

There were, of course, some occasions on which people were primarily concerned for their own safety. The parish register of Cranbrook, Kent, records for the year 1597:

Now also this year others of the plague who were buried near to their several dwellings, because they could get none to carry them into the church, for it was the beginning of this infection, so that none would venture themselves.

However, it is interesting that, as the course of the outbreak progressed, the people of Cranbrook felt more willing to bury the dead in the churchyard. After the initial shock, the deeper-rooted beliefs seem to have reasserted themselves. Plague outbreaks provide a touchstone against which to measure the strength of commitment to the traditional and customary burial rites in early modern England. It is a remarkable testimony to the intensity of feeling about decent funerals that these were still carried out despite the extreme disruption and danger posed by plague.

Children who died in pre-industrial England received, despite the shortness of their lives, burials similar to those of adults. It might have been thought that, since the death of a child was a reasonably common event, their burials would have been less elaborate than those of their elders. This is the case in some primitive societies, a fact which has led certain anthropologists to suggest that the degree of grandeur of a person's funeral directly reflects his or her status in that society, and that this, in turn, corresponds to the intensity of loss felt at the person's death.[16] However, the evidence concerning the burial of children in early modern England shows that this concept by no means universally holds true.

Even after the burial of a pauper child, a small 'drinking' was often provided by the parish. Slightly higher up the social scale, at the funeral of George Dawson, aged four, who died at Lincoln in 1625, bread, beer, 'victuals' and a winding sheet were provided. The cost was a meagre 3s, but then George's father, a waterman, himself left goods worth only £6. In 1648 a serving boy was drowned with his master, Stephen Hudson, in Kent, and was interred at a cost of £3 7s.

Rachel Flintham, the daughter of a Lincolnshire yeoman, who died 'during her minority' in 1638, received a burial costing £4 10s, while in the same year and county, Margaret and Dorothy, the children of Mary Copledike, were interred together at a cost of £14 2s 4d. A more detailed breakdown of expenditure is available for the funeral of Thomasine Stredwick of Ivychurch, Kent, again in 1638. She was coffined and buried in the chancel and a funeral sermon was preached over her corpse. Six pairs of gloves were given to those who carried her body to church, while the other guests received ribbons. After the service, wine, beer and cakes were provided; the total cost of her burial came to

£3 10s 11d.

On occasion, the burial of a child could be an extremely elaborate affair, as the funeral rites of an unnamed girl, who died in Edinburgh in 1634, clearly show. The crafts, or guilds, of the city were present at the ceremony. This was followed by a considerable drinking at which beer, wine, shortbread and tobacco were served, while a dole was given to the poor and to prisoners in the tollbooth. A black velvet pall was hired to cover her coffin, which was carried to the kirk by the city's bellman. The total expenditure on the magnificent affair came to £231 11s 6d Scots.[17]

One reason for these elaborate, or at least respectable, funerals accorded to children in the early modern period was the genuine grief felt by parents at the loss of their sons and daughters. Although such deaths were far more common than in twentieth-century Britain, they were none the less painful. This is how John Evelyn described the death and burial of his son Richard in January 1658:

> After six fits of a quartain ague with which it pleased God to visit him, died my dear son Richard, to our inexpressible grief and affliction, 5 years and 3 days old only; but at that tender age a prodigy for wit and understanding; for beauty of body a very angel; for endowment of mind of incredible and rare hopes . . . I suffered him to be opened, when they found that he was what is vulgarly called liver-grown. I caused his body to be coffined in lead and reposited on the 30th at 8 o'clock that night in the church of Deptford, accompanied with divers of my relations and neighbours, among whom I distributed rings with this motto, *Dominus Abstulit* [the Lord has taken away] intending, God willing, to have him transported with my own body to be interred in our dormitory [vault] in Wooton Church . . . to lay my bones and to mingle my dust with my fathers.

The burial of little babies, however, occasioned rather less grief than is generally the case in modern Britain. Their parents were less attached to them, obviously in part because of the shortness of their life-spans, but also by way of a deliberate policy. Since mortality in the first year of life was particularly high, the emotional suffering would have been too intense if a really firm bond were established between every child and its parents during the first precarious few months of its existence. John Evelyn, less than three weeks after the death of five-year-old Richard, made the following brief and simple entry in his diary:

The afflicting hand of God being still upon us, it pleased Him also to take away from us this morning my youngest son, George, now 7 weeks languishing at nurse, breeding teeth, and ending in a dropsy. God's holy will be done! He was buried in Deptford Church the 17th following.

The practice among richer parents of employing wet-nurses for their children, no doubt partly occasioned by an unwillingness to become too attached to a child who might then die, in itself helped to maintain the high mortality rate among babies. Lawrence Stone has estimated that the mortality rate for 'nurse children', as they were called, was about twice that for maternally fed infants.[18] Parish registers bear witness to the popularity of sending London children to wet-nurses in the country; places like Lewisham, Sydenham and Orpington were all regularly chosen. The registers of Mitcham, Surrey, record the burial of several such infants during Elizabeth I's reign; for example, in 1590, 'Elizabeth Beresley a nurse child of London her father being a joiner born in St Olave's parish, bur[ied] Nov[ember] 13'. The decline of the practice of wet-nursing from the late seventeenth century onwards is one small facet in the development of individualism and the growth of family feeling, in this instance going hand in hand with improvements in the life expectancy of young children.

Although grief may have been rather less when a small infant died in early modern England, the burial ceremonies for these babies were still decently observed. Infants who died before their mothers had been churched were buried in their chrysoms, pieces of white cloth held round the body with bands or pins. The chrysom was what the child had worn at its baptism and these babies were often referred to as chrysom children. In the registers of Westminster Abbey is recorded: 'The Princess Ann's child a chrysom bur[ied] in the vault Oct[ober] 22 1687.' While the death of small babies was an expected occurrence in early modern England and the loss felt either socially or personally was kept to a minimum, it is significant that their burial rituals still followed the traditional pattern, the customary decencies being rigorously carried out.

In stark contrast with the respectable burials of other children, or, indeed of many of the various groups of unfortunates examined so far, stands the treatment of the bodies of stillborn babies. It was necessary to include the following clause in the oath sworn by many seventeenth-century midwives:

If any child be deadborn, you yourself shall see it buried in such secret place as neither hog, dog nor any other beast may come unto it . . . you shall not suffer any such child to be cast into the lanes or any other inconvenient place.[19]

This one hinted-at exception to the almost universal rule of decent burial in early modern England underlines the fact that funerals were not simply carried out to dispose of the unwanted body. If this had been the case, all corpses would have been treated in the same manner as these unfortunate stillborn children, whose remains, clearly, were sometimes eaten by animals or left to rot by the wayside.

The treatment which their corpses received suggests that these babies were barely considered to be human beings. The vital distinction between these and other children, or indeed any of the groups of unfortunates, was that the stillborn babies had not received baptism. In early modern England, life, certainly in the recognised social sense, was felt to begin at baptism, and, at least in the cases of debtors or executed criminals, to end at burial rather than at physical death. As with funerals, the social aspect of baptism was at least as important as its religious function. One of the changes in attitude from this period onwards has been the gradual pushing back of the moment at which life is thought to begin, from baptism, to birth and, still further back, to conception. This issue, central to the late twentieth-century debate concerning the ethics of abortion, has its roots in the development, and then ascendancy, of the philosophy of individualism.

The crucial significance of baptism is shown by the power which the church vested in midwives to baptise the newly born if there were any danger of death. This action would allow the child Christian burial. At North Elmham, Norfolk, in 1555, 'the 2 children of John Brow and Agnes his wife were christened by the midwife at home the 16 day of April, and were buried that same day, it was Easter Tuesday.'

Sometimes this hasty baptism by the midwife could lead to mistakes; in Hanwell, Middlesex, in 1731, 'Thomas, son of Thomas Messenger and Elizabeth his wife, was born and baptised Oct[ober] 24 by the midwife at the font called a boy and named by the godfather Thomas, but proved a girl.' To avoid confusions of this sort, especially in dire emergencies when it was impossible to delay long enough even to choose a name, some sixteenth-century midwives called the child 'Creature of Christ' or just 'Creature', after a verse in Corinthians. It was a strange name to carry through life for those who did live; in 1579 a Creature Cheeseman married John Haffynden of Staplehurst, Kent. However, for the many who did not survive the trauma of their entry into the world, this name made all the difference between proper burial in the churchyard and, at best, being laid by the midwife in some 'secret place', or even being thrown on to the rubbish tip.

The difference in attitudes towards baptised and unbaptised infants is shown in the iconography of the memorial brass of Elizabeth Franklin, who died in childbed in 1622 and was buried in St Cross, Oxford. She is shown sitting in bed, surrounded by her dead babies. The one who had been baptised appears in chrysom clothes with a bare face, but those who died unbaptised are depicted totally enveloped in shrouds, with no visible human characteristics. Although the life-spans of these children may have varied literally by a matter of minutes, the distinction, to the people of early modern England, was immense.

From this evidence concerning the funerals of the unfortunate, it is now time to turn and look at the burials accorded to the great majority of the population. This study of the interments of those on the fringes of society in early modern England has revealed, many times over, the great emphasis placed on decent burial during this period, even for undesirables and social outcasts. It has also touched on a few of the significant differences in attitude to be found in a society where individualism was not so highly prized as it is in modern Britain. Also, some of the social functions performed by the funeral ritual have become apparent through examining these particular people's burials. These themes, and many others, must now be traced in the funeral rites of the ordinary men and women of early modern England.

Notes

1. Quoted in Linebaugh, 'The Tyburn Riot against the Surgeons', in *Albion's Fatal Tree*, pp. 82-3. This essay discusses in detail popular responses to executions and the development of anatomical dissection.

2. Ibid., p. 81.

3. Paupers' burial from overseers' of the poor accounts for Lincolnshire, Kent and Oxford. Coffin at St Alphage, London Wall, described in Cox, *Churchwardens' Accounts*, p. 173.

4. *Journals of the House of Commons*, vol. xxv, p. 274.

5. Quotations of 1721 and 1774 from George, *London Life*, p. 353.

6. Quoted in Picton, *City of Liverpool*, i. p. 234.

7. Burn, *Ecclesiastical Law*, iv. p. 289.

8. Quoted in Emmison, *Elizabethan Life*, p. 174.

9. Anon., *Prison of Ludgate*, p. 60.

10. London, British Library: MS. Lansdowne 79, No. 74.

11. Linebaugh states that more than three-quarters of those executed at Tyburn were aged between 20 and 30; Linebaugh in *Albion's Fatal Tree*, p. 116.

12. Edinburgh, Register House: RH 91/38.

13. Dyer and Blackstone, quoted in Ives, *History of Penal Methods*, p. 289.

14. Bailey, ed., *Diary of a Resurrectionist*, p. 139.

15. Quoted in Cox, *Parish Registers*, p. 164.

16. Blauner, 'Death and Social Structure', *Psychiatry*, vol. xxix.

17. Edinburgh, Register House: RH9/1/24/2.

18. Stone, *Family, Sex and Marriage*, p. 81.

19. Oxford, Bodleian Library: MS. Oxford Archdeaconry Papers, Berks. C. 162, fol. 82r. I am indebted to Charles Webster for bringing this to my attention.

4 'LET'S CHOOSE EXECUTORS'

The period from the mid-sixteenth century to, roughly, the mid-
eighteenth century, marks the zenith of the bereaved's control over the
funeral rituals of relatives and friends. The power was, at least legally,
if not always in practice, vested in the dead person's executor. Before
the Reformation, as has been seen, the dying took considerable interest
in their own funeral preparations and laid down, often in great detail,
directions to be followed by their executors. The rationale for this
concern about one's own funeral was simply swept away in the
doctrinal changes at the Reformation; with it went, for the most part,
testators' interest and control in this area. From the late seventeenth
century onwards, the development of the undertaking profession began
to curtail much of the executors' decision-making power. Although
nominally providing their clients with a range of options from which to
choose, undertakers were able to bring considerable pressure to bear on
those who availed themselves of this service, and it was the undertaker,
rather than client, who really called the tune.

The two hundred or so years during which executors were primarily
responsible for decisions about the conduct of funerals provide a
unique opportunity to study the relationship between the bereaved and
the choice of ritual carried out at a burial. Many different factors influenced this relationship; the dictates of ecclesiastical authority obviously
shaped, in the majority of cases, at least the actual interment itself. A
very powerful influence was the effect of tradition and custom on
burial practices. Indeed, it is doubtful whether many of the bereaved
actually saw themselves as making conscious choices concerning
funerals, but rather were simply carrying out what was customarily
agreed to be appropriate. However, these customs were gradually modified by the users, possibly quite unthinkingly at times, in response to
changing attitudes and circumstances. These rituals provide an indication of the prevailing *mentalité* concerning death and the disposal of
the dead, as well as reflecting particular people's attitudes.

One important factor, it might be supposed, would be any directions
the deceased had left concerning the funeral; since such directions were
comparatively uncommon, it might seem likely that they would be
respected. Usually, of course, the matter was quite straightforward and

was easily carried out by the executor, for instance a request in a will for burial in a particular parish or in a certain spot in the church or churchyard. One particularly interesting feature of these requests was a desire to be buried next to or near a relative. To give some Kentish examples, Thomas Rucke, in 1607, willed to be buried 'as near to the body of my father as conveniently I may'; Margaret Parker wanted to be interred 'near my first husband Robinson', and John Dean, a bachelor, desired 'to lie amongst his ancestors'. These requests reveal a mental map of the church very different from that which prevailed in pre-Reformation England, when testators usually described their chosen burial places with reference to the nearest altar, saint's statue or light. After the Reformation, areas of the church became identified as the resting place of particular families, suggesting a new orientation, more secular and familial, in the face of death.

Rather less frequently, requests were made in wills for a sermon to be preached, a dole to be distributed, or a 'drinking' held for relatives and friends of the deceased. These requests, too, were generally carried out more or less faithfully. For example, Richard Wible in his will, dated 1586, ordered that bread, beer and one cheese should be given to the poor at his burial; the executor's account records the purchase of the bread and the beer, at a cost of 12s 4d, but it seems that the poor did not receive the cheese.

Deathbed wishes were subject to the consent not just of the executor but of all parties interested in the will. These wishes were usually expressed verbally; often a dole for the poor was requested. It is tempting to see in these charitable bequests a belief in the efficacy of a last-minute bid for salvation, a doctrine which had officially been swept away at the Reformation. For whatever reason they were made, people seem to have been prepared to forgo some of their inheritance so that the last requests of their dead relatives might be fulfilled.

However there were certain notable occasions on which executors deliberately ignored the express wishes of the dead, even though these were clearly set out in their wills. This action, on the part of the executors, was in fact legal, since the funeral directions in a will were, and indeed still are, unenforceable in law, but merely serve to indicate the deceased's desires. One such case of flagrant disregard concerns the will of Joseph Hall, Bishop of Norwich, who was a fierce opponent of the practice of interring corpses in churches. Despite very clear directions to the contrary, his executors had him buried in the chancel of Heigham Church, Norfolk, in 1656. Another bishop, James Montague, willed in 1618 that his funeral was not to cost more than £400, and that on no account was his corpse to suffer 'any cutting or mangling'. His brother Charles, the chief executor, having distributed the legacies, wrote: 'My care is how to perform the [funeral], which God willing I will do to the uttermost of all he left, and add of my own to it if there be cause.'[1] The bishop's body was disembowelled, embalmed and then buried at a total cost of £940 18s 11d.

Examples may be found of a similar disregard for the wishes of the dead among people of rather more humble origin than the two bishops. Mary Knight of Canterbury in 1618 left in her will 5s for her coffin and a further 50s to cover the remaining burial charges and to pay for a drinking. Her son George, however, spent no less than £14 16s of her estate on the funeral. Margaret Parker of Sandwich willed in 1608, 'that there shall be bestowed upon a dinner for such as shall accompany my corpse to the grave, and other needful funeral expenses that day, twenty marks of lawful money of England'. In the event, almost precisely double that amount was actually spent.

Why should executors so flagrantly disregard the deceased's directions in this way? That it was a reasonably widespread practice is revealed by John Weever, who felt it necessary to discuss the problem in his *Ancient Funerall Monuments*; significantly, he condones the executors' decisions: 'Although all these ceremonies be despised by our parents on their deathbeds, yet should they not be neglected by us their children, or nearest of kindred upon their interments.' To Weever, those testators who asked for cheaper or simpler funeral rituals were undervaluing themselves and therefore the executor's duty was to ignore requests motivated by modesty. This certainly seems to be the sentiment which underlay Charles Montague's decision to spend so much on his brother's funeral, despite the bishop's directions to the contrary. Indeed, lavish expenditure on funerals could be seen as an outlet through which the bereaved were able to express their sorrow and feelings of helplessness and loss.

However, these altruistic motives do not comprise the whole story. Another factor influencing executors was a great unwillingness to break with tradition. This may well explain the actions of the executors of Joseph Hall. As bishops were traditionally buried within the walls of a cathedral or church, the executors were not prepared to take it upon themselves to follow his own directions and diverge from customary practice.

At the heart of all these decisions by executors lay value-judgements concerning what was due by way of funeral rites, according to the status of the deceased. Status was a complex issue, not least because of the difficulty of defining it. On one level, an executor's decision that the burial must reflect the deceased's status can be viewed as a mark of respect and concern for the dead person's memory. However, by implication, the funeral also reflected on the social standing of the surviving family, so that a public display of the deceased's status necessarily benefited the bereaved too. It is therefore impossible exactly to distinguish altruistic from selfish motives on the part of executors.

Nor was burial according to status simply the concern of individuals and their families; it had a political dimension, too. At the highest social levels, funeral rituals were symbolic of the power of the ruling class and helped to reinforce their superiority; that was why they had to be so closely regulated by the College of Arms, a matter to which Elizabeth I devoted much attention. Throughout society, funerals served to maintain the status quo and to reaffirm the traditional hierarchy of power and prestige. The conservatism of funeral practices reflected their role in maintaining social stability, through public display of social gradations. For this, and for the other reasons already mentioned, it was difficult to persuade an executor to carry out a funeral with less pomp than was commonly considered appropriate for a person of that status.

The great majority of people, of course, fully accepted and, indeed, would never have questioned the belief that funeral grandeur should be commensurate with the deceased's social status. In several funeral accounts the sum spent on the burial is qualified by such phrases as 'she living and dying a gentlewoman', 'he being an ancient minister' or, more simply, the deceased being 'of good rank', 'of good repute' or 'living in good esteem'. Both sides in the theological debate about death, outlined in Chapter 2, were united in their agreement that funeral rituals should reflect the status of the deceased. The *Directory* allowed for 'civil respects' to be shown at the burial, while Richard Hooker wrote, in reference to the display of worldly honours at funerals, that 'some man's estate may require a great deal more according as the fashion ... where he dieth doth afford'. Anthropologists have noted the correlation between social status and funeral grandeur in widely differing cultures. It has been suggested that funeral rituals, in pre-industrial societies, should be regarded as 'work' necessary to restore the breach caused by the death of a member. The higher the deceased's social standing, the more disruption is caused by his death and so the greater the restorative rituals have to be to return society to its normal functioning.[2] This analysis presupposes a cohesive social structure where individuality is subordinate to the welfare of the wider group; it is the disintegration of such a society that underlies the changes in funeral ritual traced in this book.

A fascinating insight into the way that status actually affected the decisions concerning a funeral in early modern England is given in a letter from John Chamberlain to Dudley Carleton, written on 5 January 1608. Chamberlain's brother, Robert, had recently died and John, although having declined the executorship, was involved in planning the burial. The letter reveals the necessity of fulfilling traditional expectations coupled with the need to maintain a position in a socially competitive world. Chamberlain wrote:

> I am much busied and troubled about it [the burial] with Clarenceux [King of Arms] and otherwise, but if I might have had my will there should have been less ado, for of all things I love not show or ostentation, but there be so many precedents of very fresh date of his equals and inferiors, that it could not be well avoided. But the worst is the charge will be very great and riseth above a thousand marks which is too, too much for a private man.

Others shared Chamberlain's distress over the amount of money seemingly wasted on funerals commensurate with the deceased's status. Robert, Second Earl of Dorset, making his will in the same year that John Chamberlain was despairing over his brother's funeral costs, directed that he was to be buried

> without blacks or great solemnity of funeral but in a Christian manner as other people are of meaner sort, because the usual solemnities of funeral such as heralds set down for noble men are only good for the heralds and drapers and very prejudicial to the children, servants and friends of the deceased and to the poor which inhabit there about, towards all which the deceased might otherwise be more liberal, and therefore as I said before I earnestly desire mine executors that they use no such solemnities at my burial.

Francis Willis, the third president of St John's College, Oxford, made the unusual request that he was 'not to be buried according to the estate in which I have lived but according to the proportion of my goods which I shall leave behind me at the time of my death and no other wise for I would not by my will leave my wife in debt'.

The lengthy explanations, which these two men felt it necessary to give, emphasise the strangeness of their request that wealth, rather than status, should determine their funeral pomp. In fact, money was very little considered during preparations for a funeral; as has been seen in the case of debtors, by law the funeral was to be arranged without the debts being taken into account. Most of the examples of testators' wishes being ignored, quoted above, involve the executors spending far more money than the deceased had directed. It is therefore not surprising that the Earl of Dorset and Francis Willis both expressed their wishes with some vehemence.

Their words also illustrate the fact that there was no obvious and direct relationship between wealth and status in early modern England. Particular status groupings, such as 'yeomen' or 'gentlemen', contained within them people of widely different wealth and, indeed, some yeomen were actually more wealthy than certain gentlemen, although they were still lower in social status. A similar pattern is found when considering the funeral costs of people in different social classes, at least below the ranks of the aristocracy. It is impossible to categorise, say, esquires' funerals or yeomen's funerals in financial terms at all. For example, within a group of 121 Kent gentlemen buried between 1580 and 1640, the funeral costs ranged from 15s to about £150, and were widely scattered in between. Among 25 knights and esquires in the same county there was a difference of more than £130 between the cheapest and the most expensive funeral, again with considerable variation between the two extremes. There was also a noticeable overlap between the funeral costs of one social group and another; a handful of the 101 yeomen in the Kent sample had funerals costing more than £20 when the average funeral of a gentleman cost not much over £5 (see Table 1, p. 239).

One fact which emerges clearly from an analysis of a large sample of funeral costs incurred in four counties, Kent, Berkshire, Lincolnshire and Somerset, is that those with the least in terms of worldly goods cost proportionally the greatest amount to bury; of the poorest testators' estates, between 12 and 20 per cent was expended on the funeral (see Table 2, p. 239). However, the dominant impression gained from the available statistics concerning funeral costs in early modern England is their great range and lack of standardisation.[3] This, by implication, suggests considerable freedom of choice, at least in financial terms, on the part of executors. One reason was that money alone could not procure the prestige of the funeral; this came from the numbers of people attending it and, if many came voluntarily, great kudos could be obtained at next to no cost.

The situation of the aristocracy with regard to funeral expenditure was rather different because the College of Arms was responsible for their burials. The heralds tried to enforce a clearly stratified code of funeral pomp based on status, which effectively determined the cost of burial for each different rank. The resentment this caused has already been seen in relation to the Second Earl of Dorset's will and, slightly less overtly, in Chamberlain's letter to Carleton. Indeed, resentment grew so strong that there was, during the first half of the seventeenth century, a major aristocratic revolt against the tyranny of the College of Arms in matters funereal; thereafter a less standardised regime prevailed, enabling the testators themselves or those bereaved to determine the form of the ritual.

While some people, including the Second Earl of Dorset, and Bishops Montague and Hall, favoured simpler burials than convention demanded, another group, conversely, explicitly attempted to use funerals to advance their standing in the social order. In these latter cases, however, the initiative more frequently lay with the bereaved, who had the most to gain from such shows of ostentation. As has already been suggested, it would be impossible to identify such attempts at social climbing purely in terms of the money spent on the funerals. However, there are certain specific items of expenditure which reveal that non-aristocratic families were aping their social superiors. John Weever, complaining about one such attempt, voiced distinctly the important belief that social status did not reflect wealth alone. He wrote:

> Sepulchres should be made according to the quality and degree of the person deceased . . . which is not observed altogether in these times: for by some of our epitaphs more honour is attributed to a rich *quondam* tradesman or griping usurer than is given to the greatest potentate entombed in Westminster.

Another sphere in which the upper classes were copied by their inferiors was called into question by the Puritan writer Henry Barrow: 'How can they prove it now lawful to disbowel and embalm every rich glutton where his burying place is hard by, and there is no cause either to keep or remove him?' In the instances criticised by Barrow, embalming had been divorced from its original *raison d'être* — to allow time for the preparation of an elaborate or distant funeral — and had become simply a matter of social prestige and snobbery.

The imitation of aristocratic ritual to gain social advancement is also displayed in the illegal use of heraldry at some funerals. All heraldic display at funerals was controlled by the College of Arms; if any 'arms . . . shall be set up or erected at any . . . burial or interment without such authority and assent first had and obtained . . . then it shall be lawful for [the heralds] to raze, deface and pull down the same being so used'.[4]

However, of the 28 burial accounts in the four counties during the first half of the seventeenth century which record the purchase of heraldic 'escutcheons', only six also mention the obligatory payment of fees to the heralds. Among the Kentish funerals with illegal heraldic displays was that of Mary Dunkin, in 1621, for which a painter named Parkinson supplied escutcheons; these were likely to have been small shields of arms painted on buckram and hung around the church. For the burial of George Man at St Dunstan's, Canterbury, in 1637, the painter received £1 for escutcheons and a further 10s for 'a fair escutcheon to hang over the grave', probably a funeral hatchment.

The College of Arms waged a constant battle against illegal painters of funerary shields. Although some of those people entitled to display a coat of arms were simply bypassing the heralds to avoid the fees, others were using arms to which they had no entitlement. In 1624, a painter, Robert Kirby, was imprisoned in the Marshalsea for carrying out 'work at funerals without consent and allowance of the Officers of Arms', including some which was 'performed erroneously and falsely'. When he was warned by the heralds 'that he should desist . . . he . . . did give ill language to the parties who so warned him, saying he would do it, do what they could'.[5] John Weever, speaking on the heralds' behalf, derided the 'ignorant country painter', pointing out that 'many and great errors are daily committed to the great offense and prejudice of the ancient nobility and gentry of this kingdom, and to the breeding of many ambiguous doubts and questions'. The social and political dangers attendant on the illegal use of heraldry at funerals are hinted at in the ominous tone of Weever's words. To Weever, the role played by funerals in the maintenance of social stability was unequivocal.

One other area in which some people aped their social superiors was in the adoption, during the first half of the seventeenth century, of burial by night. For the aristocracy, the development of night funerals represented a revolt against the suffocating strictures of the College of Arms and, in particular, against the heraldic funeral, repugnant both in terms of its ideology and its cost. However, lower down the social scale, there was no such motivation to adopt night burials; it was simply a fashionable craze involving, in fact, greater expense than daytime interment. An entry in the account of Barbara Mainwaring's funeral, dated 1626, reads:'Item for torches to attend the deceased's corpse to church (she being buried in the evening) 12s.'

At Clement Stronghill's burial in New Romney in 1638, 40s was spent on torches and links, 'he being interred in the night or evening time'. The illumination of these funerals was not the only additional expense; the customary burial fees demanded by the church were usually doubled if the funeral was held at night. Presumably, however, these extra expenses were felt, by some people at least, to be worth paying, to acquire the status-enhancing quality that such excursions into essentially aristocratic territory were felt to bring.

The vast majority of executors were content to follow tradition and provide funerals commensurate with the social status of the deceased. It must be remembered that anyone called upon to act as executor would have attended a great many funerals since childhood and would thus be familiar with the whole process of burial. In 1702, the Reverend Matthew Henry noted as unusual the fact that none of his close relatives had died within the last three years, adding that 'since I set out in the world, I was never so long without the death of children or others near and dear to me'.[6] The number of people present at a funeral was often very large and the guests encompassed a wide social range; one Berkshire funeral account records, simply, that 'the people of Boxworth' were present at the funeral. Extensive experience of funerals no doubt aided executors in the task that faced them, and the aspirations of many executors could be summed up in Jeremy Taylor's words, written in 1651, concerning the burial of a corpse:

> Let it be interred after the manner of the country and the laws of the place, and the dignity of the person . . . so far is piety: beyond it may be the ostentation and bragging of a grief . . . In this as in everything else, as our piety must not pass into superstition or vain expense, so neither must the excess be turned into parsimony and chastised by negligence and impieties to the memory of their dead.

The most striking difference between preparing for a funeral during the Tudor and Stuart periods and making similar preparation: today lies in the services provided by the undertaker, a profession not known until the very last years of the seventeenth century and at first found only in London. Indeed, in many rural areas there was insufficient work to support a specialist undertaker until the development of the motor car made travelling easier. Before this, undertaking was simply a sideline of another business such as carpentry. This meant that country people tended to remain, until well into the twentieth century, less affected by the changes brought about by the professional undertaker than were their urban contemporaries. A new geographical distribution of funerary practices was created overlaying, but not replacing, the older demarcation of the north and west from the south and east with a differentiation between urban and rural practices.

During the early modern period, the influence of the undertaker was principally felt in London, where the profession originated. However, the implications of the development reached far beyond the metropolis and helped to shape the funeral code of Victorian England, a code which, in some respects, is still with us today.

The rationale for relying on a single purveyor of all things necessary for a funeral was, in itself, sound and apparently beneficial to hard-pressed executors. For instance, to organise the funeral of Sir Hannibal Baskerville of Sunningwell, Berkshire, in 1670, 17 different suppliers had to be contacted for goods ranging from mourning hats and rings to cakes and beer; and this figure did not include ordering the coffin and shroud or making arrangements with the minister, gravediggers, ringers and so forth. Nor was Sir Hannibal's funeral outstandingly lavish for its time. It certainly would have been considerably easier to contact an undertaker and, in the words of one eighteenth-century advertisement, be

> accommodated with all things for a funeral as well the meanest as those of greater ability upon reasonable terms, more particularly, coffins, shroud, palls, cloaks, sconces . . . hangings for rooms, heraldry, hearse and coaches, gloves, with all other things not here mentioned . . . [7]

However, it could be argued that, psychologically, it would be better for the bereaved to have to organise the funeral themselves and so, perhaps, avoid the feelings of lethargy and uselessness not infrequently reported by the newly bereaved today. A similar sentiment afflicted William Jones, the Vicar of Broxbourne, on the death of his daughter Caroline in 1807:

> After feeling myself almost moped and melancholy with. . . contemplating the corpse of my daughter, I wandered round the churchyard, for which I was reproved, not very gently, by my *punctilious*

wife, as having done very wrong; for 'I ought not to appear out of my own doors for two or three days.'

The undertaking profession reinforced the social withdrawal of the bereaved, as favoured so strongly at the beginning of the nineteenth century by Mrs Jones, by carrying out the practical tasks which were once the responsibility of surviving relatives.

The first known undertaker, a painter and coffin maker named William Russell, entered into an agreement with the College of Arms in 1689 whereby its members would attend the funerals he organised, for a fee.[8] However, within ten years, undertakers had started to usurp the functions of heralds at funerals, acting as masters of ceremonies as well as supplying all necessary paraphernalia. Gradually, undertakers began to dictate the form of the ritual, particularly the quantity of trappings to be used, in very much the same way as the heralds had controlled aristocratic funerals in the sixteenth century. Whereas the heralds' control had only extended over a small if powerful section of the population, the undertakers' influence reached all social levels, even the poor.

The development of the undertaking profession created other problems for its clients. The creeping commercialisation of death brought with it undesirable consequences, the general principles of profitable business practice taking on a more sordid aspect when human tragedy was its lifeblood. As early as 1728, the poet Young, in his *Love of Fame*, included this couplet in describing the prelude to a funeral:

While rival undertakers hover round
And with his spade the sexton marks the ground.

Horace Walpole, in 1763, noted as being particularly mercenary the case of Sir Robert Brown, 'who, when his eldest daughter was given over, but still alive, on that uncertainty sent for an undertaker, and bargained for her funeral in hopes of having it cheaper, as it was possible she might recover'.

Undertakers sometimes went to extreme lengths to obtain clients. For example, Major John Oneby, awaiting execution for murder in 1726, was decidedly displeased to receive the following letter:

Honoured Sir,
    This is to inform you, that I follow the business of an Undertaker, in Drury Lane, where I have lived many years and am well

known to several of your friends. As you are to die on Monday, and have not, as I suppose, spoke to anybody else about your funeral, if your honour shall think fit to give me orders, I will perform it as cheap, and in as decent a manner as any man alive.[9]

Whatever the approach used by the undertaker, or its effect on those preparing the funeral, usually the executor, professional undertaking undoubtedly brought with it a change in the pattern of funeral expenditure, particularly among less wealthy people. During the sixteenth and seventeenth centuries the largest single item of expenditure for a funeral was the provision of food and drink for the guests. Usually this amounted to half the total cost of burying someone and could sometimes rise to as much as three-quarters or more of the complete expenditure. For example, the funeral of George Glandish, of Ebony Court, Kent, in 1622, cost a total of £6 6s 5d. Of this sum, £5 1s 9d was spent on a feast at Ebony Court after the interment, for which the following items were bought: 2 sides of mutton, 6 bushels of wheat, 6 pounds of currants, half a pound of sugar, 1 ounce of cloves and mace, 1 ounce of cinnamon, butter, a fat calf, 12 pounds of bacon, 40½ pounds of cheese, a fat wether, 7 dozen and 2 loaves, 23 twopenny loaves and beer. The remaining £1 4s 8d was ample to provide a simple coffin and shroud and to pay the fees of minister, clerk, sexton, bearers and bellringers, as well as any other incidental expenses.

By contrast, the following purely decorative items were all provided by a London undertaker for members of a burial club in 1800, as noted by Sir Frederick Eden. Significantly, no money was allocated for food and drink, nor would the participants in such a club have been wealthy enough to provide anything much extra; often they were hard pressed to meet the undertaker's premiums:

The deceased to be furnished with the following articles: a strong elm coffin covered with superfine black and furnished with two rows all round, close drove, with best black japanned nails and adorned with rich ornamental drops, a handsome plate of inscription, angel above the plate, flower beneath, and four pair of handsome handles, with wrought grips; the coffin to be well-pitched, lined and ruffled with crape, a handsome crape shroud, cap and pillow. For use, a handsome velvet pall, three gentlemen's cloaks, three crape hatbands, three hoods and scarves, and six pairs of gloves, two porters equipped to attend the funeral, a man to attend the same with hat and gloves; also the burial fees paid if not exceeding one guinea.

Understandably, undertakers were keen for their clients to spend as much as possible on the items they were offering, rather than on things purchased elsewhere. However, the eating and drinking after the more traditional form of funeral had a social and psychological role which far transcended in significance its mere monetary value; it was a form of communal therapy and social restoration for the bereaved and their immediate social group.[10] When undertakers succeeded in draining money and significance away from the funeral meal in favour of their own business, it was more than simply a transfer of finance that was involved. In effect, a supportive, communal activity – the funeral meal – was being eroded by a competitive, isolating and individualistic element, the display of those material commodities in which undertakers specialised. The competitive streak was already present in funeral practices, as has been shown, long before undertakers appeared on the scene, but their emergence served to increase this tendency at the expense of more socially supportive rituals. Those who suffered most from this change in emphasis, inevitably, were the clients themselves. The modern-day undertaker sometimes sees part of his role as being a grief therapist, assisting the bereaved in their sorrow. It is therefore ironic that it was the sensitive twentieth-century undertaker's commercially minded predecessors who, albeit perhaps unwittingly, helped undermine the traditional community-based comfort provided by the funeral meal. However, as with other changes in burial rituals, the process did not happen with equal speed throughout the whole country and, to this day, people in the north of England generally set far greater store by a funeral meal than is the case in the south.

The displacement of food from the burial, together with the emphasis on material goods promoted by the undertaker, altered the whole concept of a 'respectable' funeral. In early modern England, respectability would in general come from a large turn-out of voluntary mourners, perhaps partly attracted by generous provision of food and drink. By the Victorian period, respectability was conferred by the quantity of material trappings – sashes, hatbands, gloves, scarves and so on – which could only be purchased from the undertaker for cash.

The poor were particularly hard hit when there was a death in the family. Their abhorrence of pauper burials, like those in eighteenth-century London which have already been described, drove the poor to make savings which they could sometimes ill afford, to avoid such a fate. This led to the founding of burial clubs or friendly societies; particularly in the second half of the eighteenth century they greatly increased in number. Run usually by undertakers, their development parallels that of the undertaking profession. In their advertisements, undertakers played freely on their clients' concern for respectablity. An example of 1800, noted by Sir Frederick Eden, was typical of many in its appeal to gentility: 'A favourable opportunity now offers to any-one, of either sex, who would wish to be buried in a genteel manner, by paying a shilling entrance and two pence a week for the benefit of the stock.'

A writer in 1742 who traced the descent of the friendly societies and burial clubs from the guilds of the Middle Ages congratulated himself that 'when any of the members die, they are . . . buried in a very decent manner by the society, at the expense of three pounds and attended to the grave by the whole club'.[11]

A different and rather more critical viewpoint was expressed by Patrick Colquhoun to the 1815 committee on mendicity, when he complained of the friendly societies:

There is one general principle . . . which I highly disapprove, and that is, the ambition of the most miserable of them to have what they call a decent funeral; an undertaker generally endeavours to get into the society, that he may bury all of them, and that funeral takes from the funds which ought to go to the widow and fatherless . . . [12]

Although identifying the undertaker as manipulating the burial club, the brunt of Colquhoun's criticism fell on the poor themselves. His words are in direct line of descent from the Puritan attacks on ritual as being a waste of money, particularly on the part of the poor. This view of ritual is now being discredited through the work of anthropologists and social scientists, but in nineteenth-century England it definitely held sway. A few contemporaries were more perceptive and realised that the poor would not change their burial customs unless the rest of society abandoned its obsession with materialistic funeral rites. It was to this end that Charles Dickens, in his will, described undertakers' wares — 'scarf, cloak, black bow, long hatband' — as a 'revolting absurdity', and banned the genteel labels 'Mr or Esquire' from his own tombstone. At local level, the occasional cleric also raised his voice against the steady advance of the undertaker. One such opponent was William Jones, the Vicar of Broxbourne, who in 1816 mentioned that his local carpenter 'felt somewhat alarmed, lest I should hurt his "craft", as an undertaker, by my lectures in favour of plain, inexpensive funerals'. Unfortunately, the vicar somewhat undermined his own credibility in the eyes of his parishioners by ordering from the same undertaker a coffin, kept in his study, which he used to store his plentiful supply of drink.

Can undertakers really be blamed for the alteration in funeral rites which culminated in the precisely graded extravaganzas of the Victorians? What is indisputable is that undertakers aggravated the situation and played upon the emotions of their clients, both individually and *en masse*, to create a trade more materialistic in nature and more lucrative to themselves. However, the profession of undertaking could not initially have come into being if the premise on which it rested, that death was a fit candidate for commercialisation, had not been acceptable to its potential customers. The obvious convenience of the trade to the busy executor no doubt assisted its establishment, as did an increasing revulsion at performing the more intimate preparations to the corpse. Other factors aided undertakers in their task. The individualistic, competitive element in society was already present in funeral practices, as was a love of display and conspicuous show; undertakers merely served to increase these tendencies, making them, at first, desirable, and then essential, for all social ranks. The broader bonds of communal solidarity had already come under attack from the increasing emphasis on the individual and the immediate family, while in cities, urban life weakened group ties. Undertakers only had to step into a pre-existing gap. Snobbery on an individual, family and class level was a well-established force on which they readily drew. A feeling that the living and the dead should be firmly separated, both on grounds of public health and propriety, further played into the undertakers' hands. The whole process was gradual and insidious. Undertakers, precisely because they reflected so closely the already existing *mentalité*, did not meet with great opposition. The profession of undertaking was both a product of, and instrument in reinforcing, the values of the society in which it flourished.

Notes

1. *Historical Manuscripts Commission. Buccleuch and Queensbury*, i, p. 253. For will and funeral account see Oxford, Bodleian Library: MSS. North.

2. Blauner, 'Death and Social Structure', *Psychiatry*, vol. xxix.

3. For full discussion of the statistical evidence, see Gittings, 'Funerals in England', unpublished, M. Litt. thesis, Bodleian Library, Oxford, esp. Chs 1 and 2.

4. Oxford, Bodleian Library: MS. Ashmole 836, fol. 12.

5. Ibid., fol. 627.

6. Quoted in Stone, *Family, Sex and Marriage*, p. 215.

7. Illustrated in Puckle, *Funeral Customs*, facing p. 230.

8. Wagner, *Heralds of England*, p. 302.
9. Villette, *Annals of Newgate*, i, p. 373.
10. See below, Chapter 7.
11. Quoted in George, *London Life*, p. 399.
12. Ibid., p. 303.

5 'PREPARE TO FOLLOW THIS FAIR CORPSE UNTO HER GRAVE'

> It must be remembered that I always speak of middling people, among whom the customs of a nation are most truly to be learned.

This advice to his readers was given by a Swiss traveller, Misson, describing funeral practices in post-Reformation England. It is also applicable to this chapter, and the two following, which look at the funerals of 'middling people', drawing principally on the material contained in probate accounts. Many thousands of these documents survive, from the period from the mid-sixteenth to the early eighteenth centuries, covering the counties of Kent, Berkshire, Lincolnshire and Somerset. They form a unique record of how ordinary people were buried; this chapter begins the trilogy by following the corpse from its deathbed to the church.

The period loosely termed 'early modern' formed a watershed in the history of attitudes towards death in England. Elements of the older, medieval attitudes still can be discerned, for example in the ritual of waking with the corpse. These medieval attitudes were characterised by a collective, rather than individualistic, approach to the problem of death, emphasising group solidarity and support for the bereaved. However, during the early modern period, these older practices and attitudes were gradually being eroded by rituals stressing the individuality of the deceased and the importance of the immediate family, rather than the wider social group. The preaching of funeral sermons, the erection of increasing numbers of church monuments and the changes in the distribution of mourning clothes at the burial all testify to this new trend. The anxiety which resulted from growing individualism is revealed in a desire to separate the living and the dead, and in an increasing horror at the idea of physical decomposition, as shown, for example, by the growth in the use of coffins at burials. Within this survey of funeral practices in early modern England, all these elements, some reflecting medieval and others more modern attitudes, are to be found intermingled, as well as many customs which have died out or been greatly altered over the course of time and a few which have remained the same to this day.

Most people died at home, the traditional place both for entering the world and for leaving it. If a person died away from home efforts were made to bring back the corpse if at all possible; the body of William Kyte was carried across the English Channel in 1639, 'being slain in Dunkirk and brought to Dover to be buried'. A similar journey, recorded in a large painting now at the National Portrait Gallery, was made bearing the body of Sir Henry Unton, who died on a diplomatic mission to France in 1596. When John Trenner dropped dead in the streets of Canterbury in 1607 he had to be laid 'in a poor body's house all night after his death' before being carried back to his native Milton for burial.

If someone went missing and was assumed to be dead, a search would be organised for the body. The miller of Holywell, Oxfordshire, went out in his boat to recover the corpse of John Bowden MA, and was rewarded with the suit of clothes that Bowden had drowned in. By today's standards this might seem ghoulish, especially to the super-stitious, but this reward reflects a less personalised and more matter-of-fact view of death, as well as the relatively greater value of the garments themselves. The search might well take some time; when the body of John Wright, a murder victim, was at last found, covered with some earth in a wood in Berkshire, it was necessary to wrap the corpse in skins, rather than a shroud, for its belated burial.

Burial away from home was complicated to organise and could be expensive. Jane Beale of Kent said that her husband had died in 1645 'at or about Sunderland in the north parts of England', and added that more was spent on his funeral 'than needed to have been if he had died at or near home'. Burial abroad caused even more problems. When Richard Willoughby, a Dover merchant, died in Denmark in 1613, Gyles de But, his executor and partner in the ship explained that

> his funeral, which in regard he deceased in a foreign country . . . was very chargeable, especially he being a merchant and a master of the ship, in respect whereof the other officers and merchants were constrained to perform the said funeral both for the custom of the country and the reputation of our nation in a more chargeable manner than had been otherwise convenient.

In some foreign countries religious difficulties arose, too; when a Canterbury silk weaver died in Flanders in 1631 it required a dispensa-tion from the bishop 'to have him interred in Christian burial (he dying a Protestant and the people being papish in the town he died in)'. Nor were foreigners dying in England necessarily accorded better treatment, as is revealed in an entry in the parish register of St Botolph's, Bishopsgate, London, in 1626. 'Coya Shawsware, a Persian merchant that came with the Persian ambassador, was buried at the west end of the lower churchyard, without the walls in the waste ground in Petty France.'

Francis Tate, an observer of funeral customs, wrote in 1600: 'Amongst us there is not any set and determinate time how long the corpse should be kept, but as seemeth best to the friends of the deceased.' Obviously this was as short a time as possible; a delay of five days before a Lincolnshire priest was buried in 1606 was considered exceptional and worthy of comment.

One way that an executor could buy more time in which to prepare the funeral was by having the corpse embalmed. This was absolutely essential if a grand burial, such as the heraldic funeral of a member of the aristocracy, was planned. The fee for such embalming was generally quite high; £28 4s 1d was charged to embalm Henry, Earl of Huntingdon, in 1596.[1] The embalming of a gentlemen of the same period cost £5, while the services of a surgeon for 'ripping the corpse', as it was graphically called, could be bought for 5s.

Usually the standard of embalming for members of the aristocracy was very high, and some bodies remain well preserved to this day. The process of embalming is satirically described by Nashe in the *Anatomie* of Martin Marprelate:

> Having bestowed his bowels in a ditch . . . and filled up his hungry belly . . . with coal dust, for spice they would not bestow (his carrion being not worth it) and sawdust they could have none: they wrapped him in a blanket . . . for that all others are lapped in sheets (and he loved ever to be singular) . . .

In 1705, Thomas Greenhill published his *Art of Embalming*, extolling the virtues of the craft and its practitioners:

> Death's grisly terrors by your skill to charm,
> And his fell furies of their stings disarm.

His defence of embalming reflected one facet of an increasing preoccupation with the preservation of the individual after death:

> Some have spared no means to render themselves immortal . . . but finding death inexorable and irresistible, they altered their measures

by inventing a thousand ways to perpetuate their memories after their dissolution . . . It may justly be said of embalming, that [it is] . . . undeniably the most considerable and efficacious means to answer their intention. For the utmost care in erecting monuments etc. yields but an obscure and imperfect idea of the person deceased, whereas by embalming, that very person is known to be preserved . . .

At the time Greenhill was writing, the practice of embalming had not yet become widespread, and he then confessed that 'want of opportunity has been in some respect a prejudice to my business'. Interestingly, he added that 'the noble act of embalming has been entirely ruined by the undertakers', which suggests that this specialist aspect of the provision of services for the dead was already being undercut by the nascent profession very early on in its development.

Francis Tate recorded that, during the sixteenth century, the body was 'laid forth . . . upon a floor in some chamber, covered with a sheet and candles set burning over it on a table day and night, and the body continually attended or watched'. Writing in 1600, he added that the practice of burning candles was then rarely observed, being considered superstitious, while watching was declining because of the rowdiness and irreverence of such occasions. Tate was witnessing the transition from the traditional medieval custom of holding wakes to the subdued and more rigorously Protestant practices of post-Reformation England. However, this transition did not take place with equal speed throughout the whole country. While these rituals had died out in the south and east by 1600, they were still to be found occasionally in the northern and western parts of the country, long after the Restoration. For example, this was how Mr Mawtese described a Yorkshire wake to John Aubrey:

At the funerals in Yorkshire, to this day, they continue the custom of watching and sitting up all night till the body is interred. In the interim some kneel down and pray (by the corpse) some play at cards, some drink and take tobacco: they have also mimical plays and sports *e.g.* they choose a simple young fellow to be a judge, then the suppliants (having first blacked their hands by rubbing it under the bottom of the pot), beseech his Lordship: and smut all his face. They play likewise at hot cockles.

The role reversal in these games — 'the simple young fellow' acting the judge — brings to mind the Lords of Misrule appointed by the court during the twelve days of Christmas or the boy bishops and mock kings of medieval Europe. Role reversal acted as a safety valve, in this case to a society under intense pressure following the death of one of its members. Controlled disorder and a make-believe realignment of the social hierarchy gave relief from the intensity and the threatening nature of the situation, thereby stemming, rather than encouraging, a descent into chaos. Instead of weakening the established order, such licensed deviance, contained within the clearly defined limits of social ritual, acted as a strengthening and reinforcing element, a fact not appreciated by those who tried to stamp out such rituals as being superstitious.

Another feature of these games played at wakes was the overtly sexual imagery. In a chapter entitled 'Love', John Aubrey describes hot cockles, the game mentioned by Mr Mawtese, in the following way:

> I have some reason to believe that the word cockle is an old antiquated Norman word which signifies arse: from a beastly rustic kind of play or abuse, which was used when I was a schoolboy . . . so hot cockles is as much to say hot or heated buttocks or arse.

It seems that the 'heated buttocks' were the result of the players striking one of their number, who was blindfolded, in a sexual variation on blind man's buff. The playing of sexual games around a corpse reveals one aspect of the closeness of the living and the dead during the early modern period; our present-day distaste at such activities arises from our perceived polarity between the two which, in its turn, is a legacy inherited from the more Puritanical of our ancestors. It is, perhaps, not surprising that a traditional society threatened by the destructive force of death should choose to counter the threat with games that recall the power of procreation. This, of course, was a community-based rather than an individualistic form of solace, as it would be of little comfort to someone mourning the loss of a unique individual that human life in general would still continue.

The sums of money spent on wakes suggest that the number of people attending was often quite large. For example, when a Cambridge student died in 1618 his body was watched by fellow scholars who consumed wine and beer costing 5s 9d, and burnt 10d worth of candles and perfume; the payment for the perfume reflects the grisly reality of decomposition, which must have been apparent to those present.[2] However, the dominant impression left by waking is of a communal, supportive and often openly enjoyable event, preventing the bereaved from retreating into loneliness or introspection and containing within it elements of social restoration, the whole edifice resting on a basis of Catholic eschatology.

The principal objection among Protestant reformers to wakes undoubtedly stemmed from the religious aspects of these rituals though, interestingly, some Catholic bishops during the Middle Ages had complained of the 'indecent and guilty games' and of 'perverse customs'.[3] An account of religious abuses in Lancashire in about 1590 included the following complaints about wakes:

> They set forth the corpse in their houses all garnished with crosses, and set round about with tapers and candles burning night and day, till it be carried to the church. All which time the neighbours use to visit the corpse, and there everyone to say (a *Pater noster* or *De profundis*) for the soul: the bells (all the while) being rung many a solemn peal. After which, they are made partakers of the dead man's dole or banquet of charity.[4]

Considering that wakes were so unpopular with the ecclesiastical authorities both on religious and moral grounds, as well as hinting at political and social disruption, it is perhaps surprising that waking continued for as long as it did after the Reformation. For example, in Lincolnshire in 1628, bread, meat, fire and candles were provided for those waking with the body of Thomas Monye, while a strike of coals was burnt at Edmund Lasie's wake in 1633; in Yorkshire waking continued even after the Restoration. The decline of waking was partly brought about by active opposition from the clergy. Social changes also played their part, as the traditional social values on which waking depended were gradually eroded by the newer emphasis on the individual and the immediate family circle. Political upheavals, as John Aubrey shrewdly noted, indirectly affected such customs as waking, too: 'The civil wars coming on have put all these rites or customs quite out of fashion. Wars not only extinguish religion and laws but superstition and no suffimen is a greater fugator of phantoms than gunpowder.' For all these reasons, the north and west of the country gradually followed the lead set by the south and east. Inexorably, the holding of wakes became a thing of the past.

In the more 'civilised' south and east of England, by the end of Elizabeth I's reign, paid watchers were only employed in cases of suspected foul play or death by misadventure. All those who met with accidental death were watched before being viewed by the coroner; in one Lincolnshire man's case the coroner was summoned 'he dying suddenly and the neighbours doubting the cause thereof'. The two most common causes of accidental death were incidents with horses or carts and drowning; Thomas Worley in 1614 contrived to bring the latter fate upon himself by 'venturing to swim in the haven at Sandwich'. The weather also took its toll of victims, including one Kentish man 'slain with a thunderbolt'. Agricultural work could be hazardous, causing deaths through asphyxiation in hay, falls from trees while fruit picking, being 'gored by a bull' and many other ways. In 1768, a fishing trip ended in unexpected disaster for Stephen Aldridge 'who was suffocated by a flat-fish, which he inadvisedly put betwixt his teeth when taken out of the net; but by a sudden spring it made into his throat, and killed him in two minutes'. Somewhat unnecessarily, the parish register adds, 'it is here recorded as a warning to others, to prevent the like accident'.[5]

The job of the watchers was principally to see that no one tampered with the corpse before the coroner's inquest. Sometimes their vigil lasted for several days, as when William Streather, a labourer, died of exposure in 'the great snow' in Lincolnshire in 1634; it took the coroner six days to reach him. Even in normal weather conditions a Lincolnshire coroner's journey could be slow, and he had to have guides to help him pick his way through the fens. Usually a jury would assist the coroner to reach his verdict, but only very occasionally did a surgeon attend, so most judgements were made on the external appearance of the corpse alone. The coroner would expect to be paid 13s 4d for viewing a corpse and would often receive a meal too. The watchers, however, had to be content with a few pence for their pains. Sometimes the watching, and the subsequent coroner's inquest, would take place in the parish church, presumably as a further measure against interference.

The watchers were also on hand in case the 'deceased' suddenly revived, a by no means unknown occurrence in a society lacking sophisticated medical technology. Matthew Wall of Braughing, Hertfordshire, was actually carried to his grave, and it was only when one of the bearers tripped and dropped the coffin that he revived; he then lived for several years more, until 1595, most grateful for his lucky escape. Braughing still commemorates his 'resurrection' every year.[6]

In murder cases, the watchers around the victim's corpse were also looking out for any sign as to who the assassin might be. There was a widely held tradition, believed even by James I, that the corpse would bleed if its murderer approached or touched it. In the course of a murder trial at the Hertford Assizes in 1629 this sworn statement was made:

> That the body being taken out of the grave thirty days after the party's death, and lying on the grass, and the four defendants being required, each of them touched the dead body, whereupon the brow of the dead, which before was of a livid and carrion colour, began to have a dew or gentle sweat arise on it, which increased by degrees, till the sweat ran down in drops on the face; the brow turned to a lively and fresh colour; and the deceased opened one of her eyes, and shut it again three several times: she likewise thrust out the ring or marriage finger three times, and pulled it in again, and the finger dropped blood upon the grass.[7]

It is, incidentally, interesting to remember that the cost of obtaining justice in a murder case had to be borne by the estate of the deceased. Probate accounts, therefore, detail expenditure for this purpose, and often tell a fascinating tale, as in the case of William Storr of Gawdby, Lincolnshire. He was murdered, in 1602, by his wife and her lover, Richard Burrell. When the crime was discovered, the culprits attempted to flee. Burrell was captured at Crofton, tied with a cord and brought back, partly by hired boat and partly by horse, to Stamford. Meanwhile Storr's wife had been taken at Bardney. The guilty parties were then both incarcerated in Lincoln Castle to await trial, £6 being paid to the gaoler for the woman's imprisonment there. At the trial further expense was incurred in fees for counsel, the Clerk of the Assizes, witnesses and so on. Finally, after many journeys to Lincoln on the part of Storr's brother-in-law, justice was obtained, £11 14s 11d having been spent altogether.

For the great majority of people, whose relatives simply died of natural causes, any watching was becoming exclusively a family affair. The communal support provided by a wake was replaced by the solitary vigil of the close family. The grim loneliness this could entail is graphically revealed in a terse entry in Pepys's diary for 6 July 1661, concerning the death of his uncle: 'My uncle's corpse in a coffin standing upon joint stools in the chimney in the hall; but it begun to smell so I caused it to be set forth in the yard all night, and watched by my aunt.' Thomas Hardy in *Far From the Madding Crowd* uses the vigil with the dead as the setting for a dramatic revelation, when the coffin lid is wrenched up by his heroine, watching on her own.

The restriction of watching to members of the family is a further step in the separation of the living from the dead, and is part of the development culminating in the modern reaction of horror at seeing a corpse. In 1815, the growth of the feeling of revulsion was noted by William Jones, Vicar of Broxbourne in Hertfordshire. He made the connection between the love of self and the fear of death which is the central theme of this book, though he saw it more in physical than psychological terms. He wrote:

> Fine gentlemen and ladies shudder at the very idea of viewing a corpse. After all the anxious care that they bestow to pamper, adorn, perfume, etc. their own frail bodies, how mortifying must it be to them to think of the havoc of death, how soon they will be loathsome and a prey to worms.

An important step in preparing a corpse for burial was to shroud it, a process which often involved the use of flowers. Francis Tate described how 'the body is wrapt up with flowers and herbs in a fair sheet, and this we call winding a corpse'. Thomas Overbury in his description of 'a fair and happy milkmaid', wrote: 'all her care is that she may die in the springtime, to have store of flowers stuck upon her winding sheet'. One Kent funeral account, dated 1594, mentions 'herbs and flowers' used for this purpose. Generally the scents used to freshen the corpse were sweetwater or rosewater. Various accounts also record rosemary, which was sometimes carried by mourners as well as laid round the body (see Plate 1, p. 124). Another Kent burial account itemises 'rosemary dipped in rosewater and given to the neighbours', while at an Oxford funeral described by Aubrey, the assistants were called 'men of rosemary'. Coles, in his *Art of Simpling*, published in 1656, described the qualities and significance of this herb:

> They are . . . plants which fade not a good while after they are gathered and used (as I conceive) to intimate unto us, that the remembrance of the present solemnity might not die presently, but be kept in mind for many years.

Coles also added that 'rosemary and bays are used by the commons both at funerals and weddings'. Thomas Dekker emphasised a further symbolic link between burial and marriage in *The Wonderful Year*, drawing attention to the 'strange alteration' whereby 'the rosemary that was washed in sweet water to set out the bridal is now wet in tears to furnish her burial'. Of course, so far as the mourners were concerned, rosemary was not only 'for remembrance', as in *Hamlet*, but also served to conceal the smell of putrefaction. To this day, however, the use of flowers is one of the few areas where the similarity between weddings and funeral rituals still continues. As in the case of the rituals connected with wakes, the use of flowers, common to both marriages and funerals, pointed to the continuing cycle of human life in which the death of one member was compensated for by the procreation of future generations.

Flowers were not the only mementoes of life which went with the deceased into the grave; Tate records that 'sometime there is put up with it something which he [the dead person] principally esteemed'. This practice is one which stretches back into prehistory and is also to be found today. In the *Merchant of Venice*, Nerissa speaks of a particularly treasured ring:

> You swore to me, when I did give it you,
> That you would wear it till your hour of death,
> And that it should lie with you in your grave.

Similarly in his poem 'The Funerall', John Donne employs the image of an entombed bracelet:

> Who ever comes to shroud me, do not harm
> Nor question much
> That subtle wreath of hair, which crowns my arm . . .

Other items buried with the dead reflected superstitious beliefs, often with strong Roman Catholic and even pagan connotations, which caused considerable concern among the clergy. John Aubrey recalled that 'when I was a boy (before the civil wars) I heard them tell that in the old time, they used to put a penny in the dead person's mouth to give to St Peter, and I think that they did so in Wales and in the north country.' Another superstitious practice of ancient origin was that salt should be put on the body to ward off evil spirits, to stop the deceased's ghost from walking and to prevent the corpse from swelling or bursting; Brand noted a reference to this custom in a poem by Herrick: 'Dead when I am, first cast in salt . . . '

On most occasions it appears that an actual sheet, taken from the household's supply of linen, was used as the shroud. This arrangement nearly always seems to have been followed in Kent and Lincolnshire. However, in the Berkshire funeral accounts there are numerous examples of the purchase of a shroud, usually costing between 3s and 5s; that of Thomas Saunders cost 7s 4d, 'being very large'. Occasionally the material is specified; for example, 4½ ells of holland at 3s the ell, or 4½ yards of linen at 2s 6d a yard. An Oxford pauper burial, recorded in the overseers of the poor accounts, mentions four ells of white osnaburg and some thread costing, in all, 3s 4d. The shroud was tied at top and bottom. In Lincolnshire a coarse thread, called 'incle', was used. In the nineteenth century it was also tied firmly round the feet of the deceased, to prevent the ghost from 'walking', but whether this folk belief was held in earlier centuries it is impossible to say. Indeed, another tradition suggests that the shroud should not be tied too tightly lest it impede the wearer on the day of resurrection.[8]

Beneath the shroud a smock or shirt would be worn. Reginald Shrawley, a brother of the hospital of St John, Canterbury, was buried in 1638 in 'a sheet, shirt and cap' costing, in all, 4s. One Berkshire funeral account mentions the provision of 'necessary cloth fit for a woman dying in travail'. Francis Tate wrote of the winding of the corpse that 'by whom it is done, I think at this day is little regarded amongst us'. Often this, like many other of the less pleasant jobs, was given to the poor. Sometimes neighbours would perform this task; unfortunately the majority of probate accounts before the Restoration simply mention 'women' so it is impossible to form an accurate general picture. The action was variously called shrouding, winding, laying or stretching forth and, occasionally, 'steiping'; in Kent the term 'socking' was often used.

After the Restoration rather more is known about the process of shrouding the corpse, since the Act of 1678 making burial in woollen shrouds compulsory focused more attention on the whole process. Misson gives a full description:

> There is an Act of Parliament which ordains, that the dead shall be buried in a woollen stuff, which is a kind of a thin baize, which they call flannel; nor is it lawful to use the least needleful of thread or silk. (The intention of this Act is for the encouragement of the woollen manufacture.) This shift is always white; but there are different sorts of it as to fineness, and consequently of different prices. To make these dresses is a particular trade, and there are many that sell nothing else; so that these habits for the dead are always to be had ready made, of what size or price you please, for people of every

age and sex. After they have washed the body thoroughly clean, and shaved it, if it be a man, and his beard be grown during his sickness, they put it on a flannel shirt, which has commonly a sleeve purfled about the wrists, and the slit of the shirt down the breast done in the same manner. When these ornaments are not of woollen lace, they are at least edged, and sometimes embroidered with black thread. The shirt should be at least half a foot longer than the body, that the feet of the deceased may be wrapped in it, as in a bag. When they have thus folded the end of this shirt close to the feet, they tie the part that is folded down with a piece of woollen thread, as we do our stockings, so that the end of the shirt is done into a kind of tuft. Upon the head they put a cap, which they fasten with a very broad chin cloth, with gloves on the hands, and a cravat round the neck, all of woollen . . . Instead of a cap, the women have a kind of head-dress, with a forehead-cloth.

An affidavit had to be produced by the executors to say that wool alone had been used. Many of these documents, signed by the women who had shrouded the corpse, still survive. One way to avoid this regulation was to dispense with a shroud altogether and bury the corpse 'in herbs', or flowers and hay. The rich often preferred to pay the penalty for disobedience, set at £5 by the Act, rather than comply. Pope, in his *Moral Essays*, makes the dying Narcissa declare:

'Odious! in woollen! 'twould a saint provoke,'
(Were the last words that poor Narcissa spoke)
'No, let a charming chintz, and Brussels lace
Wrap my cold limbs, and shade my lifeless face:
One would not, sure, be frightful when one's dead –
And – Betty – give this cheek a little red.'

The motivation behind the legislation compelling the use of woollen cloth for shrouds, which was not repealed until 1815, reflects a mixture of pragmatism and materialism in respect of death. Although not without precedent, the Act was far more wide-reaching, and better enforced, than any previous ordinance. It is precisely this same period and *mentalité* which allowed the profession of undertaking to develop with such rapidity. In the early 1680s, the minister of Helmdon, Nottinghamshire, showed his contempt for this mercenary law by adding sarcastic comments in the parish register about his parishioners' affidavits: 'shrouded only in a winding sheet made of the fleece of good fat mutton' was one description, while 'Thomas Shortland was well wrapt in a shirt of woollen and was let down into his dormitory with that vestment about his corpse to the great satisfaction of a law enjoining that habiliment as convenient for the dead.'

The body, once shrouded, might then be placed in a coffin. These were usually bought ready-made, 'in the whole' as one account puts it, at a cost, before the Restoration, of about 6s. Edward Witton, of Berkshire, 'being a gross man', had to have a coffin costing 7s 6d. John Case's coffin was purchased in Maidstone in 1632 and then carried to Boxley where he was to be buried. Sometimes planks and nails would be bought separately and then assembled. On occasion frankincense was used to perfume the coffin and pitch was employed to seal it; sometimes the coffin was oiled.

In the west of England the coffining of the body was the occasion for a ceremony called 'chesting' to which the neighbours might be invited, with food and drink being consumed. As in the case of wakes, a much greater involvement of the wider community during the period between death and burial was to be found in the more distant and 'backward' areas of the country. This reflected more closely the communal networks of the Middle Ages than the atomistic concept of man's destiny enshrined in post-Reformation theology.

However, not everyone by any means was buried in a coffin; many people were laid in the grave wrapped only in a shroud. This arrangement seems to be envisaged in the burial service in the *Book of Common Prayer*, which speaks of the earth being scattered over the body. The extent to which coffins were used varied greatly from one county to another. In Kent these were nearly always employed, even sometimes for pauper burials from the Restoration onwards, while in Lincolnshire they only featured infrequently. In Berkshire, about half the probate accounts before the Civil War mention coffins. This variation does not reflect different prices in the different counties. The frequency with which coffins were used seems, however, to have increased in all three counties during the first half of the seventeenth century. This suggests that the graphic immediacy of shovelling soil directly onto the corpse was becoming less acceptable, the full realisation of the process of physical decay being somewhat masked by the wooden coffin. Such increased sensitivity towards human decomposition reflects a growing concept of the self and its individuality (see Table 3, p. 240).

As might be expected, the people with greater wealth tended more often to be buried in coffins. Members of those social groups enjoying higher status also had coffins more frequently. In the town of Rye in Sussex it was definitely social status which determined whether a coffin were used, and it was even regulated by order:

> No person . . . under the degree of Mayor, Jurat or Common Councilman, or of their wives, except such person as the Mayor shall give licence for . . . shall be chested or coffined to their burial, and if any carpenter . . . make any . . . coffin . . . (other than for the persons aforesaid excepted) he shall be fined ten shillings.[9]

A further factor which sometimes influenced the rich or those of higher standing in the community to use coffins was that these people were frequently buried in church. In some parishes, though certainly not all, such interment had to take place in a coffin. For poorer people a number of churches provided a communal coffin in which the body might be carried to the grave, although for the actual burial the corpse was only shrouded.

In some areas, even after the Restoration, the use of coffins had not fully taken hold and it fell to the local minister to bring about the transition, being perhaps more sensitive about the issue than his parishioners. For example, the Vicar of Bakewell between 1678 and 1724 wrought the transformation there, as the parish register records:

> The custom of interment in wooden coffins (wooden Josephs) was on the Reverend Mr Monks coming to reside here. A corpse from Sheldon was brought in swaddling clothes . . . and was detained in church until a coffin was made, and the wife then took off the flannel for her own use.

A further refinement to burial in a coffin was the post-Restoration practice of filling the bottom of it with bran, in Misson's words, 'about four inches thick . . . that the body may lie the softer'. Clearly, though, the body's comfort was hardly the real concern. The bran prevented the funeral party from hearing the corpse move as the coffin was lifted and can be seen as a further development of the process of hiding the reality of death from the living, a process which has culminated in our use of hospitals and undertakers to ensure that we never see a corpse at all.

Tate recorded:

> On the day of the interment the body is brought forth of the

chamber, where before it lay, into the hall or great chamber, and there placed till the mourners be ready and marshalled . . . the body is laid with the face upright, and the feet towards the door.

Before setting out for the church, the mourners, after refreshments, were able to pay their last respects to the deceased. The body was displayed, shrouded but with the face uncovered, and perhaps laid in its open coffin.

Tate described how the corpse was prepared for departure: 'the coffin or bier is covered with a sheet over which lieth a black cloth . . . and so he is carried towards the grave'. The black cloth, mentioned by Tate, is the pall or hearsecloth. Often it could be hired from the parish for a matter of pence or shillings; that of Snave, Kent, in 1639 cost 3s to use. The parish of St Botolph's Without, Bishopsgate, owned three hearsecloths; the best cost 12d to borrow, the second cost 8d and the old hearsecloth 4d. Sometimes, enterprising woollen-drapers would hire out palls and also a cloth for the pulpit; a Maidstone and Canterbury woollen-draper both appear in the probate accounts doing this. For grander funerals, the pall would usually be purchased, at a cost of about 10s. In the list of fees for St Botolph's Without, Bishopsgate, it states that 'if any person of note shall be buried . . . the Parson is to have the hearsecloth . . . and the Clerk is to have the pulpit cloth'.[10] After the funeral of Mary Delanney in Canterbury, in 1623, the hearse and pulpit cloths were given to the minister and clerk 'as the custom is'. This arrangement, however, was not accepted by everyone. Sir Roger Twisden, of East Peckham, Kent, noted in his account of the money spent on his father's burial in 1628: 'Mr Warrell Minister of Peckham . . . demanded the black cloth [which] lay over the hearse as his customary due but I made it appear to him we had no such custom.'[11] Usually the bier was borrowed from the church; bishops' injunctions sometimes enquire whether a parish owns a suitable bier and pall. Generally a small payment was due to whoever brought the bier, often the sexton, and only on rare occasions did the estate actually have to purchase one.

According to Tate, 'the corpse is taken up and carried either by poor people chosen out for the purpose, or by the servants of him that is dead'. John Wesley, founder of Methodism, who died in March 1791, left in his will 'six pounds to be divided among six poor who shall carry my body to the grave'.

Occasionally the dying man named those whom he wished to carry his body. At least one London church had its own bearers who had to be paid even if it was decided not to employ their services.[12] However, in the majority of cases, the accounts remain silent about who carried the dead person to the church; since no other evidence remains, it seems plausible to suggest that it was neighbours, kinsmen or friends. Usually the bearers would receive a small payment and sometimes a gift of gloves, too. Those who carried the body were flanked by people holding the edges of the pall. In May 1703, in his eighty-second year, John Evelyn was asked to bear the pall at the burial of Samuel Pepys who 'had been for nearly 40 years so much my particular friend'. Sadly, Evelyn wrote, 'my indisposition hindered me from doing him this last office'. The importance attached to the carrying of the corpse and holding up the pall is indicative of a closeness between the living and the dead still remaining in early modern England.

Certain groups of people seem, by custom, to have had particular bearers. Members of some Kentish trades were carried by their fellow workers. William Brett, a shoemaker of New Romney, was carried in 1638 by four other shoemakers, who received aprons for their services. In the previous year a Canterbury baker, Thomas Bartlet, was borne by eight of his fellow tradesmen, again each being rewarded with an apron. When James Gransden died in 1638 'according to the deceased's own often speech and appointment during his life time whilst he enjoyed good memory', four tanners were given boots and gloves for transporting him from Canterbury to his grave at Hackington. An eighteenth-century instance, at St Paul's, Covent Garden, drew 'a vast crowd of spectators' when, in 1735, 'the head cook of the Rose Tavern [was buried], the pall being supported by six cooks dressed in white napkin caps . . . white stockings and white gloves [and] green aprons'.[13] This custom is still continued today among some social groups, for instance members of the armed forces.

Another group of people who sometimes had special bearers were girls dying in their virginity. This burial custom is described in a ballad of about 1650:

A garland fresh and fair
of lilies there was made
In sign of her virginity
and on her coffin laid.
Six maidens all in white
did bear her to the ground . . .[14]

The garland was allowed at Ophelia's burial – her 'virgin crants' – even though 'her death was doubtful'. Probate accounts contain details of a number of funerals where this ritual was practised. Ellen Love of Baldesmere, Kent, specified this form of burial in her will of 1624:

> She said that she would have a coffin to be laid in and a sermon at her burial and willed four maids to carry her corpse to church and willed to everyone of these 12d a piece and bridelaces to be given at her burial.

Her funeral account shows that these instructions were carried out, at a total cost of 17s 9d. Three further accounts from Kent and Lincoln-shire record virgins being carried by girls, though, unfortunately, young women form a class which appears infrequently in probate accounts.

This burial custom was not always performed and could vary some-what in form. In one instance, a young girl was carried by men wearing white waistcoats. In another, a married woman was recorded as being carried by women; possibly she may have died during childbirth. Bachelors, too, sometimes seem to have been mourned in white rather than in black; Misson mentioned that 'for a bachelor or maid, or for a woman that dies in childbed, the pall is white'.

The burial rites of maidens and bachelors in early modern England seem alien to present-day ways of thought, which emphasise the dichot-omy, rather than the similarity, between weddings and funerals. The blending of the symbolism of wedding and funeral has already been touched upon, both in the execution of criminals and in the use of rose-mary and other flowers at ordinary people's burials: it can also be related to the idea of role-reversal mentioned in connection with wakes. In pre-industrial England, where life was uncertain and death could strike at any age, the ritual celebrating the continuation of mankind also conjured up man's end and vice versa. Perhaps the most striking example of this, from a twentieth-century viewpoint, was the custom, recorded in 1729 by Dr J.A. Blondel in *The Power of Mother's Imagina-tion over the Foetus Examined*, 'for pregnant women to be pall-bearers of their friends dead in childbed'.[15] Although physiological considera-tions were respected in this custom, requiring the pregnant women to carry only the light pall rather than the full weight of a body, concern for the psychological impact on the individual participants was subord-inated to a more generalised and communally based concept of the renewal of human life.

With the exception of the burials of children, women dying in child-birth, virgins and bachelors, at which white was used, the colour for mourning at post-Reformation funerals was black. The 'customary suits of solemn black' and 'inky cloak', worn by Hamlet, were major items of expenditure for these burials. Of course, mourning could be worn for a period of time after the actual interment; seventeenth-century widows often wore black for several years after their bereavement. Formal court mourning began in the Middle Ages and the custom gradually spread down through the ranks of society.[16] Sir Ralph Verney in 1651, a year after his wife's death, was still mourning her; his observance extended as far as 'two black taffety night-clothes, with the black night-caps, and black comb and brush and . . . slippers of black velvet'. The Verney family even owned a black mourning bed which was lent out to bereaved relatives and friends.[17] During the eighteenth century the keeping of a period of mourning became more widespread and the use of second mourning — between full mourning and the return to normal dress — became common. This, in turn, heralded the strict, formalised code of the Victorian era, affecting all social levels. The colour black was chosen for its symbolic association with night: 'Hung be the heavens with black, yield day to night . . . We mourn in black'.

In 1622, the Privy Council ordered that all mourning clothes must be made 'only of cloth and stuffs made of the wool of this kingdom, and not elsewhere nor otherwise', although this was impossible to enforce.[18] The provision of mourning clothes was an expensive business and so it was in general confined to wealthier people; the poor simply wore their ordinary clothes to a burial.

The main characteristic of women's mourning costume was that it was generally old-fashioned in style, as befitting a withdrawal from worldly concerns. The medieval barbe — a chin cloth in the shape of a beard — was still worn by women mourners in the sixteenth century, including Mary Queen of Scots. Another item of mourning costume, worn by both women and men, was the mourning hood, often pulled forward over the eyes (see Plates 5 and 6, p. 126). The back of the hood frequently culminated in a long tippet; one made for a mourner attending the funeral of George Man in Kent in 1637 cost 14s. Although women's mourning dresses were supposed to be unfashionable, they still drew hostile comments from Puritan critics, such as Henry Barrow:

> Who be more curious and nicely picked to have their mourneries fitted at an hair breadth, than these mourning women? You shall not have them more choice of any garment that ever they wear, than (for the most part) they are of this: these are signs of a very sorrowful heart.

One luxury often added to mourning dresses was lace for decoration. For example, to create mourning dresses for two women and two children attending the funeral of Matthew Mennyce at Sandwich in 1610, six yards of black cobweb lace at 6s 2d a yard were purchased.

Male mourners usually wore mourning cloaks. Besides the mourning cloak, men often wore black hats; at Henry Saker's funeral in 1614 each of his three sons wore a hat, costing 13s 6d for the three (see Plate 2, p. 124). In addition, at the funeral of Susan Omer in 1631, black suits and boots were provided for her two brothers, while one of them also received a black-hilted sword with matching hangers and spurs, costing in all 24s 6d. The total expense of providing mourning clothes could often be quite considerable; in 1636, at Ethelbert Omer's funeral, the black cloth used cost £32 3s 5d, trimmings from the mercer £12 and further 'stuff' £24 5s, including a black mourning beaver for the deceased's mother, which by itself cost £4 8s. The tailor's bill came to £5 16s 4d, but this may well have been an under-estimate since the tailor was a relative of the dead man and received a pair of boots worth 12s in which to ride to the funeral.

Generally, mourning garments, as recorded in probate accounts, were provided solely for relatives of the deceased. At aristocratic funerals the number and rank of the mourners was set out in the heralds' regulations, as was the quantity of black cloth for each of them, but the gentry, given a freer choice than the peers, often favoured family alone. Frequently this was restricted just to the widow or to the widow and children of the deceased. At other times it was extended to include more distant relations, brothers and sisters and their spouses, parents, nephews, nieces and so on. At the funeral of John Coppin of Canterbury, in 1629, his parents, two sisters and brother-in-law all wore mourning, while at Thomas Garrard's burial in 1617 black was worn by his wife, his uncle, his two brothers and one sister, his four children and his grandmother. Occasionally friends of the dead person would receive mourning; another group who were sometimes favoured were the deceased's servants. A further beneficiary might be the minister or clerk conducting the burial, which caused Barrow to insinuate: 'Could they not (let them speak of their conscience) find it in their hearts to be so set awork every day in the week.'

The use of mourning at a funeral served to single out visually the wearers from the rest of the guests, giving an indication of who were considered to be the most important participants in the ritual. The emphasis placed on the immediate kin of the deceased, through the wearing of mourning, was a reflection of the growing importance attached to close blood relations, to the exclusion of the wider social group. It was an acknowledgement that their grief was different from and by implication unsharable by the other guests. It can be seen as the initial stage in a process which was to lead eventually to the nuclear family carrying the full weight of bereavement alone, with little or no support from the surrounding community who may, indeed, positively and actively shun them.

However, as has already been suggested, the early modern period is a watershed in the history of funeral customs, between medieval and modern practices, containing elements from both eras. Although the wearing of mourning was often used to emphasise the importance of the nuclear family, there were occasions on which the medieval practice of giving mourning to the poor was still retained. Matthew Mennyce of Sandwich declared in his will that he would be buried decently and like a gentlemen, 'and also he giving to poor people of the same town . . . so many gowns as he . . . was years old'. His account records the purchase in 1610 of 37 gowns of broadcloth, embellished with escutcheons and crests. At Dorothy Hudson's funeral, in 1639, garments worth £10 were given to the poor, while 33½ yards of kersies at 3s 10d the yard were bought to provide poor men with gowns for Richard Mocket's funeral in Oxford. This practice was approved of by Thomas Becon as a form of charity, although he criticised the fact that the poor received 'coarser cloth' than the rich. Henry Barrow, on the other hand, attacked the hypocrisy of 'poor men put in mourning weeds, which never got so much by the glutton in all his lifetime, which are so far from mourning, as they are glad with all their hearts'.

The whole idea of mourning dress was anathema to those of more Puritanical belief and a lively debate was waged on the subject. One principal line of argument was the insincerity of wearing mourning; as Cartwright declared, 'there being under a mourning gown often times a merry heart'. Bolton called such black clothes 'artificial forms of sadness and complemental representations of sorrow', while Henry Barrow condemned people 'mourning only in their garments'. The *Admonition* spoke of 'their strange mourning by changing their garments, which if it be not hypocritical, yet it is superstitious and heathenish'. Cartwright produced a further argument against mourning:

> Where there is sorrow indeed for the dead, there it is very hard for a man to keep a measure, that he do not lament too much; we ought not to use these means whereby we might be further provoked to sorrow . . . it is very dangerous to provoke it.

In these more Puritan attitudes may be seen the origins of the twentieth-century denial of mourning.

The wearing of mourning also had its champions. Whitgift declared:

> For a signification of love towards them that are departed mourning is not denied to be a thing convenient . . . I see not why the wearing of mourning apparel should not be profitable to put a man in mind of his own mortality, seeing it carrieth a remembrance of death with it.

However, he, too, appreciated that the custom could be misinterpreted:

> Mourning apparel is of great antiquity . . . and I think it is no matter of religion, but of civility and order. If any man put religion in it, then no doubt it is superstitious.

Anthropologists have discussed the ideas lying behind use of mourning clothes in various cultures. Westermarch suggests that mourning is worn as a sign of regard for the dead and as a token of grief, both concepts which seem applicable to early modern England. Van Gennep describes mourning in the following way: 'It is a transitional period for the survivors, and they enter it through rites of separation and emerge from it through rites of reintegration into society (rites of the lifting of mourning).' This 'liminal period' is shown by the wearing of special garments, though in early modern England there appears not to have been a fixed length of time for this, unlike many other societies. Several anthropologists have noted, like the critics mentioned above, that ritualised mourning might be at variance with the true feelings of the survivors. However, as Malinowski explains, such rituals still have a therapeutic value since 'they create a social event out of a natural fact'. He would also disagree with Bolton and Cartwright's view of the detrimental effects of mourning rituals on the sincerely bereaved; the wearing of mourning serves to 'endorse and . . . duplicate the natural feelings of the survivors', in his opinion, a beneficial thing. Indeed, it has been suggested that the abandonment of formal mourning by twentieth-century man, together with the tendency for the small, nuclear family to become the sole unit responsible for the entire burden of bereavement, is one of the prime causes of the present-day anxiety over death.

Notes

1. London, British Library: MS. Harleian 4774, fol. 141.
2. Porter, *Cambridgeshire Customs*, p. 34.
3. Puckle, *Funeral Customs*, p. 63.
4. *State Civil and Ecclesiastical of Lancaster, Chetham Miscellanies*, v.
5. Thiselton Dyer, *Old English Social Life*, pp. 167-8. For a discussion of accidental death, see Hair, 'Accidental Death and Suicide in Shropshire', *Shropshire Archaeological Society*, 1ix.
6. Described in Jones-Baker, *Folklore of Hertfordshire*, p. 164.
7. Ibid., p. 82.
8. Gutch and Peacock, *Folklore Concerning Lincolnshire*, pp. 240 and 243.
9. Quoted in Puckle, *Funeral Customs*, p. 42.
10. London, Lambeth Palace: Arches F.7, Muniment Book 1635-1667, fols. 170 and 173.
11. London, British Library: Addit. MS. 34, 163, fol. 4.
12. London, Lambeth Palace: Arches F. 7, Muniment Book 1635-1667, fol. 172.
13. Quoted in Cunnington and Lucas, *Costume for Births, Marriages and Deaths*, p. 136.
14. Hindley, ed., *The Roxburghe Ballads*, i, p. 246.
15. Not Blondin as cited in *Folklore*, xlvii, p. 230.
16. For a full illustrated discussion of mourning clothes see Cunnington and Lucas, *Costume for Births, Marriages and Deaths.*
17. Quoted in Godfrey, *Home Life under the Stuarts*, pp. 270-71.
18. Larkin and Hughes, *Stuart Royal Proclamations*, i, no. 229.

Plate 1 *(above)* Detail of the title page of a polemical tract, *London's Lamentation,* published in 1641, showing burials in plague time. The London mourners carry sprigs of rosemary.

Plate 2 *(above)* Funeral invitation for Thomas Foley's burial in 1677. The scenes, clockwise from the top left, show the drinking at home around the coffin, the funeral sermon, the interment and mourners in hats and cloaks carrying the pall-draped coffin.

Plate 3 *(above)* Funeral procession from 'The Dance of Death', by Thomas Rowlandson,
published in 1816. Death carries a lid of feathers.

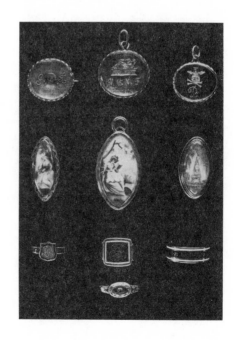

Plate 4 *(right)* Mourning jewellery,
c. 1600-1800. The earlier images
of skulls and skeletons gave way
in the eighteenth century to more
classical and romantic designs. The
giving of inscribed memorial rings
indicated a desire for worldly
remembrance.

Plate 5 *(above)* Detail of the funeral procession of Lady Lumley, in 1578, showing the pall-draped coffin, hooded mourners and heralds bearing banners.

Plate 6 *(above)* Detail of the funeral procession of Queen Elizabeth I, showing the royal effigy flanked by gentlemen pensioners with their halberds reversed.

Plate 7 *(above)* Monument to Alice, Countess of Derby, died 1636, by Maximilian Colt; Hare-field, Middlesex. The tomb is based on the design of a hearse.

Plate 8 *(above)* Monument to John Donne, died 1631, by Nicholas Stone; St Paul's Cathedral, London. Donne himself posed in his shroud for the drawing from which this monument was made.

Plate 9 *(above)* Monument to Robert Cecil, died 1612, by Maximilian Colt; Hatfield, Hertfordshire. This monument combines representations of the four Cardinal Virtues, one with her breasts bare, and the traditional late medieval arrangement of the skeleton lying beneath the figure of the deceased.

Plate 10 *(above)* Monument to Sir Francis and Lady Page, died 1741 and 1730, by Henry Scheemakers; Steeple Aston, Oxfordshire. Page ordered the tomb on the death of his wife; he even left money in his own will to have it regularly dusted.

'THE BRINGING HOME OF BELL AND BURIAL'

Misson described how the funeral procession would set out from the house in post-Restoration England: 'They nail up the coffin, and a servant presents the company with sprigs of rosemary; everyone takes a sprig, and carries it in his hand till the body is put into the grave, at which time they all throw their sprigs in after it.'

According to Tate, the body should be carried to church 'the best and most convenient way . . . and neither into the market place, nor other streets for ostentation'. However, according to a homily of 1562, this was not always easy to do because 'greedy men . . . plough up so nigh the common balks and walks' that there was not left 'a broad and sufficient bier-balk to carry the corpse to the Christian sepulture'.[1] From probate accounts it is clear that the usual distance for carrying a body to church was under a mile. Any further was considered exceptional; 'two long miles' is one heartfelt comment, in a Kent account dated 1628. Occasionally in the wilder and wetter parts of the country the body had to be taken by water; in 1599, Richard Bell was rowed three miles to burial in Lincolnshire, for which 18d was charged. Sometimes it was necessary for the corpse to cross a river, as in the case of William Jolly who was taken from Chislet via Grove Ferry to Sandwich, or George Peele who was ferried across the River Trent to Dunholm for burial in 1604.

Misson recorded what the funeral procession looked like as it wound its solemn way to the church:

> One or more beadles march first, each carrying a long staff, at the end of which is a great apple or knob of silver. The minister of the parish . . . attended by the clerk, walks next, and the body . . . comes just after him. The relations in close mourning and all the guests two and two, make up the rest of the procession.

Additional evidence about the funeral processions of ordinary people during the late seventeenth and eighteenth centuries comes from the small woodcuts which sometimes decorate funeral invitations.[2] In eighteenth-century examples, an extraordinary figure makes his appearance, often placed just before the body. This was the 'featherman', who bore on his head a coffin lid covered in plumes of black

feathers — an undertaker's delight! (see Plate 3, p. 125.) The featherman and his 'lid of feathers' were hired, in the late eighteenth century,
for about 2s a time and the practice continued during the nineteenth
century, provoking the scorn and sarcasm of Charles Dickens. 'Because
there were not feathers enough yet, there was a fellow in the procession
carrying a board of 'em on his head, like Italian images.'[3]

On occasion, the body would not be buried in its own parish but
would be carried to another for burial. This was an expensive business,
not only because of the cost of transport, but because burial fees had
to be paid in both parishes. Usually the double payment was referred
to as 'a customary right' being paid 'according to demand and due',
although one disgruntled accountant explained that he only paid twice
over 'to avoid troubles and suits of law'. When people were buried
outside their normal parish of residence this was usually for family
reasons, either at their own request or that of their close relatives. To
give some Kentish examples, Henry Farerway of Staplehurst was buried
in Cranbrook as his wife desired, Ingram Elvey of Lympne asked to be
buried at Allington where he had been born, while John Dean of
Whitstable was interred at Hernehill among his ancestors, and Edward
Sayer of Bilsington, at Allington 'among kindred and friends'.

Of course, if the distance were great, it was impossible for people to
carry the corpse to burial on their shoulders and so wheeled transport
had to be hired, while most of the mourners travelled on horseback.
These great funeral processions are found fairly frequently among the
accounts of the higher gentry in Kent; after the Restoration the word
'hearse' begins to be used in its modern sense. The joiner making the
coffin for Anne Undean of Canterbury in 1639 charged 15s for his work,
'being a fair strong one because her body was to be far carried in a
coach to burial by her own appointment in her will'. The coachman
made two journeys to Molash, her chosen resting place, one with the
body and one transporting her relatives and friends. Two coaches were
hired in 1631 to carry the corpse of Susan Omer, and her friends, from
Beakesbourne to Ash, while her two brothers rode on horses with black
saddlecloths and bridles. At least 32 people on horseback accompanied
the coach bearing Ethelbert Omer from the George, Canterbury, to
Ash, in 1636, with bells ringing in the parishes on the way; in 1629,
20 people rode with the body of John Coppin from Canterbury to
Deal. An interesting variation on the mourning coach was provided in
1608 at Margaret Parker's burial — the mourning boat. The corpse had
to be carried by water from Sandwich to her appointed place of burial,
Moncton. The boat was hired to carry the body and the mourners, with

four men to row it, at a charge of 20s. 'A great quantity of black cloth' was hired 'to cover or tilt the boat', at a cost of 33s 4d. The remaining mourners rode to the burial and had to be ferried across the water, for which 5s was charged.

These processions with coaches and riders were smaller and cheaper versions of the funeral processions of the aristocracy, which could take several days to reach their destination, involving many people staying at inns along the way, and the ringing of the bells in all the parishes through which they passed. Gradually, the carrying of the body gave way to wheeled transport for people of all social levels, thus further separating the living from the dead. However, by one means or another, the corpse was brought to the church and was then ready for the actual interment itself.

A funeral taking place would be known to all in the vicinity by the sound of bells. Bell ringing was an important feature of the process of death in early modern England. As a man lay dying, a passing bell would be tolled for him, so that he and all his neighbours should know his end was near. This contrasts very strongly with our own hospitalised form of dying, where often the imminence of death is not revealed to the patient at all, or is even denied. The passing bell consisted of nine strokes for a man, the 'nine tailors', six for a woman and three for a child, followed by one stroke for each year of his or her age. In Lincolnshire, it was sometimes called the soul peal, on which Bishop Hall commented: 'we call them soul-bells for that they signify the departure of the soul, not for that they help the passage of the soul'. Sometimes, however, the sick man would revive and the passing bell would have to be rung again on another occasion when he actually died. There are frequent references in probate accounts to the passing bell being tolled twice and sometimes even three times. Before Thomas Finch finally died, in Kent, the bell was tolled for him on four different occasions.

The effect of the passing bell on its hearers was described by the Bishop of Chichester in his injunctions of 1638, enquiring, 'is there a passing-bell tolled, that they who are within the hearing of it may . . . recommend the . . . departing soul into the hands of their Redeemer . . . out of a fellow-feeling of their common mortality?'

It was this bell which inspired Donne to write perhaps the finest passage in his *Devotions*:

Who bends not his ear to any bell which upon any occasion rings? but who can remove it from that bell which is passing a piece of himself out of this world? No man is an island, entire of itself; every man is a piece of the continent, a part of the main. If a clod be washed away by the sea, Europe is the less, as well as if a promontory were, as well as if a manor of thy friend's or of thine own were: any man's death diminishes me, because I am involved in mankind, and therefore never send to know for whom the bell tolls; it tolls for thee.

'Excessive and superstitious ringing' at funerals was one of the remnants of Roman Catholicism which post-Reformation bishops tried to stamp out, though seemingly with little success. They desired to limit it to two short peals, one before and one after the burial, with no superfluous ringing or handbells. However, the knell, or 'forthfare' as it was sometimes called, was known to extend for the whole day; one London parish register, that of St Peter, Cornhill, mentions six hours of ringing at a funeral, again suggesting the spirit of a wedding rather than a burial. Certain parishes, for example Faversham, Kent, and Grantham, Lincolnshire, had their own peculiar ringing customs which continued to be practised. When a man died and was buried at sea his knell would still be rung in his home parish when the news reached there. Generally, the ringers would be paid 6d or 1s for their services and given food and drink too. That bell-ringing was profitable to the church may be seen from the vestry minutes of All Saints, Newcastle. Between 1643 and 1655 no passing bells had been tolled, being considered superstitious. However, on 21 January 1655 it was decided to reinstate the custom because of the loss of revenue suffered by the church during its suspension.[4]

When a body was carried through another parish on its way to the grave, it was customary for those bells also to be rung. Certain towns had their own bell-ringer who would walk the streets with a handbell when anyone of note died. The fees of the bellman of the city of Oxford were graded according to the rank of the deceased and were to be paid 'albeit any man or woman being executrix shall be unwilling to have him go abroad'.[5]

Anthony à Wood noted an unusual practice at Oxford University in 1661:

Dr John Oliver died. Buried Oct. 30 . . . The day before his burial the university bellman went from college to college with the doctor's scarlet [robes] and square cap on (according to ancient custom in these matters) to give notice when he should be buried. This custom had been prohibited by the Parliamentary Visitors, 1647 or 1648.

The bellman dressing in the dead man's robes seems not to have been considered in any way strange or distasteful by his contemporaries, although it must have given the appearance of the deceased issuing invitations for his own funeral.

Even in plague time the bell-ringing customs were maintained, their sound being felt to drive away evil. Pepys, in his diary, noted on 26 July 1665: 'Sad news of the death of so many in the parish of the plague . . . The bell always going.' The lengthy bell-ringing involved in every burial kept death firmly in the mind of pre-industrial man.

For those who could afford it, the use of black cloth in funeral rituals was not restricted to mourning clothes. At grander funerals the inside of the church would be swathed in black; as Henry Barrow said, the 'church must also . . . be solemnly arrayed and hanged with black, that even the very stones may mourn also for company'. To buy the necessary quantity of cloth would have cost an immense amount, so generally it was hired, even for the funerals of peers. For Thomas Mennes's burial in Sandwich in 1633 his house was also hung with blacks, since the mayor and jurats were entertained there to supper, following the funeral. For Richard Mocket's burial in Oxford both the chapel at All Souls and the University Church were festooned with cloth; 86 yards of cotton and 57 yards of baize were hired at 1d a yard. The University Church was also hung, again with hired cloth, when John Fleming of Wadham College was buried in 1617. At Dame Mary Gardner's funeral in Abingdon the black cloth was loaned for 5s and a man was paid 6d to hang the chancel with it, using a hundred tenter-hooks, costing 3d.

At the funerals of Oxford and Cambridge academics, their bereaved colleagues would pen verses which were pinned to the black hangings in the church and to the pall. For John Fleming's funeral in Wadham Chapel, 1s 6d worth of pins was needed to secure the verses, which must have been quite considerable in number. At the funeral of Ralph Gray, a commoner of Christ's College, Cambridge, the necessary pins cost 4d. Unfortunately a ladder was broken in putting up the verses, for which a further 6d had to be paid.[6] For the funeral, in 1609, of Dr Soame, Master of Peterhouse and Vice-Chancellor of Cambridge University, there were sufficient verses composed to adorn the University Church and the chapel, court, hall and parlour of the college. A copy was made of some of the lines pinned to the pulpit in St Mary's; the verse conjured up a conflict between St Peter and Abraham as to which should have the pleasure of Dr Soame's company:

> Peter and Abraham were of late at strife
> Which of them two should entertain his life . . .
> Peter possession pleaded, Abraham right . . .

However, the matter was settled in the 'highest court' of heaven and so

> Abraham enjoys what Peter had before,
> In Peter's house he sojourned as a guest,
> In Abraham's bosom now his soul shall rest.[7]

When George Walker was buried in Lincoln Cathedral, in 1598, the 'choir men' performed at the service, receiving 40s for their pains. The same sum was paid 'to the singing men for their fee', at the funeral of John Fleming in Wadham Chapel, while another Oxford academic, Richard Mocket of All Souls, also had choral accompaniment at his burial. The luxury of a sung office for the dead struck one contemporary as rather strange:

> It is a custom . . . to attend the funeral of their deceased friends with whole chantries of choice choir singing solemnly before them: but behind follows a troop all clad in black, which argues mourning: much have I marvelled at this ceremony, deeming it some hidden paradox, confounding thus in one things so opposite as these signs of joy and sorrow.[8]

Sir Thomas Browne realised the power of music 'to excite or quiet the affections . . . according to different harmonies', saying of music at classical funerals that 'the secret and symbolical hint was the harmonical nature of the soul; which delivered from the body, went again to enjoy the primitive harmony of heaven'. Something of this harmony may be experienced by listening to the music which Purcell composed for the funeral of Queen Mary in 1695.

If the priest were not already walking in the funeral procession on its way to the church, he had, according to the directions in the *Book of Common Prayer*, to meet the corpse at the gate of the churchyard and walk before it to the church, with all the guests following the body 'in token', as Veron put it, 'that they shall all go after, at the time appointed of God'. Misson recorded that in post-Restoration England: 'The common practice is to carry the corpse . . . into the body of the church where they set it down upon two trestles, while . . . a funeral sermon is preached, containing an eulogy upon the deceased.' (See Plate 2, p. 124.)

Funeral sermons followed a set pattern. In the first half, a suitable text would be expounded, reminding the hearers of their own mortality. The second half consisted of a biography of the deceased, displaying his merits and virtues to the full and lamenting his sad departure from the world. The separatist critic Barrow satirised this:

> All this while we have said nothing of the excellent virtues of the party deceased, for the priest (I trow) hath said enough for him in the pulpit: though he were the veriest profane atheist, profuse glutton, greedy extorter . . . though he never had any knowledge, love or fear of God in his life.

The preacher's duty was 'to make him by his rhetoric a better Christian in his grave than he ever was in his life'. A very different view of the purpose behind funeral sermons is put forward by Thomas Becon: 'I would gladly have . . . a sermon, wherein the people may be admonished of their mortality . . . that, when the time come, they may yield up a good soul into the hands of the living God.' Funeral sermons looked towards the afterlife yet acknowledged the sadness of losing an individual from this world; as the different viewpoints suggest, these two aims might not always be entirely compatible.

Certainly, at least on occasion, the funeral sermon was truly heartfelt. Mr Atkinson, a preacher, 'would take nothing for his pains taking in preaching at the funeral' of Katherine Cartwright of Normanby, Lincolnshire in 1609, and so the accountant sent Mrs Atkinson a strike of wheat and two of malt. At the funeral of Dr Whitaker in Cambridge in 1595 the sermon was 'pathetically preached' by the Vice-Chancellor. 'His tears were so mannerly (or religious rather), that, observing their time, they obstructed not his sermon till come to a competent length, when the spring-tide of his weeping stopped his preaching.'[9] Further evidence of the good relations between a preacher and his congregation may be found in the account, dated 1636, of John Botting of Goudhurst, which itemises 'a cup of wine for the preacher's comfort after the sermon ended'.

Quite frequently a sermon would have been appointed by the deceased in his will; Thomas Rucke of Kent even specified the text to be expounded: John, chapter 4, verse 14. The sermon for Mary Dixon, so her Kent account of 1616 records, was preached 'by the appointment of the parish', while sometimes death-bed requests were made for sermons. On occasion, the chosen preacher was an outsider, in which case the minister also had to be paid for allowing the sermon in his church. The usual fee for a funeral sermon was 10s before the Restoration and £1 after. The number of sermons preached increased during the seventeenth century (see Table 4, p. 240). They were particularly popular in Kent; not surprisingly they were predominantly preached for the wealthier and higher in status. This drew not unjustified criticism from Puritans like Cartwright who said that funeral sermons were preached 'at the request of rich men, and those which are in authority, and are very seldom at the burial of the poor, [by which] there is brought into the church . . . an acceptation of persons, which ought not to be'.

Funeral sermons were extremely lucrative for the clergy, who were as 'greedy of funerals as vultures after dead carcasses', in the words of one of their detractors.[10] This caused a rift between the English and Scottish ministers during the Civil War period; one Scot wrote home from London that 'our difference about funeral sermons seems irreconcilable . . . it's here a good part of the minister's livelihood, therefore they will not quit it'.

To those, like this Scottish minister, who were Puritanical in outlook, a funeral sermon smacked of popery and resembled praying for the dead, as it 'nourisheth an opinion that the dead are better for it'. Whitgift, putting the viewpoint of the established Church, fiercely denied this: 'Surely there is as much difference betwixt our funeral sermons and the papistical masses . . . as there is between cold and hot, black and white, light and darkness, truth and lies, heaven and hell.'

It is obviously impossible to tell with any certainty what was in the minds of the people who ordered funeral sermons. Perhaps the only light shed on this by probate accounts is in the case of Henry Broughton, a Lincolnshire man who in 1600 ordered not one, but three funeral sermons; it seems reasonable to suggest that he might have felt that three would benefit him more than one, like the Roman Catholic masses for the dead. An additional point to consider is that, particularly from the late seventeenth century onwards, funeral sermons reached a much wider audience than simply those people who gathered in the church to hear them preached. With growing frequency, funeral sermons were printed and sold as popular pamphlets; they were therefore the forerunners of newspaper obituaries.

During the burial service, the body would be laid to rest either in the churchyard or in the church itself. Misson noted that

> if the body is not buried in the church, they carry it to the church-
> yard belonging to the same, where it is interred in the presence of
> the guests, who are round the grave, and do not leave it till the
> earth is thrown in upon it.

Either place was anathema to Puritans, who opposed the whole
notion of interment in consecrated ground; as one Scot wrote, 'where
learned you to bury in hallowed churches and churchyards, as though
you had no fields to bury in? . . . it is neither comely nor wholesome'.
A number of superstitions were connected with graveyard burial, for
example that the north side of the churchyard should be reserved for
suicides, excommunicates and other undesirables. In 1657, a minister,
Mr Benjamin Rhodes, decided to challenge this custom and 'requested
to be interred in the open churchyard, on the north side (to cross the
received superstition, as he thought, of the constant choice of the south
side)'.[11]

The grave was traditionally dug, at a depth of six feet, from east to
west, the head lying to the west, in the words of Thomas Browne,
'that he may rise with his face to the east'. Three Kent accounts talk of
'rearing up the grave', presumably meaning making an earth ridge over
it. At a time when very few churchyards had tombstones to mark the
graves, this must have been an attempt to delay the process of oblivion,
into which all the dead inevitably sank. Another Kent account
mentions a payment for 'greening the grave'; possibly the naked earth
was too harsh a reminder of the recent loss.

Bodies buried in the churchyard were liable to be disturbed to make
room for new graves; in densely populated urban parishes this was
completely inevitable. When this happened, any bones which were
found were usually placed in a charnel house. In the churchwardens'
accounts of St Mary, Warwick, for the year 1653-4, John Glendall 'and
his boys' were paid 1s for 'piling up the bones in the bonehouse'. At
St Margaret's, Westminster, the problem of old bones clogging the
churchyard had become so acute in 1616 that £2 2s had to be paid
'to several men for four days work apiece in digging a large pit of twelve
foot deep, thirty foot long and about ten foot broad to bury the bones
in the churchyard'.[12]

Even in country churchyards, the overcrowding of bodies could be
chronic. The old churchyard of St Andrew's, Widford, Hertfordshire,
measures less than half an acre, but bodies were being buried there con-

tinuously for at least 900 years. Between 1559 and 1658 there were 384 interments, while from 1659 to 1800 there were a further 600 bodies buried. In all, before its closure in 1903, this small country churchyard must have received the mortal remains of at least 5,000 people.[13] The situation in urban churchyards, particularly in London, was, of course, far worse. The *Journals of the House of Commons* for 1747 recorded the fact that in the parish of St Andrew's, Holborn,

> the two churchyards . . . which . . . are not one acre, are so full of corpses, that it is difficult to dig a grave without digging up some parts of a corpse before decayed . . . and . . . that it was so offensive in the year 1720, that the churchyards were shut up by order of the King and Council.

Nor were churchyards reserved entirely for graves. Those bishops who cherished 'the beauty of holiness' had to issue injunctions against the feeding of cattle in churchyards, the playing of games, depositing dung, the emptying of chamber-pots or 'easing of nature', fighting, performing plays and hanging out washing to dry. This list of activities suggests a closeness between the living and the dead almost unknown today.

A more peaceful grave might be obtained by paying to be buried within the church itself. Even there, bodies were not immune from being moved, as Pepys noted on 18 March 1664:

> To church, and with the gravemaker chose a place for my brother to lie in, just under my mother's pew. But to see how a man's tombs are at the mercy of such a fellow, that for sixpence he would (as his own words were), 'I will jostle them together but I will make room for him;' speaking of the fullness of the middle aisle, where he was to lie.

The overcrowding may have been one reason why the practice of burial inside churches was on the decline during the first half of the seventeenth century, both in Kent and Lincolnshire.

The extent of burial within a single church can be calculated for All Hallows, Honey Lane, London, where the site of interment is recorded in the parish register. Of 340 burials in the parish between 1580 and 1640, 118, or 35 per cent, were inside the church: 26 in the chancel and 92 in the body of the church. The making of graves could cause considerable disruption to church furniture, pews having to be taken down and then re-erected after the interment. At the very least it meant the removing of sections of tile and paving from the floor, which had to be replaced. If a vault were constructed, the process was even more complicated; in one Kent case in 1636, 'bricks and irons to lay over and fasten' had to be purchased for 37s 10d. On occasion, disputes would arise over repairs to these graves and they would be left open for some time, even if they contained an uncoffined body. A mixture of concern for hygiene and a desire to maintain proper social distinctions led Bishop Middleton of St David's to attempt to limit the practice within his own diocese. In an injunction to the clergy of 1583, he ordered

> no corpses to be buried within their parish church or chapel (for that by their general burying there great infection doth ensue) except those of the best sort of the parish.

In 1643, the General Assembly of the Church of Scotland displayed a much more single-minded approach to this obvious health hazard, when it prohibited all persons 'of whatsoever quality' from being buried 'within the body of the kirk, where the people meet for hearing of the word'. Behind the hygienic argument against burial in church lay the belief that the living and the dead should be kept apart; 'churches were for the living and churchyards for the dead'. It also reflected, in some measure, the more Puritanical view of the body as a thing loathsome and abhorrent.

However, the practice was also attacked by clergy of a very different persuasion, who, in the words of Joseph Hall, Bishop of Norwich, 'do not hold God's House a meet repository for the dead bodies of the greatest saints'. Archbishop Sancroft expanded on this view, saying that it was 'improper that the House of God should be made the repository of sinful man'.[14] This condemnation of the practice of burial in church, coming, as it did, from eminent people of very different theological persuasions, must also have assisted to bring about its decline. As with many other traditional burial customs, however, it continued to be carried out more frequently in the north than in the southern counties of England (see Table 5, p. 241).

As might be expected, burial in church was on the whole confined to those of greater wealth and higher standing in the community. One Berkshire account explains that Anne Woodward was buried in New Windsor Church, 'being an ancient woman of good reckoning'. William Marten of Wellington, Somerset, was buried in the church porch in 1617; perhaps this was a compromise between being buried in the churchyard or paying to be interred in the church itself. An often quoted epitaph makes a similar point:

Here I lie at the chancel door,
Here I lie because I'm poor:
The further in, the more you pay:
Here lie I as warm as they.[15]

Intramural interment was indeed expensive; usually 6s 8d for burial in the church and 10s in the chancel. These charges were strongly attacked in the early seventeenth century. Henry Spelman quoted a typical set of burial fees, declaring that

no ground in the kingdom is now sold so dear as a grave . . . the church-wardens of parishes . . . sell graves in the church and church-yard like ware in their shop . . . The grave is the only inheritance that we are certainly born to . . . how do the dead rest from their labour, if they be vexed with payments?

For a simple funeral, fees were due to the minister, clerk and sexton of the parish. The clerk or sexton would receive about 4d for digging the grave; one Lincolnshire account gives a payment of 1s for 'grave making in the frost'. The minister would claim a few shillings for performing the burial and the clerk received about 1s for his attendance. A mortuary or 'corpse present' also would be due, calculated according to inventory sum; even when the living was vacant this still had to be paid, being collected by the patron instead. In Abingdon, an extra fee of 2d was charged for registering the death. As Henry Barrow remarked: 'Neither rich nor poor, neither young nor old, can get burial without money in the Church of England: no penny, no *Pater Noster* there'. Any extra ceremonies, as the writer of *The Curates' Conference* shows, cost more:

So much for burials, so much for the knell, so much for the grave, for the corpse more, if coffined; more yet, if in such a churchyard; more than that, if in the church; higher yet, if it be in the chancel; beyond all these, if buried with torches, and sermon, and mourning with attendance; but it is put upon the highest strain, if it be a stranger.

Almost exactly this progression of fees is to be found in the table of burial charges for St Botolph's Without, Bishopsgate, London.[16] Complaints about the expense seem to have had some justification; between 1598 and 1626, £100 14s was paid in various burial fees to one London church alone, that of All Hallows, Honey Lane.

A number of Kentish people who appear in probate accounts were buried in the cathedral at Canterbury, principally Doctors of Divinity living within the precincts. The cathedral duties were even higher than those for a parish church; Francis Foxton paid £3 13s 4d in fees for his brother's burial in 1632. The passing bell and knell cost 10s and the peal at the burial a further 10s, while for breaking the ground 20s was charged and the 'vergerers' also had to be paid for their attendance. Sometimes, rather than being actually buried in the cathedral, a person might have the cathedral bell rung on their funeral day, although the burial was elsewhere. When John Manwaring was buried in St Mary Magdalen, Canterbury, in 1622, the cathedral bell was tolled for him for a fee of 5s and, while Anne Undean's body was being carried to Molash, the cathedral ringers, charging 17s for their services, rang peals.

For a brief period, at the close of the seventeenth century, death duties also had to be paid out of the estate. The Marriage Duties Act of 1694, repealed in 1706, ordered that 4s was to be paid as a burial tax. John Evelyn noted the general unpopularity of the Act in his diary on 14 July 1695:

> No sermon at church, but after prayers the names of all parishioners were read, in order to gather the tax of 4s for marriages, burials etc. A very imprudent tax, especially this reading of the names, so that most went out of the church.

The tax was certainly efficiently collected in Kent, where several probate accounts mention the payment of 'the King's duties' or 'the Queen's duties'. This experiment in the taxation of death, not to be tried again until the 1850s, was, significantly, initiated during the same decades that attempts were made to force people to use woollen shrouds to assist the economy and when the first undertakers were establishing their businesses. The burial tax was a further facet of the materialistic outlook towards death which, as has been suggested, underlay the success of the undertaking profession.

For the vast majority of burials, the last shovelful of earth, and perhaps the replacement of the turf, was the finishing touch for the grave. Very few graves, particularly in churchyards, had tombstones before the late seventeenth century. The position of a particular grave would only be remembered by close relatives or, as in *Hamlet*, by the gravedigger; it was an exceptional incumbent who bothered to record the location. Among the rich, the erection of permanent funerary monuments was well established and indeed increasingly prevalent, as Francis Bacon noted in 1592, in his *Observations on a Libel*: 'There was never the like number of beautiful and costly tombs and monuments, which are erected in sundry churches in honourable memory of the dead.'

Gradually, the growing desire for worldly memorials to the dead led to the setting up of tombstones to ordinary people as well as their social superiors. Throughout the seventeenth century, a small, but mounting number of Kentish people had such memorials placed over their graves. Some were content with wooden markers called bed-heads or leap-boards, very few of which have survived into the twentieth century, but others wanted to be remembered in durable stone. Many of these people were buried inside the church and some of their memorials remain to this day. It is therefore possible to get some indication of what particular memorials cost during this period. For example, the following entry appears in the probate account of Edward Hales, Esquire, of Faversham, in 1634:

A tombstone to lay over the deceased's dead corpse with two brass pieces thereupon, one for his arms thereon engraven and an other for an inscription of the time of his death and to declare to aftertimes who lay there buried £5 14s 2d.

This brass is still to be found in Faversham Church. It is similar to many thousands of others laid down during the sixteenth and seventeenth centuries when memorial brasses began to commemorate a wider social range than they had during the Middle Ages.

Rather more was spent by the executors on the tomb of William Goodwin, D.D., Dean of Christchurch, Oxford, a wall monument, though not large in size. It was erected in 1620 and cost £13. The painted stone bust of the dean shows him in academic dress, holding a book, while his coat of arms surmounts the monument. Beneath the tomb is a Latin inscription, partly in verse, and in the sides of the architectural surround are emblems of mortality. This type of monument, too, was popular in the sixteenth and early seventeenth centuries, again reflecting a widening of the social group commemorated by sculptured tombs.

The executors of Edward Crayford, Esq., of Great Mongeham, Kent, decided that money was better spent on a stone monument than on transitory obsequies. The tomb, which cost £40 in 1615, is of considerable size. It is a wall monument containing figures of him and his wife at prayer, while their children kneel below; above the architectural surround are his coat of arms and two large obelisks. The side columns are flanked by two putti and beneath the monument is an inscription. His funeral, by comparison, cost only £30.

On occasion, it was the deceased himself, rather than the executors, who decided upon having a tomb. A fascinating example is to be found in the will of John Brooke of Ash in Kent, made on 1 May 1582. After giving precise directions about the place in the church where his body was to be buried, he continued:

> And I will there a large marble stone to be laid over me
> with my arms engraved upon the same and under them this
> epitaph which followeth and also what day and year I died:
> ' J John Brooke of the parish of Ash
> O Only he is now gone:
> H His days are past, his corpse is laid
> N Now under this marble stone.
> B Brookstreet he was the honour of
> R Robbed now it is of name
> O Only because he had no seed
> O Or child to have the same.
> K Knowing that all must pass away
> E Even when God will none can deny.
> He passed to God in the year of grace
> A thousand five hundred   it was
> The   day of   I tell you plain
> The   year of Elizabeth's reign.'
> And I will that the same stone thus engraved to be laid over
> me by my executrix within two years next after my decease
> or else she to forfeit twenty pounds to the churchwardens
> of Ash.

It is tempting to speculate whether Brooke's failure to leave heirs, the traditional way to keep one's memory alive, prompted him to be so particular about his memorial.

The amount spent on tombstones by these people, always, of course, the more wealthy of those represented in the Kent probate accounts, ranged from a few shillings to many pounds. After the Restoration, payments began to appear for churchyard tombstones; for example, in

1681 the 'stone placed at the head of the deceased's grave' cost 30s, the deceased being Abraham Lees of Ashford, while its carriage from Canterbury cost a further 4s. Usually, for monuments set up inside the church, several pounds at least were spent, as these Kentish examples show; George Man's tomb cost £5 in 1637, Richard Clerk's, £7 3s 4d, and Richard Dawkes', £8. A memorial could well cost more; for Jacob Turner's tomb £13 was charged and for John Manwaring's, in 1622, £13 6s 8d. A number of probate accounts give further details concerning the purchase of tombs. Henry Saker's tombstone was carried from London to Faversham in 1614 at a cost of 12s. The stone which covered the bodies of Anne Undean and her husband in Canterbury was quarried in Maidstone; it was a particularly large slab and was commissioned in 1639 by her son-in-law Thomas Shede at a cost of £9. Ethelbert Omer's tomb had to be carried to Ash and set up by a mason, costing £9 12s 1d in all. At the same time the memorials to his father and brother were re-erected and repaired, for which 2s 6d was charged.

All these sums of money invested in tombs testify to the growing desire for earthly remembrance of the individual, already noted, for example, in connection with funeral sermons. A contemporary rationale for the erection of tombs, displaying this same feeling, is provided by William Wyrley in *The True Use of Armorie*, published in 1592. He posits that, next to the love of God, what inspires men to 'laudable actions' is the thought that

> their doings shall be had in a reverent remembrance with . . . all good men . . . well may their just virtues . . . be remembered with funerals, obsequies, and monuments, after their decease . . . a fair example is thereby given [to others] to imitate the regiment of their predecessors.

This increasing emphasis on worldly commemoration might be seen as symptomatic of a developing unease in the face of death itself, and an attempt to avoid oblivion.

Not surprisingly, the erection of tombs was criticised by some contemporaries. Barrow wondered if members of the established Church could

> show warrant by the Word, for the exquisite sculpture and garnishing of their tombs, with engraving their arms and achievements, moulding their images and pictures, and to set these up as monuments in their church.

Daniel Featley, writing in 1636, stated that 'superfluous expense upon the supulchres of the dead . . . is an abuse of our age'. He added, 'if that which hath been luxuriously . . . and ambitiously, if not superstitiously, consumed in erecting . . . tombs or monuments for the dead' had instead been employed on church building, the reproach of neglecting churches would have been removed from 'the men of this age'.

Others revealed their disapproval of tombs by actions rather than words. Wyrley, writing long before the destruction of monuments during the Civil War and Commonwealth, recorded: 'of late, travelling through . . . this land . . . I found that many monuments . . . were . . . broken and defaced'. Weever, noting the same fact, lamented that 'nothing will be shortly left to continue the memory of the deceased to posterity', which led him to compile his famous collection of epitaphs.

In his book, *Ancient Funerall Monuments*, Weever quoted William Camden's summary of the purposes of epitaphs: 'In them love was shown to the deceased, memory was continued to posterity, friends were comforted, and the reader put in mind of human frailty.'

All these various elements may be traced in the epitaphs of early modern England, but during the course of the period a distinct shift in emphasis occurred, as a chronological survey of inscriptions shows. In earlier inscriptions, the reader is often most forcefully 'put in mind of human·frailty'; 'such as I am so shall you be' is a commonly met sentiment. The comforting of friends, however, occurs more frequently in the memorials of the seventeenth and eighteenth centuries, rather than the sixteenth century. Those who mourned for nine-year-old Meneleb Rainsford, buried at Henfield, Sussex, in 1629, were consoled with an inscription which included these lines:

Cease then for thy dear Meneleb to weep
God's darling was too good for thee to keep
But rather joy in this great favour given
A child on earth is made a saint in heaven.[17]

Expressions of love for the deceased also became more overt in the course of the sixteenth and seventeenth centuries, together with explicit acknowledgement that a particular individual, once dead, can never be replaced on earth, as in this memorial, dated 1674:

Death parts the dearest lovers for a while,

But makes them mourn who only used to smile:
But after death our unmixed loves shall tie
Eternal knots betwixt my Love and I . . .

The type of remembrance of the deceased fostered by epitaphs also underwent a striking change during the early modern period. The typical Tudor epitaph simply described the dead person in genealogical terms, listing any offices they held. In the seventeenth century, a more personal tone appeared, as in this inscription of 1640:

These nine years lived he with his lady fair
A lovely, noble and like virtuous pair.
Their generous offspring (parents joy of heart)
Eight, of each sex . . .

By the eighteenth century, epitaphs had become so fulsome in their praise of the deceased's personal virtues that they severely strain credibility. For example, we are told that the husband of Rebecca Leyborne, who died in 1756,

. . . never saw her once ruffled with anger,
Or heard her utter even a peevish word . . .
Resigned, gentle, courteous, affable:
Without passion, though not without sense,
She took offence as little as she gave it;
She never was, or made, an enemy;
To servants mild; to relations kind;
To the poor a friend; to the stranger hospitable;
Always caring how to please her husband . . .

The expression of individualism became so fully developed in eighteenth-century epitaphs that some even described the physical features of the deceased, again, of course, in flattering terms. The epitaph to Mary Ward, who also died in 1756, recorded:

Her person was tall and graceful
Her features handsome and regular
But her mind pious, modest, delicate and amiable
Beyond the credit of description . . .

During the early modern period a distinct alteration also took place in the iconography of churchyard memorials and church monuments, particularly affecting the way that death was represented. A matching development occurred in the design of another form of commemoration too, mourning and memorial jewellery. In the sixteenth and seventeenth centuries, both tombs and memorial jewels were frequently decorated with skulls or skeletons.[18] These acted as *memento mori*, providing a direct and unequivocal reminder of physical decomposition. The general acceptance of this representation of death, repugnant to twentieth-century sensibilities, is emphasised by the fact that these emblems of death were actually worn as decoration (see Plate 4, p.125).

However, this easy tolerance of such harsh reminders of the effects of death did not continue, by and large, after the mid-eighteenth century. The winged skulls, so popular on earlier tombstones, gave way to the far softer image of flying souls or cherubs. Classical forms began to appear on tombs: urns, weeping willows, sorrowing ladies and so on. These likewise became the dominant themes in mourning jewellery, often beautifully painted in miniature on ivory, sometimes even incorporating some of the deceased's hair in the design.

What is perhaps most surprising about this shift towards classicism is the swiftness with which the older, more direct representation of death was completely ousted by the gentler, more sentimental images. This change in style was not simply an alteration in fashion. It also reflected a rapidly growing unease at the whole process of physical decay, and a desire to swathe the reality of decomposition in a romantic aura, masking and denying the actuality of death. Additionally, it meant that on those occasions when, from the later eighteenth century onwards, skeletal imagery was used, for instance in 'gothic' novels, it was intended to arouse shock, disgust and fear, the stock reactions to 'horror' today. This increase in apprehension about bodily death permeated many of the different aspects of the funeral rituals of early modern England; the tombstones of that era bear witness to a major shift in attitudes, which even now continues to shape our response to death.

Notes

1. Quoted in Wilson and Levy, *Burial Reform*, p. 92.
2. Oxford, Bodleian Library: John Johnson Collection, Funerals, Box I.
3. Cost from Hardy, *Benenden Letters*, pp. 222-4; Dickens, quoted in Morley, *Death, Heaven and the Victorians*, p. 21.
4. Bourne, *Antiquitates Vulgares*, p. 6.

5. Salter, ed., *Oxford Council Acts 1583-1626*, p. 77.

6. Porter, *Cambridgeshire Customs*, p. 34.

7. Cooper, *Annals of Cambridge*, iv, pp. 322-3.

8. Brand, *Observations on Popular Antiquities*, ii, p. 268.

9. Cooper, *Annals of Cambridge*, ii, p. 542. For a discussion of funeral sermons, see Collinson, 'A Magazine of Religious Patterns', *Studies in Church History*, xiv.

10. *Curates' Conference*, p. 499.

11. Samwaies, *The Wise and Faithful Steward*, p. 27.

12. Quoted in Cox, *Churchwardens' Accounts*, p. 170.

13. Wilson and Levy, *Burial Reform*, p. 13.

14. London, British Library: Addit. MS. 5805, fol. 100. It has been calculated that, in the later Middle Ages, 54 per cent of Lincolnshire testators were buried within churches; Ariès, *The Hour of Our Death*, p. 92.

15. Grigson, ed., *Faber Book of Epigrams and Epitaphs*, p. 170.

16. London, Lambeth Palace Library: Arches F.7, Muniment Book 1635-1662, fols. 169-73.

17. Quoted in Gittings, *Brasses and Brass Rubbing*, p. 67.

18. For an illustrated account of tombstones, see Burgess, *English Churchyard Memorials*, esp. pp. 165-7. A large collection of memorial jewellery may be seen at the Victoria and Albert Museum, London, Jewellery Gallery, case 27, sides A and B.

7 'WITH MIRTH IN FUNERAL'

Many of the funeral rituals so far examined have reflected more of the modern than of the medieval approach to the problem of death. Increasing emphasis on the individual and the nuclear family, growing abhorrence of the process of physical decomposition and a desire to separate the living and the dead have been noted in connection with several changes in burial customs, while only a few rituals have recalled the communal solidarity of the Middle Ages. This chapter serves to redress the balance by looking at the rituals of eating and drinking and the distribution of gifts at the burial which, *par excellence*, illustrate the survival of medieval attitudes and customs. It was, significantly, in the secular, rather than the more ecclesiastical aspects of the funeral that this survival principally took place, since these were less easily influenced by the reforming zeal of the orthodox clergy or by those of more Puritanical inclination.

It is worth considering first how many people might attend any one funeral. Probate accounts provide some answers to this question. A few accounts actually state figures: 'about 100' people, 'about 50 persons attended the corpse to the church', 'about or well near an hundred people at the funeral', 'being an hundred persons at the least' and 'there being 300 people or thereabouts at the . . . burial'. Other accounts simply say 'there being very many in number', 'much company', 'great concourse of people' or other similar expressions.

At attempt is made by some accountants to explain the size of the gathering in terms of the deceased's standing in the community. Stephen Worley of Dymchurch was described in 1626 as 'a man of credit and good fashion and well beloved and esteemed of'. Stephen Norton was called 'a gent. of good sort', while the large attendance at George Stronghill's funeral in 1606 was put down to the fact that he was captain of the soldiers at Lydd. At the burial of Robert Coffen of Kent, in 1648, the company was 'great and costful' due to him being 'a bachelor of good account and his sisters liking well of him'.

What is most significant is that these well-attended funerals were not particularly expensive by comparison with many others. Even the burial of Stephen Hills, a yeoman of Eastchurch, in 1618, at which three hundred people were present, only cost £7, which was certainly not an inordinate sum. The guests at Elizabeth Cruttenden's funeral, which took place in Kent in 1636, consumed only £2 worth of food and drink between a hundred of them. These sums would suggest that to have a hundred or so people at a burial was certainly not an uncommon event in seventeenth-century Britain. Indeed, in 1681 the Scottish Parliament passed an act attempting actually to limit the number of guests at a funeral to one hundred. At some Nonconformist burials in the late seventeenth century, the numbers of guests ran into thousands rather than just hundreds, as Anthony à Wood's diary records.

Who were all these people who flocked to a burial? Unfortunately, no attendance lists survive for the funerals of ordinary people, as they do for some aristocratic burials, so the evidence is very slight. In Berkshire administrators' accounts, the usual formula employed is simply 'neighbours, kindred and friends'. One Lincolnshire account talks of 'the meeting of friends and neighbours' at the burial. Some Kent accounts single out, from a larger group, 'kindred and familiar acquaintances' as meriting special treatment at the funeral. One important group attending burials in all these counties were the poor, whose role will be discussed later in this chapter.

Sometimes people travelled long distances to a funeral; when Peter Tangett was buried in Canterbury in 1621 his sister, brother-in-law, and the entire Company of Tailors at Faversham made the journey to see him buried. Some of the friends attending the funeral of John Case of Boxley, Kent, in 1632, had to stay the night there, it being too far for them to return home that evening. Generally a messenger would be sent to invite the guests. When Ellen Cooke of Canterbury died in 1681 the nurses who laid her out then took the invitations to the guests.

Occasionally at Kent funerals the local militia would be present. They frequently attended the burial of their own officers and sometimes of outsiders, too. They would come 'in their furniture' with black ribbon tied in fancy knots, and black cloths to decorate their drums. Their purpose was, as one account puts it, 'to tender their respects in countenance of the deceased's funeral' and they must have been an impressive sight. The men would be paid for their presence, usually about 10s; food and drink were also provided for them. Displays such as this served to enhance the status of the deceased and quite possibly attracted an even bigger crowd to the funeral. Another group of people who might be invited to a burial, for the same effect, were the local mayor and councillors. Elizabeth Mayott in 1614 paid the Mayor of Abingdon and his brother to attend her husband's funeral. This was clearly a blatant piece of social snobbery but would, no doubt, have increased the show and drawn the crowds.

A very different function, it could be suggested, was served by the attendance of children at funerals. In Kent accounts, children, where mentioned, are always those of the deceased; often they are specially singled out by the wearing of mourning. They show publicly that, although a death has occurred, the particular family line still continues to flourish; they also mark the family as the primary unit which copes with death. However, in Berkshire and Lincolnshire accounts, references are found to the presence of the young at funerals, which are phrased to imply that these children were not related to the deceased. For example 'poor children' attended the burial of Anne Peele in 1605, while two Berkshire accounts mention 'young folks' or 'young people' at burials, 'according to the custom'. At one London church the attendance of 'youths' at a funeral was a well-established practice:

We the youths of the parish of St John of Jerusalem whose names are hereunder written do willingly subscribe to the order following: *vide* that we shall be ready at an hour's warning for any burial or marriage . . . In witness whereof we have hereunder set our hand the 21st of September 1635.[1]

This linking of youth with death, a concept alien to twentieth-century ideas, is clearly related to the connections between weddings and funerals discussed in previous chapters. It appears in contemporary literature, as in the opening stanza of Herbert's 'Mortification':

How soon doth man decay!
When clothes are taken from a chest of sweets
To swaddle infants, whose young breath
Scarce knows the way;
Those clouts are little winding sheets,
Which do consign and send them unto death.

However, the presence of children at funerals also had a definite practical purpose. It seems reasonable to assume that the Berkshire and Lincolnshire children, being unrelated to the deceased, were not significant for their ties of kinship and inheritance, as in the Kentish examples. Rather, their importance may be seen in their symbolism as an age group; although death might remove a member, the community still continued to exist through the procreation of children. Children represented a means of circumventing death through the survival of the species; the fear of death aroused by a funeral might therefore be mitigated by their presence. This custom showed a community rather than a family-based approach to the problem of death; it also pointed to a secular alternative to the Church's teaching on how death was to be overcome.

Some indication of the major role played by eating and drinking during funeral rites in early modern England may be gauged from the fact that the consumption of food, on many occasions, both initiated and terminated the whole proceedings. This was particularly so after the Restoration, when the deceased's home became the setting for much of the total funeral ritual, the guests actually spending longer there than they did at the church. On one level, this clearly reflects the importance of the secular aspects of funeral rites at this time. The relocation of much of the ritual away from the communal church in favour of the deceased's own house served to differentiate more forcefully for the guests one burial from another, stressing, by the setting, the individuality and uniqueness rather than the similarity between different people's funerals.

Samuel Pepys, describing the burial of his brother, on 18 March 1664, provides an eyewitness account of the proceedings while the corpse was still lying in the house 'waiting to be carried to the church':

> I dressed myself... and so to my brother's again: whither, though invited, as the custom is, at one or two o'clock, they come not till four or five. But at last one after another they come, many more than I bid: and my reckoning that I bid was one hundred and twenty, but I believe there was nearer one hundred and fifty. Their service was six biscuits apiece, and what they pleased of burnt claret . . . the men sitting by themselves in some rooms and the women by themselves in others, very close, but yet room enough.

One pre-Restoration Kentish funeral account mentions that cakes were provided for the guests before the funeral, while in Somerset, at the funeral of Mary Gibbons in 1646, wine was served, in the words of the account, 'at her carrying forth'. The idea of eating and drinking in the presence of the corpse, which to us might seem unacceptable, appeared perfectly natural in a society where death was imbued with less horror and where the living and the dead were not so rigidly separated (see Plate 2, p.124).

This ritual is illustrated in a crude woodcut decorating an eighteenth-century funeral invitation; a large chalice-like cup is shown actually placed on top of the coffin, with a man and a woman standing on either side of it.[2] This is probably attributable to the engraver's lack of skill rather than a true representation of the event, but in wilder and more inaccessible parts of the country a very strange ritual did still take place where the coffin or corpse served as a table for food and drink. This was the practice of sin-eating, a phenomenon which greatly interested John Aubrey:

> In the county of Hereford was an old custom at funerals, to hire poor people, who were to take upon them all the sins of the party deceased. One of them I remember (he was a long, lean, lamentable, poor rascal) lived in a cottage on Ross highway. The manner was that when the corpse was brought out of the house and laid on the bier, a loaf of bread was brought out, and delivered to the sin-eater over the corpse, as also a mazard bowl [of maple] full of beer, which he was to drink up, and sixpence in money, in consideration whereof he took upon him . . . all the sins of the defunct, and freed him or her from walking after they were dead.

This custom was widely practised in seventeenth-century Wales, and, as recently as the early nineteenth century, was recorded in the Cambridgeshire fens; it reflects an even closer interrelationship between the fates of the living and the dead than was to be found in the doctrine of purgatory, officially abandoned at the Reformation.[3] The use of the sin-eater, itself a survival from the Middle Ages, reveals how Roman Catholic beliefs could be altered and distorted in popular folk tradition to produce a ritual which all orthodox Christians, Catholic and Protestant, would have found repugnant. Indeed it relates more closely to the rituals of certain tribes studied by anthropologists than to Christian practices.

After the completion of the burial service the assembled company would attend what was often referred to as a 'drinking'. It is interesting to note that this festivity also took place after the funeral of a pauper whose burial costs were met by the parish; the drinking for Joane White, an Oxford pauper, was held 'at the burial', and cost 18d. Indeed, as has been described, this ritual even occurred during plague-time following the burial of a victim, despite attempts by the authorities to ban such gatherings for fear of spreading the infection. Clearly the drinking was an essential part of the funeral ritual, whatever the circumstances; the brothers and sisters of the Kentish hospitals automatically held a drinking when any one of their number died.

Usually, at least prior to the eighteenth century, the drinking would take place in the churchyard, a further example of an intimacy between the living and the dead commonly unthinkable to twentieth-century man. Indeed, there were times when the drinking seems to have been held in the church itself. In 1603, Bishop Thornborough issued an injunction against 'feasts or drinkings' taking place within the churches in his diocese, while a Norfolk will of 1506 requested 'a drinking for my soul to the value of 6s 8d, in the church of Sporle'.[4] Sometimes the company repaired to a local tavern. William Modsley of Faversham owned two inns, the Lion and the Ship; after his funeral in 1625, cake-bread, wine, sugar and beer were served at each, costing £11 in all. Beer was the usual drink, although sometimes wine and claret were also served and, on one recorded occasion, metheglin or spiced mead. Food, too, was often provided, bread, cakes, biscuits and buns being very popular. In Kent a speciality called cakebread was frequently baked; from the probate accounts it is evident that the ingredients were flour, butter, currants, sugar, spices and rose water.

After the Restoration, 'Naples biscuits' became a popular funeral fare. For the funeral of John Andrew of Wingham, Kent, in 1668, Naples biscuits were purchased from an alderman in Canterbury and sent to Wingham in a box which later had to be returned; there must have been a considerable quantity of biscuits since the bill came to 37s 4d. The funeral account for John Brissenden of Biddenden in 1703 suggests that, on this occasion at least, the biscuits were not actually consumed at the burial but were wrapped in paper and taken home by the guests. At the post-Restoration funerals, tobacco too was sometimes provided for the guests. Sixpence worth was given away at the funeral of Jacob Rayner of Canterbury in 1714, while at Christopher Churchman's burial in the following year the tobacco and pipes for the guests cost 2s 6d.

A particularly grand drinking was held after the burial of Dame Mary Gardner of Abingdon in 1641. The beverages consisted of literally gallons of sack, white wine and claret. To eat, there were 60 pounds of cumfits, 15 pounds of biscuits and 40 dozen cakes. This was supplemented with dried fruits, pears, pippins, quinces, plums, gooseberries and almonds and other delicacies, including macaroons, marzipan, violet cakes and 'green dry lettuce'. The wine cost over £5, and the food, more than £11.

If, after a funeral, a more substantial meal were provided, it would generally take place at the dead person's house. A Lincolnshire land-owner, John Hasslewood, was commemorated by dinner for all his tenants after his burial in 1576. One Berkshire account differentiates between the poorer neighbours, who drank at the church, and the richer neighbours, who were entertained at home; in a similar vein, the account of Isaac Menton in 1638 in Kent specifically states that food was provided only for 'the better sort'. This could still amount to a large number of people; after Lady Mary Oxinden's funeral, in the same year and county, dinner was provided for 'thirty persons invited, besides others that came voluntarily thereto'.

The funeral dinner is often, especially in the Kent accounts, referred to as a 'banquet', not an unjust title for the proceedings. At the funeral feast of Charles Tripp, in 1630, amongst other delicacies, swans were provided. After the burial in 1610 of Matthew Mennyce, Mayor of Sandwich, the following items were served:

An whole vealer, 6 geese, four pork . . . five couple of capons, one dozen and one half of chickens, 2 woodcocks, 4 snipes, one dozen of larks . . . ten couple of rabbits, one dozen of three penny brown bread, three dozen of white and ravel bread and seven pigs . . . 6 dozens of pigeons, eighteen pounds of suet and four turkeys . . . and four score and seven pounds of beef.

Other necessary purchases for this banquet included butter, eggs, six bushels of wheat and grocery wares. A cook from Canterbury was paid 20s to dress the meat, and the spits were turned by poor people. However, this was not the total expenditure on food by any means, since a further 48 of the guests were given dinner at a local inn. In some areas the funeral feasts continued to be held on a grand scale, well into the eighteenth century. At the funeral of a farmer near Whitby, York-shire, in 1760, the guests consumed '110 dozen penny loaves, 9 large hams, 8 legs of veal, 20 stone of beef, 16 stone of mutton, 15 stone of Cheshire cheese, and 30 ankers of ale'.[5]

Food was definitely the most expensive single item in a funeral account, usually accounting for about half the total sum spent. The banquet for Matthew Mennyce cost almost exactly half his total funeral charge of £84 8s 3d. Sometimes the proportion spent on food could rise as high as three-quarters or more of the complete expenditure. Cer-tainly in terms of the proportions in which the money was expended, funerals in the early modern era were more for the living than for the dead.

The drinking or dinner served various purposes within the funeral ritual itself. It was, on one level, a display of the social standing and wealth of the deceased. One Berkshire account mentions 'a funeral feast or remembrance'. This choice of words might seem to imply that the recipients should pray for the deceased, in return for the food, as had been the case before the Reformation. The deceased left the world in a style commensurate with that in which he had lived, in order to preserve his memory in the minds of all who attended. Other accounts refer to eating and drinking after the funeral as an 'entertainment'. Certainly there must have been an element of enjoyment in this ritual, mitigating the sorrow aroused by the interment. It is on these grounds that Richard Hooker defended the tradition. 'For the comfort of them whose minds are through natural affection pensive in such cases no man can justly mislike the custom which the Jews had to end their burials with funeral banquets.'

Critics of the established Church, however, such as Thomas Cartwright, took a different stance: 'This device of man's brain . . . driveth quite away a necessary duty of the minister, which is to comfort with the word of God the parties which be grieved at the death of their friends.' Barrow satirised the practice of feasting after a funeral: 'After all is done in church, then are they all gathered together in a costly and sumptuous banquet. Is not this jolly Christian mourning? Who would not mourn thus every day in the year?'

A more personal criticism of the practice of feasting after a funeral was made in 1809 by William Jones, Vicar of Broxbourne:

> Yesterday the body of old Mr Milward was buried; and the doctor and myself sat down with the executors and a very large party at the Bull, Hoddesdon. Much wine was drunk at and after a very plentiful and elegant dinner. Twice or thrice only, in my professional life, have I joined such a set of *merry mourners*. I have no wish to be of such a party soon again. I was urged to eat and drink more than I was inclined to and I felt very uncomfortable afterwards!

A very different picture is presented by a description of the obsequies of Dr Whitaker of St John's College, Cambridge in 1595 where 'a banquet of sweetmeats, soured with so sad an occasion (at the sole charge of the college), was rather seen than tasted by the guests, formerly surfeited with sorrow'.[6] It is interesting to note this conflict between the ways of reducing the pain of death, on the one hand by Christian teaching and on the other by secular, community-based rituals.

The type of analysis employed by anthropologists studying burial rites in different primitive cultures can also provide ways of understanding funeral rituals in pre-industrial England; as Malinowski has said, mortuary proceedings are basically very similar throughout the world. He also stresses the potentially destructive impact of a death within a community, the 'disintegrating impulses' aroused by death, an event which 'threatens the very cohesion and solidarity of the group'. The rituals which evolve to cope with this desperate situation, such as communal eating and drinking, are primarily for the benefit of the living, rather than for the dead. In the view of anthropologist Raymond Firth, these customs have two functions: they stress the importance of the individual in his own society and they assist in the reintegration of the community shattered by a death. Van Gennep makes this same point when he says that the effect of such funeral rituals is 'to reunite all the surviving members of the group with each other . . . in the same way that a chain which has been broken by the disappearance of one of its links must be rejoined'.

The anthropologist Marcel Mauss suggests that the act of giving in itself has an important function since it can prevent a break in social relationships, besides maintaining the status of the individual. A comparison might be drawn between the funeral feasts of seventeenth-century England and the North American Indian potlatch which Mauss describes. Both are a display of status and also self-perpetuating ceremonies, as Mauss explains, containing the obligation to give, 'the obligation to receive and the obligation to make a return', thereby ensuring the continuation of the custom. The anthropological concepts concerning similar rituals help to illuminate the purposes behind the funeral feast or drinking, suggesting why the consumption of food and drink played such an important part in early modern burial practices, occupying a far longer time than the funeral service itself.

This analysis, drawing on anthropological concepts of the funeral feast or drinking, can also illuminate another feature of these funeral customs, the giving of luxury goods to the guests at a burial. This, too, involved the display of status and the reintegration of the social group through a shared, pleasurable experience, which inherently contained the obligation to perpetuate the custom. The usual gifts were gloves or ribbons. Often these were distributed in large quantities; three and a half dozen gloves were supplied at the funeral of Isaac Hamon in 1642, while ribbon was purchased in dozens of yards. At burials, lace was given, as were points, thread and, in Lincolnshire, incle. Sometimes the ribbons would be white as well as black, while in Kent 'bridelaces' occasionally appear in accounts, again suggesting the link between weddings and funerals. At post-Restoration funerals, scarves, often made of crape, were given. At the Rector of Aldington's funeral in 1680, £10 worth of gloves, scarves and ribbons was distributed, while those who attended the burial of Arthur Lees in Maidstone received crape scarves and kid leather gloves, five dozen pairs for the men and two dozen for the women present.

Another custom which became extremely popular after the Restoration was the giving of rings to guests at a funeral. These were often gold, set with black enamel, giving the name of the deceased and date of death. On Pepys's death in 1703, 123 rings were distributed to his friends, although he himself seems to have had little sentimental regard for rings given to him at funerals; as he recorded after one burial, on 29 March 1669: 'had a very good ring which I did give my wife'. Some probate accounts mention the purchase of rings; for example, at the funeral of Thomas Marshall at Maidstone in 1714, ten rings, costing 10s each, were distributed, while at Richard Greenhill's burial in Canterbury in 1710 £12 was spent on rings for his relatives and friends. Mourning rings, with their personalised inscriptions, are further evidence of the growing desire for worldly remembrance to be found in early modern England (see Plate 4, p. 125).

Sometimes these gifts were reserved for specially selected guests, 'kindred and familiar acquaintances' being singled out to receive gloves at the funeral of George Moore, while on other occasions they were designated for the preacher or for those carrying the body. Some accounts record that only the relatives were favoured, as was commonly the case with mourning clothes. At the funeral of Mary Delanney in Kent in 1623 her family received stockings and garters as well as ribbons and gloves. At the burial in 1639 of John Dean, a bachelor of Whitstable, young bachelors and maids were presented with ribbon, in the words of the account, 'as the manner is where he died'. This custom suggests a symbolic role played by unmarried people, at the funeral of one of their number; their presence, like that of children, promised future marriage and procreation, thereby circumventing the annihilating powers of death.

One group in Berkshire who were specifically designated to receive ribbons and laces were young people, 'according to the custom' or 'according to the use of the country'. The giving of ribbons to the young further strengthens the idea that they fulfilled a symbolic function at funerals. The obligation they incurred in receiving these gifts was, in their turn, to grow up into a new generation of adults, thus preventing death from totally destroying human life. It is also interesting to consider the effect of this ritual on the children themselves. Their participation might be seen as a method of reducing their fear of dying, through pleasant association, a form of 'conditioning' which, by linking funerals with the receiving of gifts in the minds of the young, alleviated some of the terror surrounding death. This idea features prominently in Aldous Huxley's vision of the future, *Brave New World*, where children are encouraged to play in the wards of the hospital for the dying and receive extra sweets on 'deathdays'. This new 'death conditioning' imagined by Huxley is ironically very similar in fact to what actually happened for many centuries at English funerals.

One large and important element at a late sixteenth- or early seventeenth-century funeral was the poor, attracted by the promise of a dole. Only one of the probate accounts mentions the number of indigents actually present; 180 people each received a penny dole at the burial of Thomas Beake of Wickhambreux, Kent, in 1569. The account of Anne Bisborough says that there were 'a great company of poor people which attended the burial', who received 20s, distributed among them by the churchwardens. When the dole was given in bread it seems reasonable to suppose that each poor person would receive one or two loaves. If this were the case, then, for example, between 50 and 100 paupers would have been fed at the funeral of George Moore of Canterbury and between 85 and 170 at the funeral of George Young of Thannington, Kent. Although it is impossible to be certain, it would seem that a crowd of about a hundred poor people, in addition, of course, to the ordinary guests, would not be an unusually high figure for an early seventeenth-century burial.

Funeral doles, which have been described by W.K. Jordan the historian as one of 'the most perfectly typical forms of medieval alms', persisted well into the post-Restoration period. As late as 1760, at the funeral of a Yorkshire farmer, a thousand people were fed and received a dole.[7] White, an Elizabethan cleric, complained in a sermon of 1589 that 'the dead do give more than those that are alive, and therefore if God will have the poor provided for, I think he must provide to take away more of the rich men'.[8] Such literary evidence as to the prominence of funeral doles, however exaggerated it may in fact have been, is given considerable support by surviving probate accounts, particularly those for wealthy people, but sometimes also of humbler folk. While there was a gradual decline, throughout the sixteenth and seventeenth centuries, in the proportion of accounts mentioning a dole, change was slow and uneven. A higher proportion of Lincolnshire accounts mention doles than do those for Berkshire and Kent; in this, as in other respects, the north clung more firmly to old ways (see Table 6, p. 241). Throughout the country, however, comparatively steady provision of alms in monetary terms needs to be seen in the context of the prevailing inflation, which reduced the value of such bequests in real terms.

Doles were usually given in money or, if in bread, in the form of penny loaves. These were sometimes distributed in truly enormous quantities; 28½ dozen at the funeral in Kent in 1637 of Mary Abeare, and 60 dozen at Dame Mary Gardner's burial in Abingdon in 1641. Other food might also be provided; beef and a sheep both occur in the Kent accounts, while George Young specifically stated in his will that the poor were to receive cheese at his burial. Exceptionally, cakes were provided for the poor, though quite often beer was served to wash down the food. Alternatively, the dole might be given in staple commodities, wheat or sometimes malt.

The distribution almost always took place at the church after the burial; one account records that it was given 'at the church door'. Sometimes the churchwardens would supervise the distribution of a dole and control the crowd. Occasionally, either the deceased or his administrator stipulated which poor people were to benefit from the dole, most frequently 'the poor of the parish' or 'the poor of the place where the deceased had lived'. The dole for Christopher Ponet of Warehorne, Kent, was shared among the paupers in six different parishes at the direction of his executor. Members of the Dutch and Walloon churches in Kent customarily left money to the poor of their own congregation and sometimes to the English poor of the parish in which they had lived. Two accounts, one from Lincolnshire and the other from Berkshire, specify that a dole was given to poor children. Presumably this would have increased the number of that age group present and heightened their symbolic function.

More rarely, a 'month's mind' would also be held at which the poor would again receive alms. This was a pre-Reformation ceremony, held a month after the burial, 'that the dead may be remembered and prayed for'. It was forbidden by episcopal injunctions; Bishop Hooper of Gloucester and Worcester, in 1551, enquired 'whether they keep and use any month-ends . . . which is the maintenance of the purgatory, and false belief and state and condition of the dead'. However, the phrase, 'to have a month's mind', meaning 'to have a great longing' was still in current use during the reign of Queen Elizabeth and the actual practice had not been entirely stamped out. At the month's mind of Thomas Beake of Wickhambreux, in 1569, the poor received 7s, while meat and drink worth 20s were consumed in memory of the dead man. It is quite possible that when, as in one Berkshire case, a third of the dole was given at the burial and the remainder the following Christmas, this was a relic of the older custom.

The function of the funeral dole was slightly different from the other forms of giving at funerals. It was, of course, status enhancing, since a substantial dole would attract large numbers of poor people and swell the crowd at the funeral. One account describes a dole as 'a remembrance of the deceased'; clearly, as with largesse at the drinking, the idea was to impress the recipients sufficiently so that they would not forget the dead person for a long time and, possibly, even pray for him, despite numerous bishops' injunctions to the contrary. The anthropologist Mauss describes almsgiving as a 'contractual sacrifice': 'The gods and spirits consent that the portion reserved for them and destroyed in useless sacrifice should go to the poor and the children.'

The same sentiment, translated into Christian terms, may be found in contemporary sermons. According to Richard Mariott, 'the poor man's hand is the rich man's treasury, what he lays up there, he shall find in heaven,' while another preacher described alms as 'not only comfortable to others, but also profitable to our selves, and acceptable to God'.[9] The giving of doles could even be seen as a way of propitiating the dead themselves; although Bishop Sandys claimed that 'the gospel hath chased away walking spirits', belief in ghosts and their malicious actions remained prevalent long after the Reformation.[10] John Aubrey suggested a different supernatural connection: 'Me thinks, doles to poor people with money at funerals have some resemblance to that of the sin-eater.' According to Aubrey, it appears that the poor actually took on the dead person's sins, although, no doubt, the poor themselves were more concerned to satisfy their own hunger and thirst than to reflect on their precise role as recipients of funeral doles.

Whether to propitiate God or to cast off their sins on to the poor, provision for a dole was not only a common request in the wills of the period, but also by far the most frequent death-bed request recorded in the accounts. Certainly people contemplating death may have felt that to give a dole to the poor would assist them in some way, as believed before the Reformation. This turning to charity at the last moment was attacked by a number of religious writers. Thomas Becon, in *The Sick Man's Salve*, wrote:

> I have not been of the mind that some are, which, so long as they live, greedily gather together, and bestow nothing at all upon the poor: but when they see nothing but present death, then lash they out, and liberally give unto the poor, *scilicet*, because they can keep it no longer.

Henry Barrow made the same point when he condemned the sort of man who left provision for a dole, 'though in his lifetime the poor might go naked and starve for any help and relief they found of him'. It is, perhaps, surprising that the giving of funeral doles did not come under greater attack from Puritan critics; it is described as 'idolatrous' and 'unlawful', but on the whole is little discussed. Quite possibly this is because funeral doles, like the other rituals examined in this chapter, were, in the words of the *Admonition*, 'rather used of custom and superstition, than by the authority of the [prayer] book'.

The funeral rites discussed in this chapter reveal a strong custom-based tradition which continued, in the main, to flourish long after the Reformation. The powerful healing effects of these acts should not be underestimated; the sharing of food, the presence of certain groups at the funeral and the giving of gifts, all helped to mitigate the consequences of a death within the community. Since more time and money was devoted to these rituals than to the actual burial service, it is reasonable to assert that early modern funerals were rather for the living than for the dead. These secular customs, embodying, as they did, forces to restore a society shattered by death, were a legacy of the Middle Ages that the efforts of reformers were unable to destroy. The communal rituals, although gradually being eroded, helped to diminish the impact of the acute problem posed by death, engendered by the individualistic philosophy which was steadily gaining ground throughout the period.

Notes

1. London, County Hall: P.79/JNI/22.

2. Oxford, Bodleian Library: John Johnson Collection, Funerals, Box I (seen in 1975 but missing 1983).

3. Porter, *Cambridgeshire Customs*, pp. 26-7.

4. Quoted in Glyde, *Norfolk Garland*, p. 27.

5. Quoted in Wright, *Rustic Speech and Folklore*, p. 281.

6. Cooper, *Annals of Cambridge*, ii, p. 542.

7. Wright, *Rustic Speech and Folklore*, p. 281.

8. Quoted in Jordan, *Philanthropy in England*, p. 169.

9. Ibid., pp. 169 and 202.

10. Quoted in Thomas, *Religion and the Decline of Magic*, p. 591; Chapter 19 of his book, pp. 587-614, discusses belief in ghosts, giving many fascinating examples.

8 'THE TRAPPINGS AND THE SUITS OF WOE': THE HERALDIC FUNERAL

Paradoxically, those people in Elizabethan England with the greatest wealth, the members of the aristocracy, arguably had the least freedom of choice concerning the funerals of themselves or their relatives.[1] Their burials were closely controlled, either directly by the Queen and Lord Burghley, or through the College of Arms. The reason for this was political; the death of a powerful subject weakened the social hierarchy and had to be compensated for by a display of aristocratic strength. Although a duke might have died, there were still eleven other dukes to follow him to his grave; the emphasis was on continuity rather than loss, on strength rather than bereavement. When first introduced in the late Middle Ages, the heraldic funeral could be interpreted as a manifestation of increased individualism; the same ritual, however, grew to become a suppressant of individuality, eventually leading to its decline during the seventeenth century and virtual extinction in the eighteenth.

While the heraldic funeral placed considerable strictures on the participants it should not be thought that all those involved viewed the ritual with disfavour. In 1638, William Calley wrote to Richard Harvey: 'My brother Danvers, coming lately from Littlecote, made such a relation of Mr Popham's funeral as would make any man but a coward hug death to gain so stately an interment.'[2] This chapter discusses elaborate heraldic funerals of this kind, as carried out before the Interregnum; later heraldic burials will be examined, together with the rituals which eventually supplanted them, in the next chapter.

To prepare a heraldic funeral was a lengthy business. The corpse of Francis Talbot, Earl of Shrewsbury, had to wait 24 days, while preparations were made for its interment in 1560. On occasion, the waiting period could be substantially longer. This made embalming a necessary and inevitable feature of the heraldic funeral ritual.

When Nicholas Bacon's corpse was opened after his death in 1578, three doctors were present, but the actual incision was made by two surgeons who were given aprons and sleeves to perform the job; all five men were paid 40s each. Five surgeons then seared and embalmed the body; they were paid a total of £7 8s 4d, while the bill for spices and perfumes came to £9. Four women dressed and 'trimmed' the corpse before the embalmed body was wrapped in seven ells of canvas and placed in a coffin made of lead. An inscription was engraved on the lead coffin and then it was placed inside a wooden coffin 'with hooks and hasps'. The wood coffin cost only 15s, but the lead one was £5 4s 9d, with a further 43s 4d for the inscription.

The body of James Montague, Bishop of Winchester, was embalmed by Mr Rowland, the surgeon, who was paid £2 and was assisted by two other surgeons who each received 12s. Payment of 10s was made to 'a woman to attend the surgeons with water, mops, cloths and other things'. The bowels were then buried at night by torchlight and a £1 dole was distributed to the poor. However, the embalming was not properly carried out and it became necessary 'to new embalm the body'; 'one that undertook the doing of it' received £1 while his helper was paid 10s. All this occurred despite the bishop's clear directions in his will that his body should undergo 'no cutting or mangling'. This instruction had to be ignored if a heraldic funeral suitable for the status of the deceased was to be performed.

A few corpses totally defied the embalmer's skill and had to be hastily buried, often by night. After Ludovic Stuart, Duke of Richmond and Lenox, had died in 1624,

> on the next night at ten of the clock, necessity not permitting to defer his burying, he was carried by his own servants, and accompanied with a great number of knights and gentlemen unto the Abbey Church of Westminster, and there in King Henry VII's chapel . . . honourably buried by the reverend Bishop of Lincoln . . who read himself the burial of the dead.

However, this was by no means the end, but rather the beginning of 'the pompous funerals of the gracious Prince Ludovic'. Two months later a magnificent funeral procession of a thousand mourners filed from Richmond House to the Abbey, bearing a lifesize effigy of the dead man. On reaching the Abbey, the Bishop of Lincoln preached a sermon on the text 'And Zabud the son of Nathan was principal officer and the King's friend'; then the full heraldic funeral ritual took place, with the officers of the dead duke's household breaking their staves over the effigy, rather than over the coffin as was usually the case. Nor was Ludovic Stuart the only nobleman whose funeral had to be held around an effigy rather than the actual body; when the funeral of Gilbert, Earl of Shropshire, was performed in Sheffield in 1616, six gentlemen bore a 'representation' rather than the body itself. These funerals without the actual corpse epitomise the idea that funerals are for the living rather than the dead. They also underline the perceived importance of carrying out the rituals, even when the *raison d'être*, the burial of a body, had already passed; what remained was a political and social requirement.

After the corpse was safely embalmed, or hurriedly interred, the serious business of planning the funeral began. Generally the main onus fell on the executor or executors, although others were sometimes involved, as when the Duke of Richmond's widow 'appointed . . . three commissioners, men of honour, and worthy of great respect, who diligently prepared for the funeral pomps, in the space of two months'.

However, organisers of aristocratic funerals, particularly during the lifetimes of Lord Burghley and Queen Elizabeth, were not simply left to their own devices. At all times, the requirements of the College of Arms had to be taken into consideration. The officers had to be notified 'of the death of all noblemen, knights, esquires and gents and their wives'.[3] Heralds would then attend all the aristocratic funerals and issue a certificate giving the pedigree of the deceased, together with details of his or her death and burial. The intervention of Elizabeth I and Burghley went beyond regulating the details of heraldic practices supervised by the College of Arms and entered the realm of political considerations. A heraldic funeral was a tremendous display of the power of the aristocracy, and so one important decision in which Elizabeth and Burghley sometimes interfered was where the burial should take place. It was easier to organise the whole proceedings in London, since problems of transporting goods were substantially diminished, while the difficulties and expense of accommodating guests were virtually eliminated. Certainly in London, grand funerals, such as that of Queen Elizabeth herself, recorded in Stow's *Chronicle*, made their mark upon the urban population: 'the whole streets being full of common people, the windows, leads and tiles full on both sides of the better sort'.

However, it was also politic for these displays to take place regularly in the provinces, despite any practical inconvenience it might cause. When Lord Burghley and the Queen had made up their minds that a funeral was to be performed in the country, they were not easily deflected from their course. Henry, Lord Cobham, wrote in 1597 from Cobham Hall, Kent, to Lord Burghley's son, Sir Robert Cecil:

> I could have wished your father would have allowed . . . my father's
> funeral to have been performed at London . . . for neither house nor

the church is fit for the performing of it here. Your father's will amongst us must stand for a law without any further dispute, otherwise this place is so unmeet for it, as whereas I had hoped to have had honour in burying of my father, I shall now receive shame.

Not content with that, Lord Cobham added a postscript to his letter reiterating his feelings on the matter:

PS Do but imagine what trouble I am put unto, for of necessity I must bring all the staff from Blackfriars and from Canterbury hither, which I should not need of if the funeral might be at London . . . I am heartily sorry my lord will not allow the burial to be at London.

The additional expenses incurred in having things sent from London are revealed in the accounts for various aristocratic funerals. For example, £20 was spent on 'carriage down of all the stuff' when Walter, Earl of Essex, was buried at Basing in 1576, while a further £40 was spent on 'riding charges of officers [heralds] going and coming'. Of course, the Queen did not have to battle with all her aristocratic subjects over the last resting place of their relatives, as many preferred to lie among their ancestors in the local church. However, if one received a letter from Lord Burghley, as did George, Fourth Earl of Huntingdon, in 1596, concerning his brother's burial, which ended with the words 'I think the Queen will expect your speedy resolution', there was little recourse but to comply.

If an aristocrat died somewhere other than their chosen resting place, the body had to be transported in suitable style across England. Sir Henry Sidney, Lord President of the Council of the Welsh Marches, died in the west in 1586 and had to be carried back to his family home, Penshurst in Kent, 'the corpse being attended upon by divers of the Council of the Marches, some of his kinsmen, allies and servants to the number of 140 horses at least through all the journey'.

On 9 June, 28 of Sir Henry's servants travelled down to Worcester from London to assist the corpse and a coach was got ready for the journey. On 14 June a supper and dinner was held at Worcester 'for the Council and all the officers of the court as for the townsmen and strangers'. On the following day, the journey began: bells were rung in Worcester, the poor received a dole and all the bills were paid. 'Divers poor men' helped lift the corpse into the coach and it then travelled to Evesham, with bells ringing and the distribution of doles to the poor on the way. That night, while the 'whole train' ate and slept, the town watchmen guarded the body. On the 16th, the procession moved on to Oxford via Chipping Norton where dinner was eaten and the horses properly fed. At Oxford, that night, the council were entertained by musicians, while the poor scholars of the university received the benefits of the mourners' charity. Also, the council listened to the recitation of epitaphs on the dead man. None of these particular verses has survived, but the lines composed on the death in the same year, 1586, of Sir Henry's more famous son, Sir Philip Sidney, illustrate the genre:

> England, Netherland, the Heavens and the Arts,
> The soldiers and the world have made six parts
> Of noble Sidney: for who will suppose
> That a small heap of stones can Sidney enclose?

> England hath his body, for she it fed,
> Netherland his blood in her defence shed.
> The heavens have his soul, the arts have his fame,
> The soldiers the grief, the world his good name.[4]

From Oxford, Sir Henry Sidney's body was carried in three days to Penshurst, where a magnificent funeral was prepared.

These long funeral journeys brought a display of the power of the aristocracy to many people along the route, serving a political purpose and perhaps a spiritual one, too. James Montague, Bishop of Winchester, willed to be buried 'if it be possible in the great Church of Bath'. He actually died in London in 1618 and evidently had no notion of the costly and ostentatious way his body would be carried down to Bath, for he wrote in his will that 'being to be buried in a remote place I see no great reason to be [buried] at any extraordinary charge'. The corpse lay at Winchester House in London for a month, while the funeral was prepared; in the coach-house and tackroom every piece of saddlery and all the coach's exterior and its upholstery were covered in black. Meanwhile, servants were sent down to Bath to organise the food there and to hang three houses and the Abbey with black cloth. Finally, the procession set out, the chief mourners being the dead bishop's brothers. At Kingston, a coachwheel broke and had to be repaired, but they reached Reading safely that night and sat down to a sumptuous meal at the George, which included mutton, veal, rabbits, ducks, chicken, pigeons and artichokes. For breakfast the following morning, further mutton, rabbit and chicken appeared, together with a calf's head. The servants and commoners were put up at the Cardinal's Hat; at both inns the horses were fed and reshod if necessary, while the coach was greased. The next night an equally sumptuous supper was eaten at the White Hart in Marlborough where trout, too, was served and there was tongue for breakfast; the less favoured company slept at the Bear, where a sick mare was treated and the coach repaired. On arrival in Bath, the three houses were ready for the mourners; the fowler had provided a wide range of delicacies such as plovers, quail, snipe and partridges. Further meals at Bath included roast ox, roasting pigs and pheasant. After the funeral itself, the mourners returned to London in similar gastronomic splendour.

The finer points of the organisation of a heraldic funeral rested with the College of Arms, who followed, in great detail, established regulations and precedents. One aspect of their task was to make sure that both the church and the rooms in which the body lay in state were suitably adorned with black cloth. They also had to supervise the erection of the hearse, the degree of elaboration of which varied according to the rank of the deceased. The hearse for Francis Talbot, Earl of Shrewsbury, buried at Sheffield in 1560, was 'twelve feet in length and in breadth, having a close roof with hatchments, rounding from the top, by the square, to the four corners'. Along the top of the hearse were large escutcheons of 'paste-paper', interspersed with 'pencils', small triangular flags of paper or buckram. The posts of the hearse were covered with black velvet and a 'breadth of black velvet' went around the outside of the structure, just below the 'close roof', 'and to all the nether edge of the said velvet was fastened a valence of sarsenet, written with letters of gold SIC TRANSIT GLORIA MUNDI. The valence was fringed with a fringe of black silk, a quarter deep.' The floor of the hearse was covered with black sarsenet, while outside the main structure ran two rows of low rails which, like the rest of the hearse, were hung with black cloth and 'garnished with escutcheons'. Between the two sets of rails 'stood nine stools and cushions, which were covered with fine black cloth'.

The preparation of all this had to be supervised by the heralds, in addition to the hanging of both the church, and the porch, wall and great chamber of Sheffield Castle, with black broadcloth, decorated with escutcheons. The actual work was carried out by carpenters; for Bishop Montague's funeral the timber for the hearse cost £2, while 'nails and pins to set it up' cost £1 10s. A further £1 19s 6d was spent on 'timber rails to hang blacks about the church', the carpenter receiving £2 'to frame the hearse', in addition to 19s 4d for erecting the rails. The amount and type of cloth to be used on the hearse was closely regulated by the College of Arms; for Catherine, Countess of Huntingdon's funeral in 1576, the black material for each pillar of the hearse had to be two yards long; black velvet carpets for the floor had to be four yards each and the black silk fringe on the valence had to be 'the depth of a quarter and a nail'. It is not surprising that at Bess of Hardwick's funeral in 1601 a thousand black pins were needed, costing altogether 1s 10d.

The heralds also had to supervise the work of the painters, who prepared coats of arms ranging from huge hatchments to the thousands of small 'pencil' flags which seemingly adorned every available space in the house and church. The precise numbers, designs and materials for these were again determined by the rank of the deceased. The painters also made funeral armour, the crest, helmet, sword, spurs and gauntlets carried at the burial and then hung up in the church, some of which remain there to this day. Of course, these, too, varied according to the dead man's status; a helmet of 'steel gilt' for an earl's funeral cost £1, with a further £1 for the crest, while a helmet for a knight cost 16s and his crest 13s.[5]

Part of the heralds' duties included making sure that the deceased's relatives did not attempt to use heraldic accoutrements to which they were not entitled. If this happened at a funeral carried out without the heralds' prior knowledge, then the College of Arms could fine the offenders after the event. For example, in 1648 the College investigated the proceedings at the funeral of a baronet, Sir John St John of Battersea, collecting the testimony of various witnesses and writing a report on the case. It began with a statement of the principle that the funeral rites of different social ranks should differ in their grandeur and 'that from time beyond the memory of man the same distinction and observation hath been had'. Then various witnesses were quoted. They asserted that two rooms 'were hanged to the ground and floored with blacks and the said rooms were hung unusually thick with rows of escutcheons of . . . arms'. The design of the hearse was that reserved for barons and earls:

> The deponent for his part never saw or heard of such or so many pennons used at the funeral of any person of the degree of the defunct but for number they were as many as should have been used at the funeral of a Duke of the Blood Royal.

On the day of the funeral, the heralds had to organise the procession; at Lady Berkeley's funeral, 'the whole train being . . . assembled by ten of the clock in the forenoon, were by Garter King at Arms and Chester Herald set in order and directed thus to proceed from the . . . house to the church'. Strict protocol had to be observed in the procession, with position determined by status. No doubt the task of marshalling the mourners was made easier for the heralds if, as at the funeral of Sir John Stowell, the guests had already been grouped at the house, according to their rank, as the notes or 'remembrances' show:

> Put the overseers in mind that some attend to conduct the best sort of men mourners and others of the chief rank into the drawing room. The better sort of the next mourners and others to be conducted into the great dining room: the inferior sort, and servants, to remain in the hall. If there be any ladies and gentlewomen they are to be disposed of in the little dining room.

While waiting, the mourners were offered 'banquets', with wine and beer served in the hall.

Gradually, the heralds managed to get everyone into their places and the procession would set out for the church 'with slow steps and frequent pauses', in the words of the account of Lady Berkeley's burial. Although these funeral processions varied in their details, the basic order and organisation remained the same. To give but one example, at the funeral of Francis Talbot, the 'manner of the proceeding to the church with the corpse, was thus'. First came the conductors, with black staves, followed by the poor, in twos, wearing black gowns. The number of poor people in the procession was usually determined by the deceased's age, with one for each year of his or her life. The account of the funeral of the Earl of Derby in 1572 makes it clear that the poor had to wait outside the church during the actual interment, lined up ready for the return procession. Next, at the funeral of Francis Talbot, came the choir, singing, and then the hooded standard bearer alone, followed by all the gentlemen attending the funeral, 'two and two, in long gowns, with hoods on their shoulders'. Then came, in order, the dead man's chaplains, all the esquires, and the household officials of the deceased, carrying their white staves of office. The bearer of the banner was hooded, as were the heralds who followed him; Lancaster carrying the helm and crest, Chester the target or shield, and Garter King of Arms carrying the deceased's coat of arms. The heralds wore tabards of the royal arms over their black mourning gowns. The reasons for this are set out in contemporary heraldic instructions:

> The Officer of Arms weareth the King's coat of arms at the inter-
> ment of a nobleman not only for the well ordering of the funeral
> but also for this intent that it may be known unto all men that the
> defunct died honourably, without any spot of dishonesty, the which
> might be dishonour unto his blood, and the King's majesty's good
> and loyal subject.[6]

The heralds' role at the funerals of the aristocracy was more than
purely functional; on a symbolic level they represented the authority
of the monarchy, a salient reminder to all present of the origin of aristocratic power (see Plate 5, p. 126).

Then came the corpse on an open coach, surrounded by four banner
bearers. The body was immediately followed by the chief mourner,
wearing a long train, carried by a gentleman usher; then came the eight
other principal mourners, in pairs, while the rear of the procession consisted of yeomen, also two by two.

The funeral procession of Lady Berkeley varied slightly in its details
from that of Francis Talbot. Because the deceased was a woman, the
chosen poor people were women, 70 of them in all, and they were followed by the servants of all the people taking part in the procession,
arranged according to the rank of their masters or mistresses. The coffin
was carried by eight gentlemen and yeomen, and Garter King of Arms
walked behind it with two gentlemen ushers. All the principal mourners
were women; the chief 'mourneress' wore a Paris hood and barbe and
had a train which was borne by a woman 'apparelled as an esquiress
in her gown, lined hood of black with a pleated kerchief and barbe of
lawn'; the chief mourner had two male assistants, one of them the
deceased's son, supporting her by the arms.

At even grander funerals, further refinements were added to the
procession. Trumpeters were sometimes employed, while four horses
trapped in black were led in the procession. The horse nearest to the
coffin would be decked out as the horse of honour, often using black
velvet covered with escutcheons. In addition to the usual accoutrements
borne by the heralds, gauntlets and spurs might also be carried; on
occasion, even the complete armour of the dead man would appear,
worn by a champion mounted on the horse of honour. At the grandest
of funerals the mourners were on horseback. For instance, at the funeral
of the Earl of Derby in 1572, after 100 poor men and 40 choristers
came 80 gentlemen, 'mounted on comely geldings', together with 50

esquires and knights, on horseback, as were the heralds and principal mourners. The body itself was carried on a chariot, covered with black velvet, which was drawn by four horses, trapped in black cloth decorated with escutcheons, while a pageboy, also in black, rode on each horse. At the rear came 500 yeomen and all the servants of those taking part, bringing the total to almost 1,000 participants, no mean feat of organisation for the officers of the College of Arms.

Enforced participation in the staging of these extravagant displays placed the relatives of the deceased under several constraints. Not the least of these was the financing of such events, during which many widows and heirs must have seen their potential inheritance evaporate in a whirl of black mourning cloth and heralds' fees. Equally galling, in a different way, were the heraldic regulations about who might act as chief and principal mourners at such a funeral. The ruling was that the mourners had to be of the same sex as the deceased, which meant, of course, that no one could act as mourner for their own spouse.[7] In an age which saw the growth of affectionate relationships between husbands and wives — 'affective individualism', in the words of Lawrence Stone — this ruling on the sex of mourners went against the emotional tide of the era. Because of the regulation that the principal mourners had to be of the same status as the deceased, only the eldest of any sons could act as mourner to a dead father, and daughters could rarely mourn officially for their own mothers. While the chief mourner would be the dead aristocrat's heir, it could on occasion become quite difficult to find sufficient members of the higher social echelons to act as principal mourners for one of their number: dukes and marquesses had to have eleven, earls and viscounts nine and barons seven principal mourners. Little regard could be paid to their relationship to the deceased; all that mattered, from the heralds' point of view, was to get the right number of mourners of the correct rank. The ironic situation therefore arose where, at its worst, most of the official mourners had little regret at the passing of the deceased, while the truly bereaved were excluded from any major part in the ceremony.

This conflicting situation arose chiefly because the heraldic funeral was not, in many ways, concerned with the deceased at all. Indeed, in political terms, the main reason for holding the ritual was to stress the continuing power of the aristocracy and to prove that it remained unaffected by the death of one of its members. This view of society, in which no one was indispensable and everyone could simply be replaced by another person of similar rank, was greatly at odds with the growing feeling of individualism, with its emphasis on personal uniqueness. The heraldic funeral, with its rigid regulations and essentially political orientation, was totally unsuited to the needs of a society in which individualism was taking root and where the loss of a particular person posed increased emotional tension.

On entering the church, the principal mourners all sat inside the rails around the hearse, on the stools provided for them, with the chief mourner at the head. The coffin itself was placed inside the hearse, the helmet, shield and other accoutrements being laid upon it; a psalm was sung while this was taking place. Next there might be a funeral sermon, although sometimes this was delayed until later in the proceedings. The sermon would be in two parts, the first being on the subject of death, the second concerning the life of the deceased. A popular text, used at the funeral of Francis Talbot, was 'blessed are they that die in the name of the Lord'. The preacher at Lady Berkeley's funeral

> towards the end of his learned sermon took a fit occasion to speak of her learned and virtuous life (a lady never known to dissemble or heard to swear) which speech (modestly carried) sealed also with the knowledge of many hundreds there present, wrought such effect, that seldom hath been beheld a more sorrowful assembly at a subject's funeral, nor tears more dropping down.

The sermon ended, another psalm was sung, after which the mourners all processed once around the hearse and returned to their places.

It was then that the officers of the College of Arms supervised the most dramatic and important part of the whole heraldic funeral, the offering. In this extraordinary ritual, the symbolic blessings of Church and state were merged in passing on the accoutrements and power of the dead aristocrat to his heir. The ceremony combined the usual offertory made at mass or communion with a ritual of succession, marking the return to normality of the aristocratic ranks, temporarily disarrayed by the death of a title holder. First, the chief mourner, accompanied by the most senior of the officers of arms present, went up to the altar and offered money 'in commemoration of the defunct', which the minister received in 'a silver basin'. At the Earl of Shrewsbury's funeral, the chief mourner 'making [a] reverence, gave a purse of gold for the offering. The which chief mourner had a cushion and a carpet laid by a gentleman usher, for him to kneel on'. This ritual, natural as it might seem in terms of the Roman Catholic practice of intercession for souls in purgatory, accorded oddly with Protestant beliefs; like other such customs, it was an anachronism which continued to be practised long after the *raison d'être* had been swept away.

The chief mourner, after returning to his stool, would then go up to the altar again, this time to make an offering on his own behalf. At the Earl of Shrewsbury's funeral, the chief mourner, when offering for himself, had 'neither train borne up, or cushion, or carpet to kneel on'. This was to emphasise the difference between his acting for the defunct and the humility which he adopted when playing the role of a mourner.

At this stage, both the chief mourner and senior herald would remain at the altar to receive the achievements. First the coat of arms would be carried to the altar by two principal mourners, attended by a herald. The minister, after receiving it, handed it to the heir, 'with reverence', symbolically investing him; the heir would then pass it to the senior herald, who would place it upon the altar. The next two principal mourners carried the sword, point downwards, and shield; these too, having been given to the minister, and then to the heir – the sword now with the point upwards – were also laid on the altar by the senior herald. When all the accoutrements had been offered by the principal mourners, each pair conducted by a herald, the various banners, pennons and standards carried in the procession were offered, again in pairs, and left 'leaning against the [communion] table'. When all these had been offered, the chief mourner returned to his stool, and then all the men present in the church made their offerings of money, in pairs, according to their rank.

When an armed champion, mounted on a charger, took part in the procession, the horse would actually appear in the church. For example, at the funeral of Thomas, Duke of Norfolk, in 1524, at Thetford, after the offering of the coat of arms, shield, sword, helmet and crest

> Carlisle Herald . . . went to the church door of the Abbey, where he conducted a knight up to the offering, wearing the armour of the duke departed, riding on a courser trapped with fine cloth of gold, garnished with his arms, bearing in his hand the said duke's axe, with the point downwards, and so riding to the choir door . . . then came to the sexton of the Abbey challenging the said horse for his fee, on which the knight alighted, and was led up to the offering . . .

These emblems of war were considered unsuitable to be used at the funerals of ladies. As an Elizabethan heraldic document suggested, 'it agreeth not to say a woman of arms'; it declared the practice 'not convenient' and 'not lawful today'.[8] Instead, the principal mourners offered palls which were later made into vestments, although these were not permitted if the deceased were 'under the degree of Countess'; in the case of lower ranks, the principal mourners simply offered money. The banners and other heraldic flags were offered in the usual way at a woman's funeral, and could be received by her male heir who, it will be remembered, assisted the chief mourner in the procession. At Lady Berkeley's funeral, 'her eldest son was by Mr Garter led to the offertory and there by him invested with the honour of his deceased mother, by delivery and acceptance of the banners and other ceremonies'. The ritual of the offertory at women's funerals, too, symbolised a transference of power with the approval of the Crown, as represented by the presiding herald, and of the Church, in the person of the officiating cleric.

Either just before or directly after the offering, the King of Arms or senior herald present would proclaim the 'style' of the deceased, listing their titles and publicly announcing their death. This pronouncement, a cross between a prayer and a declaration, made 'in a loud voice', marked the official demise of the public person of the deceased.

Perhaps the strangest aspect of the whole ritual, and certainly one of its most telling features, was that the company of mourners had generally left the church before the actual interment itself took place. The account of the funeral of the Earl of Derby in 1572 makes it very plain that this was what happened:

> The offering ended, the 100 poor men were placed to proceed homeward on foot, and after them the knights, esquires and gentlemen, on horseback; then Garter principal King of Arms, then the principal mourner, with the other eight mourners two and two, and then the yeomen on foot, two and two.

> After whose departure, presently the body was by . . . eight gentlemen and four yeomen . . . carried to the grave.

It is certainly clear from this, if further evidence were needed, that the heraldic funeral was concerned with a great deal more than simply burying a dead body. The corpse represented the private persona, while the titles and achievements signified the aristocrat's public existence. The whole ritual of the heraldic funeral revolved around the legitimate transfer of titles and power; the private persona counted for very little indeed. Once the titles and honour had been passed on to the successor, attention passed to him and away from the body, which now held little significance in the political show. Whatever private sorrow he may have felt at the loss of his father, the heir could not stay to see him interred, but had to return in the procession, so as to demonstrate publicly that the ranks of the aristocracy were once again restored to their full complement. The political purposes of the heraldic funeral overrode all private emotions and the participants, despite their feelings, were required to comply with the regulations.

A few people however did remain to see the actual interment and hear the service for the burial of the dead. At least one herald would attend, as the funeral certificate had to be signed, stating that the deceased had been correctly interred. Also present were the deceased's household servants, whose obligation to serve the dead person officially ended only when the coffin was lowered into the grave. For these men, the burial of their master could be a time of genuine personal sorrow, perhaps tinged with anxiety as to their own futures. At the Earl of Derby's funeral, the household officers, steward, treasurer and so on, 'when the body was buried, kneeling on their knees, with weeping tears, broke their white staves and rods over their heads and threw the shivers of the same into the grave'.

These particular men, so the account of the funeral suggests, were more fortunate than some, for on returning to Latham Hall, 'they received their offices and staves again of the new Earl, their lord and master'. Before the vault was finally closed, the achievements and banners were laid upon the coffin again; having symbolised the transference of power, the actual objects were no longer needed. A token handful of dust would be sprinkled on the coffin and then the burial ceremony was complete.

On returning to the family seat, the mourners would be treated to a sumptuous banquet. 'On the day of interment' of Thomas Howard, Duke of Norfolk, 'was a magnificent entertainment, consisting of four hundred messes'. After the funeral of Francis Talbot:

> At the castle was prepared a great dinner, that is to say, there was served from the dressers (besides my lord's services for his own board, which were three messes of meat) 320 messes, to all manner of people who seemed honest, having to every mess eight dishes; that is to say, two boiled messes, four roast, and two baked meats, whereof one was venison. For there was killed for the same feast, fifty does and twenty nine red deer . . . And after the same dinner every man was honourably contented for his pains.

For Bess of Hardwick's funeral feast in 1607, among other purchases, were green lemons, pickled oysters, sturgeon, quinces, West-
phalia bacon, spices, dried fruit, nuts, dates, rice, olives, anchovies and
pickled cucumbers. Not surprisingly, these feasts were expensive, £200
being a not untypical amount to be spent at the burial of an earl, as,
for instance, Henry, Earl of Huntingdon, in 1596. Even for the funeral
feast of a mere knight, such as that of Sir Roger Aston in 1612, over
£20 was spent on the feast, at which were served capons, pullets, geese,
chickens, 'tame pigs' and quails, not to mention eggs, butter and other
necessaries.

The purpose of the funeral banquet was to cement the relationships
altered by the death, and to display the largesse and, by implication, the
wealth and power of the new titleholder. The mourners, by accepting
the new man's food, were under an obligation to him. One aspect of the
display was that far more food should be provided than the guests could
actually consume. The leftovers were then given to the poor, again to
stress the wealth and generosity of the newly succeeded aristocrat. As
the account of the funeral of Francis Talbot records: 'After the dinner,
the reversion of all the said meat was given to the poor, with [a] dole
of two pence a piece, with bread and drink [in] great plenty.' The
feast after Lady Berkeley's funeral 'had [been] so plentifully provided that the excess herein appeared, when such dishes as for the
most part passed untouched at former tables, more than one thousand
poor people were plentifully fed the same afternoon'.

The total cost of these extravaganzas was, as might be expected, very
substantial. In gauging the actual sums of money spent, it should, of
course, be remembered that this was a period of quite rapid inflation.
This meant that later, more costly funerals were not in fact more
expensive in real terms than the rather cheaper burials found earlier in
the period. To give an example, the funeral of Thomas, Second Duke of
Norfolk, in 1524, cost £1,340, a sum unsurpassed in real terms by subsequent known aristocratic funeral costs. Some of the more expensive
heraldic funerals were those of Edward, Third Earl of Rutland in 1587
at £2,297 and, the following year, of Robert, Earl of Leicester, at a cost
of £3,500; at Elizabeth, Countess of Shrewsbury's funeral in 1608,
£3,257 was spent, while the burial of the Sixth Earl of Rutland in 1632
cost £3,544. Not all aristocratic burials were quite this extravagant, for
example the funeral of Henry Sidney with its journey across England
cost £1,571 in 1586; Lord Burghley's funeral in 1598 cost about
£1,100 and that of his son, Robert Cecil, buried at Hatfield in 1612,

cost £1,977. A few, of course, were considerably cheaper than these, but if a major aristocrat were to be buried in reasonable style, with a proper heraldic funeral, the executors could expect to spend at least £1,000, certainly after about 1580.[9]

What was bought for all this money? The largest bill that had to be paid was that submitted by the draper, or more accurately, drapers, for such a yardage of black cloth was involved, that no single merchant could possibly supply the total amount needed for such a funeral. Usually about half a dozen different suppliers were involved and the cost could represent a very large proportion indeed of the total funeral expenditure; of the £1,977 paid for Robert Cecil's burial, no less than £1,544 was spent on black cloth.[10] Other examples of the black cloth costing about three-quarters of the total expenditure are not hard to find; at Nicholas Bacon's funeral in 1578 the black cloth cost £669 out of a total sum of £910, while at Henry, First Lord Hunsdon's funeral in 1596, £836 was spent on 'blacks' out of a final bill of £1,097.

Nor was it easy, at a heraldic funeral, to reduce this bill by economising, for the heralds' regulations laid down the exact amounts of cloth that had to be used. Although the black cloth for hanging the church and family seat or London residence could be hired, the cloth given to the mourners had, of course, to be purchased in the quantities dictated by the heralds. The amount and quality of cloth to be given to each participant was dependent on their rank, as was the number of their servants who also had to be clothed in black. The cost of clothing the procession rapidly mounted up when, as in the instance of Nicholas Bacon's funeral and others of similar rank, each principal mourner had to receive 12 yards of cloth at 30s the yard for his own clothes, together with 7½ yards at 16s a yard for two gentlemen, and 1½ yards at 12s a yard for three yeomen, making a total cost of £26 14s just to equip one man and his retinue.

Another important item of expenditure after paying for the black cloth and the funeral feast was the payment to the College of Arms for the services and attendance of the heralds at the funeral. The heralds' bill covered a variety of items; their own fees and riding charges per mile, each graded according to the rank of the officer involved, the black cloth for their garments, the purchase of materials for, and preparation of, the hearse under their supervision and providing materials and overseeing the work of the painters who made all the heraldic banners, flags and accoutrements. Because many of these individual amounts were quite small and difficult to record exactly, it was usual practice for the College of Arms and the executor to agree beforehand on a composite fee covering all these different items. It was not un-common for this sum to be £100 for the funeral of an aristocrat during this period. In addition to the money, the heralds also received the hearse with all its rich trappings as their perquisite. The money and material would then be divided between the various officers involved in the funeral, the distribution being recorded, after 1618, in the parti-tion books at the College of Arms. Not surprisingly, with such lucrative rewards, the heralds were keen to participate at the funerals of the aristocracy and a system of 'turns' had to be instituted by the College to give each member a fair share of the funeral bounty.[11] John Donne, in a sermon preached at St Paul's, noted the heralds' love of funerals:

> Go to the heralds' office, the sphere and element of honour, and thou shalt find those men as busy there about the consideration of funerals as about the consideration of creations; thou shalt find that office to be as well the grave, as the cradle of honour.

Despite their keenness for order, precedence and adherence to the minutiae of rules and regulations, the heralds themselves did not always live up to the high standards which they imposed upon others. Violent squabbles rent the College of Arms, bringing the heralds into disrepute; also their fondness for spending other people's money did nothing to win them favour. On occasion, a particular herald would attempt to pocket the entire fee for a funeral, instead of sharing it according to the agreed procedure of the College of Arms. A particularly unsavoury scene occurred at Sir Henry Sidney's funeral in 1586, centring on Sir William Dethick, who was later 'put from his office' of Garter King of Arms because of the number of complaints about him. 'At the funeral of Sir Henry Sidney at Penshurst he beat the minister in the church, and in the Abbey of Westminster (after a funeral of a great estate) he struck with his dagger one Browne . . . and wounded him'.[12] Such be-haviour did nothing to endear the heralds to an aristocracy, many of whom were already growing disenchanted with the tyrannous con-strictions of the heraldic funeral and the rapacious officers who stage-managed these events.

Whatever the opinions of individual aristocrats, the College of Arms had, during her lifetime, a keen supporter in the person of Queen Eliza-beth. The importance she placed upon the performance of the heraldic funeral even led her, from time to time, to pay for the interments of her relatives and friends herself; among others, £640 2s 11d was pro-vided to bury Lady Knollys in 1569 and £1,047 6s 1½d for the funeral of Henry, Lord Hunsdon, in 1596. However, her preferred technique was, with the assistance of Lord Burghley, to put pressure on her nobles to comply with the heraldic requirements whenever their relatives died and she took a keen and close interest in all such ceremonies. The reasons for her concern have been outlined: from what has been said it is clear that the passing of the Queen herself would have a profound impact on the funeral practices of the English aristocracy.

After the funeral ceremony itself had ended, the hearse was often left standing in the church for some months as a memorial to the deceased, while a funeral hatchment would remain hanging outside the deceased's home for a period of up to a year. Generally, however, a more lasting monument would also be provided in the form of a sculptured tomb, complete with the figure of the deceased and memorial inscription. A detailed study of such tombs would occupy a massive volume in its own right; all that is possible here is to examine a handful of specific monuments, as opposed to encompassing many in broad generalisations, and to ignore aesthetic considerations in favour of social practice. However, despite these limitations, some points can be made which are pertinent to the themes discussed in this book and to the changes in funeral rituals themselves. If justification were needed for discussing tombs in the context of funeral practices, it lies most visibly in the use of tombs designed to represent the deceased actually lying in the hearse. Perhaps the finest and most famous of these particular monuments is that made by Maximilian Colt for Alice, Countess of Derby, who was buried at Harefield, Middlesex, in 1636. The monument shows the countess, to whom Milton dedicated his *Arcades*, lying on a black pall decorated with escutcheons and fringed with gold. Above her rise four black pillars supporting a domed roof simulating cloth of gold, with hanging curtains tied around the pillars, each fold and crease delicately carved in stone. Around the base kneel ladies in mourning; the whole monument, although not an exact replica of an actual hearse, gives a good impression of the sumptuousness of these constructions (see Plate 7, p. 127).

In any discussion of monumental sculpture, the balance of influence between the patron who orders the tomb and the sculptor who makes it is obviously of prime importance. From what is known about the relationship between patrons and sculptors in Elizabethan and Jacobean England it would seem that the patron got what he wanted, although how far the sculptor could mould his patron's taste remains unknown. Sir John Gage's order for the brass to commemorate himself and his two wives shows just how determined and opinionated a patron could be. In 1595, he commissioned the monument which now lies in Firle Church, Sussex, from Gerard Johnson or Jansen. Johnson drew up a plan of the proposed design and sent it to Sir John, only to have it sent back with Gage's comments in the margin, beginning:

> Where you have set out my two wives with long hair wired, my request is that they shall be both attired with French hoods and cornets, some hair showed under the cornets, the pattern of the cornet I have sent you by this bearer in a box bowed and dressed as it shall stand upon their heads.

He then went on to demand that his wives should not appear wearing fashionable farthingales, or with their ankles showing.[13]

Indeed, not only is it reasonable to suppose that the patron approved of what he got, but also in some instances, as in the case of Sir John Gage, that he would actually be the person commemorated, prudently organising his own monument before he died. Contemporary accounts reveal that if this important job were left to the heir, there was a chance that the tomb might never materialise, possibly, of course, in part because of the expense of the funeral itself; in Shakespeare's slightly sweeping words: 'If a man do not erect in this age his own tomb ere he dies, he shall live no longer in monument than the bell rings and the widow weeps.'

Elizabeth, Countess of Shrewsbury, left nothing to chance, perhaps realising that few would weep for her, and in her will wrote that she was to be buried

> at All Hallows Church in Derby at the place in the same church where it is appointed and determined that my tomb and monument shall be erected and built (which at the present time is finished and wanteth nothing but setting up).

Her tomb was made by Robert Smythson, who also designed the other great monument to her, Hardwick Hall.

The usual type of tomb erected to the memory of an Elizabethan or Jacobean magnate reflected the same values and emphasis as the heraldic funeral. The deceased would appear, often lying on a table tomb, in the robes of their office or rank, with all the emblems of their public persona that could be mustered. From the tomb would rise pillars, supporting an entablature surmounted with the arms of the deceased, while further coats of arms might well appear decorating the sides of the tomb. Possibly there would be a row of children in mourning, distinguished one from another only by their diminishing stature, and by the skulls in the hands of those already dead, a visual pedigree not dissimilar to the family trees which the heralds drew up. Often the monument would be protected by a heavy iron grille, making it very difficult to see the face of the figure with any clarity; it was the total effect that mattered, as a symbol of power and wealth, rather than the more private and personal details of the facial features. This is not to say that such tombs were not exquisitely carved, for the finest sculptors of the day were employed in making monuments of this type. A similar set of values characterised the inscriptions carved on these monuments, which commemorated the deceased principally as a public rather than a private person, listing their titles, offices and pedigree, but revealing little or nothing of their character. However, as with heraldic funerals, the ideology apparent in these stereotyped monuments and inscriptions was beginning to wane from about the beginning of the seventeenth century.

The exact cost of these monuments for the most part is unknown, but some few contracts survive to give an approximate idea of the price of a tomb. James Montague, Bishop of Winchester, left £300 to pay for his memorial in Bath Abbey. As he wrote in his will, he hoped by being buried there, 'to stir up some more benefactors to that place'. His tomb, made by William Cure and Nicholas Johnson, while certainly very splendid, cannot be said to reflect any great spiritual quality; rather, it might be felt to demonstrate the wealth and worldly power of the episcopacy. At least the bishop's directions were adhered to in terms of the amount of money to be spent on the tomb, unlike his directions for funeral charges; making the tomb with its surrounding railing, carrying it from London to Bath and erecting it there, cost exactly the £300 allowed, with merely an additional £10 spent on engraving the epitaph; however, the original contract with the sculptors was only for £200. This monument was not of exceptional splendour: others grander and more expensive are to be found.

It is appropriate to conclude this chapter on heraldic funerals by considering the monument to Henry, Lord Hunsdon, who died and was buried in Westminster Abbey in 1596. His burial was one of those paid for by his cousin, Queen Elizabeth herself, and had all the usual features of the heraldic funeral; 1,232 yards of black cloth given to the mourners, 70 poor men dressed in mourning gowns, both Somerset House and the Abbey swathed in black, the heralds' bill for £100 and so on. To pay for his tomb, he left £1,000, almost as much as the Queen spent on the funeral itself. Its design epitomised the display of public status and wealth, allowing no hint of the private man, which characterised the enforced funeral rites of the aristocracy. It was, and has remained, the tallest tomb ever to be erected in the Abbey, being in all 36 feet high. In place of an effigy is a stone sarcophagus, presumably chosen because any human figure would appear dwarfed by the sheer bulk of the monument. Around the sarcophagus stand four obelisks garnished with coats of arms, while additional arms, a crest and supporters, stand massive and prominent above. His pedigree is revealed for all to see. Further obelisks are decorated with emblems of war, signifying his public career as an eminent soldier who subdued the Northern Rebellion, while Latin inscriptions provide extra testimony to his success, both in military and in civil life, as Lord Chamberlain. It is, however, principally a monument to an ideal which no real person could fully emulate; in fact, it was rumoured that Lord Hunsdon's final illness was brought on by his chagrin at not being created Earl of Wiltshire, a title which he expected the Queen to confer upon him. It is, perhaps, significant testimony to the nature of that ideal that no human figure could appear upon this monument; like the heraldic funeral, it was created for political ends and not as a reflection of an actual human being.

Notes

1. The sources for the principal funerals discussed in this chapter are as follows:

Thomas, Duke of Norfolk, 1524; Blomefield, *History of Thetford*, Appendix VIII.
Francis, Earl of Shrewsbury, 1560; Peck, *Desiderata Curiosa*, pp. 252-6.
Lady Catherine Knollys, 1569; *Historical Manuscripts Commission, Salisbury*, i, p. 415.
Edward, Earl of Derby, 1572; Collins, *Peerage of England*, iii, pp. 72-92.
Catherine, Countess of Huntingdon, 1576; Oxford, Bodleian Library: MS. Ashmole 836, fols. 53-4.
Walter, Earl of Essex, 1576; London, British Library: MS. Lansdowne 23/67.
Sir Nicholas Bacon, 1578; Oxford, Bodleian Library: MS. Ashmole 836, fols. 21-38.
Sir Henry Sidney, 1586; London, British Library: MS. Lansdowne, 50/88.
Henry, Lord Hunsdon, 1596; London, British Library: MS. Lansdowne, 82/56.
Lady Katharine Berkeley, 1596; Smith, *Lives of the Berkeleys*, ii, pp. 388-91.
Henry, Earl of Huntingdon, 1596; London, British Library: MS. Harleian 4774, fol. 141. *Historical Manuscripts Commission, Hastings*, ii, p. 45.

William, Lord Cobham, 1597; *Historical Manuscripts Commission, Salisbury*, vii, p. 117.

Sir John Stowell, 1604; Oxford, Bodleian Library: MS. Top. Yorks, d 7, fols. 2 and 41.

Elizabeth, Countess of Shrewsbury, 1608; Chatsworth House, Derbyshire: H/29.

Sir Roger Aston, 1612; Oxford, Bodleian Library: MS. Eng. Hist. c. 480, fols. 275-83.

Gilbert, Earl of Shropshire, 1616; London, British Library: MS. Harleian 1368, fol. 35.

James Montague, Bishop of Winchester, 1618; Oxford, Bodleian Library: MS. North b 12, b 25, c 29.

Ludovic, Duke of Richmond and Lenox, 1624; Cleland, *Monument of Mortality* and Chamberlain, *Letters*, ii, pp. 551 and 554.

Sir John St John, 1648; London, British Library: MS. Harleian 5176, fols. 191-4.

2. *Calendar of State Papers, Domestic Series 1637-8*, p. 169.
3. Oxford, Bodleian Library: MS. Ashmole, 836, fol. 11.
4. Quoted in Ravenshaw, *Antiente Epitaphes*, p. 34.
5. Oxford, Bodleian Library: MS. Top. Yorks, d 7, fols. 23 and 33.
6. Oxford, Bodleian Library: MS. Ashmole 1116, fol. 51.
7. Oxford, Bodleian Library: MS. Ashmole 818, fol. 24.
8. London, British Library: MS. Egerton 2642, fol. 205.
9. For these and other funeral costs, see Stone, *Crisis of the Aristocracy*, pp. 784-5.
10. Ibid., p. 785.
11. Wagner, *Heralds of England*, p. 111.
12. Ibid., p. 201.
13. Firle Place, West Sussex: MS. drawing with annotations.

'YIELD DAY TO NIGHT . . . WE MOURN IN BLACK': NOCTURNAL FUNERALS OF THE ARISTOCRACY

The seventeenth and eighteenth centuries saw far-reaching changes in the funeral rituals of the aristocracy. The heralds' control was steadily undermined and a new form of burial, the night funeral, became prevalent. The whole ethos of nocturnal burial reflected a far more individualistic response to death than the show of political strength enshrined in the heraldic funeral ritual. By the eighteenth century, the heralds were more or less a spent force in funerary matters, making possible the emergence of new influences on burial rituals, including the rationalist philosophy which came to dominate the thought of the later eighteenth century. The effects of rationalism during this period reveal some of the fundamental problems raised by death in an individualistic society, problems which still confront us today.

In December 1618, John Chamberlain reported to his friend, Sir Dudley Carleton:

> It is grown altogether in fashion to bury now by night, as on Sunday last the Lady Haddington had a solemn convoy of almost a hundred coaches (and torches in abundance), that accompanied her from Westminster to Whitechapel on her way to Newhall in Essex where she is to be buried.

Nor was it simply the procession, now in coaches, rather than on foot or horseback, that took place at night; the whole funeral ceremony was held nocturnally. On 25 January 1623, Chamberlain described how

> the Lady Cave . . . was buried by night at St Paul's, accompanied with 65 coaches and great store of other company. The corpse was drawn in a coach covered with black velvet, as likewise the horses, with black feathers.

The popularity of night funerals led the heralds to complain to the Archbishop of Canterbury that 'of late there hath crept into the kingdom an unusual manner of burying the dead, especially the better sort, by night'. By 1631 the situation was such that John Weever could lament, if with some exaggeration, that

> funerals in any expensive way here with us are now accounted but as a fruitless vanity, insomuch that almost all the ceremonial rites of obsequies herefore used, are altogether laid aside; for we see daily that noblemen and gentlemen of eminent rank, office and quality are either silently buried in the night time with a torch, a twopenny link and a lantern, or parsimoniously interred in the day-time.

Parish registers also testify to the widespread practice of nocturnal burials; for example, at the Temple Church, London, in the years 1641 and 1642, out of a total of 21 burials, no fewer than nine took place by night. Nor did the custom cease until the last years of the eighteenth century. In 1737 the frequency of night burials was causing difficulties in Wellingborough, Northamptonshire, according to an entry in the parish register:

> There hath been and still is a custom and usage within the said parish of burying the dead at the hour of eight or nine at night in the winter, and sometimes later, which is found to be a very inconvenient and prejudicial custom both to the minister and inhabitants.

By this period, a ritual which had once been only an aristocratic practice had spread down the social scale to encompass anyone who was prepared to pay double the usual burial fees, the penalty for the inconvenience caused.[1]

In the first instance, aristocratic women seem to have been especially instrumental in bringing about this revolution in the funeral rites of the elite. In part, the fact that they were able to do this probably reflected their lower status in society; the College of Arms would be more likely to insist on a man being buried with full heraldic honours, but might show slightly less determination over the burial of his wife. The young children of aristocrats, too, were sometimes permitted nocturnal burials for the same reason. A precedent might be found in those cases where an aristocratic corpse had to be interred very fast, although during Elizabeth's reign this would later be followed by a full heraldic ceremony, sometimes with an effigy substituted for the body. A very different group of people who also contributed to the rise of night burials in the early seventeenth century were the Scottish courtiers of James I, who were not, of course, subject to the control of the English College of Arms. On 20 April 1616, John Chamberlain described how Sir John Grimes or Graemes, a Scottish courtier of some eminence, 'was solemnly buried in the night at Westminster with better than 200 torches, the Duke of Lenox, the Lord Fenton, the Lord of Roxborough and all the grand Scottish men accompanying him'.

At this date, night burial was a sufficiently rare occurrence to arouse comment, for 'in impish imitation . . . certain rude knaves [including Scots] buried a dog with great solemnity in Tothill Field by night with good store of links'. James I cannot have appreciated what problems would arise from allowing his Scottish attendants to practise what was, for England, a novel form of burial.

The great popularity of night burial among aristocrats can be explained by a variety of reasons. Some of these have already been hinted at in discussing the constraints which the heraldic burial ritual placed upon the participants.

One such cause underlying the change in style of funeral rituals was a revolt by a number of aristocrats, particularly, but not exclusively, women, at the prospect of submitting their dead bodies to the embalmers' unpleasant ministrations. As early as 1572, Mary, Countess of Northumberland, expressed this view in her will, directing 'not in any wise to let me be opened after I am dead. I have not loved to be very bold afore women, much more would I be loath to come into the hands of any living man, be he physician or surgeon.'

Lucy, Lady Latimer, in 1582, decreed that her body, 'the creature of God', was 'without opening or cutting . . . to be buried in the earth in decent order immediately after my decease'. In her will, proved in 1639, Frances, Duchess of Richmond and widow of Ludovic Stuart, ordered 'that I may be speedily buried and not opened for so my sweet Lord out of his tender love commanded me that I should not be opened. I may be presently put up in bran, and in lead before I am fully cold.' In the same year, Lady Verney was directing: 'let no stranger wind me, nor do not let me be stripped, but put a clean smock over me . . . and let my face be hid'.

All these ladies, and others too, shared a concern with their dead corpses which has strong undertones of sexuality about it; this eroticising of death was one characteristic and significant aspect of the changing attitudes towards death which underlay the more noticeable alterations in the funeral rituals of the period.

The new night funerals took very little time to organise and so were the obvious answer for those people who did not want to be embalmed. Clearly the great long processions from one side of the country to the other were not possible with an unembalmed body; in any transporting of the corpse, speed became of the essence. The coach wheels had to begin rolling through the night on the evening of the actual day of death if the body was to travel any distance. This placed certain restrictions on where bodies could be buried, as a really long journey was impossible. Almost all the night burials mentioned by John Chamberlain, who lived in London, occurred either in the capital itself, or in nearby Essex; for example, on 6 December 1623, he recounted that the Countess of Warwick 'was convoyed out of Holborn to be buried in Essex by more than two hundred horse, all with torches, and above three score coaches, among whom were both the Duchesses [of Richmond and of Buckingham]'.

However, the same need for haste also ruled out any argument over the chosen resting place, as had occurred between magnates and the Crown during Elizabeth's reign. Consequently, the wishes of the deceased or nearest of kin were likely to be fulfilled without dispute.

Another important difference between night funerals and heraldic burials lay in the choice of mourners. Whereas with the older ritual the exact number and rank of the mourners was controlled by the heralds, attendance at night funerals was purely voluntary, thereby placing new emphasis on personal ties with the deceased rather than on political considerations. Frances, Duchess of Richmond, directed that her burial, to take place on the first night a clear 24 hours after her death, should be 'without . . . any great persons to be invited but if they come of their own good will let them be respectively and dutifully used'.

Members of the aristocracy did still attend each other's funerals even though it was no longer compulsory for them to do so. John Chamberlain described Sir John Howe, who died in 1623, as being 'buried privately on Tuesday night, though there was a great deal of company'. At Lady Haddington's burial, so Chamberlain reported, were to be found besides 'the Countesses of Bedford, Exeter and Devonshre . . . the Lady Verulam with a world of other ladies'. Although sentiment was one criterion, an element of social snobbery also permeated attendance at night funerals. The niceties of rank, together with some use of heraldry, were not completely eschewed, but attendance at night funerals, motivated by whatever force, was at least voluntary, without the interference or coercion of the College of Arms.

This newly found freedom in funeral practices had two additional repercussions: the regulations as to the sex of mourners could no longer be applied, while mourners could witness the whole burial service, including the interment. A husband could now act as chief mourner for his wife and vice versa. Eventually, even the heralds were forced to give way on this latter point. When in 1662 Queen Elizabeth of Bohemia was buried in Westminster Abbey, her son Prince Rupert acted as chief mourner. The night funeral, therefore, provided public recognition of the bond of affection uniting close members of families, while cutting across the lines of rank and title. The loss of the loved individual was now fully incorporated into the ritual; the actual interment formed the climax of the proceedings, rather than being almost an afterthought, following the departure of the mourners from the church.

The recognition of loss was, perhaps, the most important respect in which the night funeral differed from the heraldic burial ritual, with its emphasis on the simple replaceability of one aristocrat by another. This sense of the irreversible loss brought about by the death of a unique individual is present in the will of Frances, Dowager Countess of Thanet, who in 1646 ordered that 'my body may be buried at Raynham, where the body of my dear Lord Nicholas, late Earl of Thanet, deceased, doth lie, and that it may be buried in the night season as his was'.

The concealment provided by darkness, at night funerals, dramatised the sorrow of the bereaved, while the flickering torches acted as constant reminders, in a society adept in the language of symbols, of the frailty of human life. The same nexus of images — death, darkness, burial and irreversible loss — occurs in contemporary literature; in his poem, 'A nocturnall upon St Lucies day', John Donne employed all the available images to convey

A quintessence even from nothingness . . .
Of absence, darkness, death, things which are not.

This new attitude towards bereavement was revealed in a somewhat extreme form, in the person of the Duchess of Richmond, who was widowed in 1624. Chamberlain, reporting the duke's death, wrote, on 21 February: 'His Lady takes it extréme passionately, cut off her hair that day with divers other demonstrations of extraordinary grief'. To the sensibilities of the time, this was 'immoderate grief' of the kind for which Hamlet was reproached. In a later letter, written on 10

April 1624, Chamberlain returned to the subject, commenting that the funeral of the Duke of Richmond was

> like to be performed with more solemnity and ado than needed: but that it so pleaseth her Grace to honour the memory of so dear a husband, whose loss she takes so impatiently and with so much show of passion that many odd and idle tales are daily reported or invented of her, insomuch that many malicious people impute it as much to the loss of the court as of her Lord, and will not be persuaded that having buried two husbands already and being so far past the flower and prime of her youth she could otherwise be so passionate.

However, despite gossip and rumour, the duchess persisted in her grief, and in her will, proved 15 years later, she reiterated her sorrow, declaring: 'With the loss of my Lord all earthly joys ended with me and I ever computed his funeral day my burial.'

With some of the directions for her own funeral, Frances Stuart, Duchess of Richmond, passed beyond the merely romantic into the realm of eroticism. She willed: 'Let them wind me up again in those sheets . . . wherein my Lord and I first slept that night when we were married.'

Like others who objected to embalming, the Duchess of Richmond seemed to have had an intense preoccupation with her dead remains. Indeed, it could be argued that the whole ritual of burial by night, which she desired for her own interment, itself contained at least a suggestion of eroticism, a drama of great emotion played out by torchlight against a backdrop of darkness. Freudians have argued that the eroticism of death is linked with the development of individualism, a nexus which first began to take shape in the late Middle Ages; they have suggested that 'one effect of the incapacity to accept separation, individuality and death is to eroticise death'.[2] Certainly there seem to be quite strong connections between these various different elements during the early seventeenth century and all, indeed, are to be found in the character of Frances Stuart, Duchess of Richmond.

The eroticising of death occurred in contemporary literature too. Indeed, the word 'die' itself had a sexual meaning, while Juliet's father describes her as being 'deflowered' by death, who has 'lain' with her. The connection between the bridal bed and the grave is also found in *Hamlet*; it appears too on a monument at Haccombe, Devon, to Thomas and Anne Carew, who died within two days of each other in

1656:

> They die but not depart who meet
> In wedding and in winding sheet
> Whom God has knit so firm in one
> Admit no separation.

The whole genre of revenge tragedy contains many references to the eroticising of death. One of the most striking and blatant manifestations of this tendency appears in the play *The Second Maiden's Tragedy*, where the plot revolves around necrophilia. The Tyrant, when the heroine chooses death rather than submit to him, has her body removed from its tomb and hires a painter to add colour to her dead face. In fact, the painter is the hero in disguise and uses poison in his tinctures so that the Tyrant dies when he kisses her. The painter then throws off his disguise and addresses the dying villain:

> Cannot the body, after funeral
> Sleep in the grave for thee? Must it be raised
> Only to please the wickedness of thine eye?
> Do all things end with death, and not thy lust?

This same tendency to eroticise death may also be traced in tomb sculpture, although necessarily in a far less overt form than in literature. Perhaps the word eroticism is a little strong, but a distinct sensuality emanates from certain sculptures of the early seventeenth century, especially some of those carved by Nicholas Stone. This sensuality would have been all the more striking to contemporaries, in comparison with the solid, stiff effigies of medieval and Tudor England. Stone's carving, at its best, has not unjustly been likened to Bernini's, whose work Stone was aware of from drawings and through the travels of his own son. Indeed, two of Stone's best monuments, those to Lady Elizabeth Carey at Stow Nine Churches, Northamptonshire, in 1617, and the tomb of Mrs Arthur Coke at Bramfield, Suffolk, carved ten years later, both have affinities with Bernini's famous St Theresa, although they both predate this Italian masterpiece. A rather different sensuality emanates from what was, perhaps, Stone's most notable commission, the figure of John Donne in St Paul's Cathedral. The original picture from which Stone worked was itself the product of a distinctly morbid and individualistic idea on the part of Donne himself. Izaak Walton, in his life of Donne, described what occurred:

Several charcoal fires being first made in his large study, he brought with him into that place his winding sheet in his hand, and having put off all his clothes, had this sheet put on him, and so tied with knots at his head and feet, and his hands so placed as dead bodies are usually fitted, to be shrouded and put into their coffin, or grave.

He was then drawn 'with his eyes shut and with so much of the sheet turned aside as might show his lean, pale and death-like face'. Donne kept the picture at his bedside 'where it continued and became his hourly object till his death'; it was then 'carved in one entire piece of white marble'. This sculpture rekindled for a while a minor fashion for similar shrouded effigies on monuments (see Plate 8, p. 128).

John Weever, writing in 1631, remarked on a further guise in which sexuality was creeping into tomb sculpture, through the detail of the ornamentation, rather than the actual effigies. He complained of 'the pictures of naked men and women . . . bringing into the church the memories of heathen gods and goddesses'. Although not actually naked, the buxom virtues, one with bare breasts, who support the figure of Robert Cecil, Earl of Salisbury, at Hatfield, equally demonstrate Weever's point. These figures, carved by Maximilian Colt in 1612, kneel around a skeleton, juxtaposing sexuality and death at close quarters. The tomb itself is a marriage of contemporary foreign influence — notably that of a similar monument in Breda, Holland — and the English late medieval type of composition where the deceased appears twice, once as in life, and also as a skeleton (see Plate 9, p. 129).

The reasons so far advanced for the sudden fashion for nocturnal burial in early seventeenth-century England have all centred on the internal purposes and symbolism of the ceremony itself, tracing a relationship between the emergence of the new ritual and a gradual alteration in the sensibilities of the time, resulting in increasing emphasis on individualism. However, more mundane explanations for this novel style of funeral can also be found, particularly in terms of their cost. Clearly a night funeral would cost less than a heraldic funeral, at the very least because no money had to be paid to the embalmers or to the heralds, neither would it have been an appropriate time to hold a feast after a nocturnal ceremony. Another element of the usual burial ritual which was often omitted if the interment was by night was the funeral sermon; the heralds in their petition against night burial, addressed to the Archbishop of Canterbury, made much of this loss:

It is a cause that those godly and devout exhortations and sermons which were heretofore usually made at the funerals of the dead whereby their virtuous lives were had in memory for the honour of the parties deceased and the instruction and comfort of the living are now utterly lost and grown out of use, and the ministers likewise of God's word have thereby lost a great part of their livelihood.

The heralds then went on to complain that charity, customarily distributed at funerals, was also, with the advent of night burials, 'utterly neglected'.

Some burials, it is certainly true, were held by night specifically to save money. For example, Sir Thomas Bludworth, making his will in 1680, directed that he should be buried 'without any pomp in some evening, [it having] pleased God to lessen me in my estate by that dreadful fire of London'.

However, other wills make it clear that financial considerations were not uppermost in the testator's mind when requesting a night funeral and that the heralds' complaints about the neglect of sermons and charity were not fully justified. For example, Dame Anne Pemberton in 1625 wished to be buried by night, 'without pomp or glory of the world', but added that

to the end the poor may not lose by the privateness of my funerals, I do will that three score and eleven poor women shall have twenty shillings a piece given unto them in lieu of so many mourning gowns and twelve a piece for their dinners. And that a sermon shall be preached at some convenient time after my funeral, at which time those poor women to be present, and then to have the said twenty shillings a piece given unto them.

Frances Stuart, Duchess of Richmond, actually requested that 200 poor people should attend her night burial in Westminster Abbey in 1639, wearing mourning gowns that were not too short and each bearing a torch. She also ordered that the Archbishop of Canterbury, the parsons of four London parishes and her houshold servants should receive black garments to act as mourners at her interment and that a funeral sermon should be preached on the first or second Sunday after her actual burial. Being buried by night allowed Frances Stuart to exercise far more control over the ritual than if she had been given a heraldic funeral, but the ceremony was by no means cheap; the duchess left £2,000 to pay for the burial and to keep her household in mourning for three or four weeks after her death.

A further way that a night funeral would be less expensive than burial with full heraldic honours was the far smaller amount of black cloth which had to be purchased by the executors for the ceremony. The heralds, realising that their interests and those of the drapers were closely aligned in funeral matters, added to their list of the evil consequences of night funerals that 'it is a great hindrance to many poor tradesmen and workmen that were wont to vend divers commodities as clothes for the furnishing of their solemn funerals which were heretofore used'. In fact, here, too, the heralds rather overstated their case. What was no longer needed was all the black cloth to hang the church, but as this had generally been hired anyway, there was no great loss of trade involved. People still wore black to funerals; the main difference was that the participants at a night funeral provided their own mourning costume instead of having it paid for out of the deceased's estate. The effect of this alteration was to change the nature of the relationship between the mourners and the deceased's family, with the replacement of an obligation formed through the receipt of largesse by a far more individualised relationship based on emotional links, without the element of coercion which characterised attendance at a heraldic funeral.

Although cost was one factor which influenced the adoption of burial by night by certain aristocrats in the early seventeenth century, it was by no means the only or central consideration for many nobles. The key factor, arguably, was a steadily mounting disenchantment with the values expressed in the heraldic burial ritual – the replaceability of one person by another, the emphasis on status rather than personal relationships and the obligation based on largesse – which no longer reflected the feelings of the participants. In contemporary terminology, this new outlook is reflected in a dichotomy between the two types of funeral, 'public' and 'private'. It was a desire to emphasise private loss in the ritual, rather than any public display of strength, which led to the fashion for burial by night.

Further factors contributed to this movement. One was the general unpopularity of the College of Arms; Robert, Earl of Dorset, specifically mentioned in his will that he did not want heraldic burial because 'the usual solemnities of funerals such as heralds set down for noblemen are only good for heralds and drapers'. A committee of the House of Commons discussed funeral fees in critical terms in 1624, while a few people, among them Sir Roger Twisden, a Kentish gentleman, refused to pay any fees to the College of Arms until finally forced to do

so by the Earl Marshal's court, the Court of Chivalry.[3] Rather ironically, the College of Arms during the first half of the seventeenth century was rather less strife-torn than in previous decades; it numbered
among its members several excellent and conscientious antiquarians,
including William Camden. However, funeral fees still rankled, for in
broader terms ill feeling against the College of Arms was simply one
aspect of the general and growing dislike of all prerogative courts, of
which the Court of Chivalry, used by the heralds, was one.

It is also possible that some of the heralds and their antiquarian
friends may unwittingly have contributed to the adoption of night
funerals, through descriptions of classical burial practices in their
writings. Burial by torchlight was itself a Roman tradition and books
like John Weever's *Ancient Funerall Monuments* and Sir Thomas
Browne's *Urne Buriall* spread knowledge and interest concerning past
mortuary rituals. That classical precedents actually affected contemporary practice is shown in the case of Egerton, Lord Keeper of England,
who, according to a letter written by John Chamberlain on 29 March
1617,

> gave order in his will to have no solemn funeral, no monument, but
> to be buried in oblivion, alleging the precedents of Seneca, Warham
> Archbishop of Canterbury and Chancellor, and Budé the learned
> Frenchman, who all took the like course.

Another group of people who may also have influenced the new
fashion were those Puritan writers, such as Henry Barrow, who had casti-
gated the worldliness of heraldic burials:

> But if [the deceased] be of any great degree, or but stepped into
> the gentry, then he hath accordingly his mourners, yea, his heralds
> peradventure, carrying his coat armour and streamers before him
> with solemn ado and pitching them over his tomb, as if Duke
> Hector, or Ajax, or Sir Launcelot were buried.

Some members of the established Church, too, were less than happy
about the heraldic ritual; James Pilkington, Bishop of Durham, wrote
that

> if civil policy add some solemnity to princes and noblemen, as their
> coat, armour, flag, sword, head-piece and recognizance, I dare not
> utterly condemn it; and yet would wish it more moderately used

than many times it is.

However, critics of the heraldic funeral, although they may have helped to end its dominance, were unlikely to have been entirely happy with the alternative, nocturnal burial ritual.The initial response of John Chamberlain reflected the fear which was felt about night burial and showed a contemporary interpretation of its symbolism. He had this to say, on 16 February 1615, about the funeral of Sir Thomas Cheke's wife:

> She . . . was buried by night with above thirty coaches and much torchlight attending her, which is of late come much into fashion as it should seem to avoid trouble and charge, but I rather think it was brought up by papists which serve their turn by it [in] many ways.

The same fear was played on by the heralds in their petition to the Archbishop of Canterbury, in which they argued that in holding night funerals 'we may seem to draw near unto popery and heathenism'. This adverse religious interpretation of the ritual, however, did not prevent its widespread acceptance; gradually the accusations of popery were forgotten.

The growing popularity of night funerals did not pass unchallenged by the heralds. In 1618, the College of Arms, supported by the Earl Marshal, produced a series of measures to try and halt the slide towards greater freedom in the funeral practices of the aristocracy. James I directed the commissioners for the Earl Marshal to enquire into the heralds' complaints; it would seem that the king had by now realised more fully the importance of the role played by funerals in maintaining the social framework. The measures adopted included a requirement that funeral certificates should be registered at the College of Arms, obligatory attendance of the officers at all funerals involving heraldry and the setting out of a precise list of payments for all items of funeral decoration, which were only to be carried out by licensed painters. Also a scale of fees was established to be paid to the heralds for registering a funeral, ranging from 40s for a gentleman's burial to £45 if a duke, duchess or archbishop were interred. In addition, the College of Arms tried to establish control over the use of heraldry on tombs, requiring all sculptors to submit drawings of their designs for approval; in the event, only the King's carver, Maximilian Colt, seems actually to have complied with this order.[4]

These regulations resulted in the prosecution of some illegal painters, but had little effect on the general trend in funeral practices. In 1635, apropos of the planned nocturnal burial of Sir Richard Deane, a former Lord Mayor of London, the Earl Marshal urged that:

> Forasmuch as his Majesty hath lately signified his express pleasure and command for the prohibiting all nocturnal funerals whatsoever . . . I . . . earnestly desire . . . the executors . . . to see the ancient and reverend ceremonies at the interment of this gentleman . . . to be decently celebrated and duly observed.

However, Charles I's prohibition of night funerals seems to have had little or no effect; nocturnal burial was by now a well-established custom.

The collapse of royal control over the burials of the aristocracy, as exercised through the heralds, had subtle but important political implications. It represented one aspect of the loosening of the bonds which linked the power of the aristocracy directly to the authority of the Crown, a further crumbling of old-style feudal obligations. It should not be thought that, in adopting night burials, grand subjects were being consciously rebellious; rather it could be seen as part of what were largely unconscious alterations within the structure of society. Neither, of course, did funerals cease to play an important part in maintaining the social hierarchy, with the dwindling of the heraldic funeral. What was different was that the crown could no longer, as it had in Elizabeth's reign, dictate where these displays of power should take place or, indeed, use them as vehicles for establishing royal control through, for example, the use of the monarch's coat of arms. Instead, individual aristocratic families were able to use the ritual to promote their own particular interests with a far freer hand.

The same changes in outlook which led aristocrats to adopt burial by night, in place of the heraldic funeral, may also be traced in the tomb sculpture of the seventeenth century; the connection between death and eroticism in both funeral practices and funerary monuments has already been mentioned in this context. Monumental inscriptions display a more personal tone, with the emphasis on the character of the deceased aristocrat, rather than simply listing his genealogy and offices held. Love between couples came to be mentioned on inscriptions, as in this example from Lord Tanfield's tomb at Burford, Oxfordshire, which was composed in 1625 by his wife:

> Here shadows lie
> Whilst earth is sad;
> Still hopes to die
> To him she had.
>
> In bliss is he
> Whom I loved best;
> Thrice happy she
> With him to rest.
>
> So shall I be
> With him I loved;
> And he with me,
> And both us blessed.
>
> Love made me poet,
> And this I writ;
> My heart did do it,
> And not my wit.

Growing individualism in tomb sculpture was also shown by the increased realism of monuments in the seventeenth century; Donne's posing for his own monument has already been described. It is this naturalism which makes tombs of this period so much more attractive than the somewhat blank expressions of many Elizabethan effigies. Alongside the new realism in facial expression went a greater freedom of composition, allowing the subject to be portrayed in a more naturalistic pose. These alterations are nicely summed up in some early eighteenth-century lines of verse about the monuments in Westminster Abbey:

> Upon their backs the ancient statues lie,
> Devoutly fixed, with hands uplifted high,
> Entreating prayers of all the passers-by.
> At length they changed the posture by degrees,
> And placed the marble votary on its knees,
> There warriers rough devoutly heaven adore
> And statesmen kneel who never knelt before . . .
> Next a less pious posture they provide

On cushion lolling, stretched with careless pride . . .[5]

The same progression was alluded to by Webster, in *The Duchess of Malfi*, in the words of Bosola, disguised as a tomb-maker:

Princes' images on their tombs do not lie, as they were wont, seeming to pray up to heaven; but with their hands under their cheeks, as if they died of the toothache: they are not carved with their eyes fixed upon the stars; but as their minds were wholly bent upon the world, the selfsame way they seem to turn their faces . . .

The new realism in expression and posture, which itself reflected the increased worldliness of this period, can well be appreciated in the fine series of monuments in the small church of Lydiard Tregose, near Swindon. They include the delicately carved mother and child on the tomb to Sir John St John, the flamboyant standing figure of the golden cavalier, and a delightful conversation piece, with Sir Giles Mompesson and his wife seated facing each other.

Another new trend in tomb sculpture, which mirrored the changes in funeral practices, was the open expression of sorrow and loss. This is clearly shown in the tomb, made in 1618, by Epiphanius Evesham to Lord and Lady Teynham at Lynsted, Kent; the lady, dressed in mourning costume, kneels in prayer beside the body of her dead husband. The sorrow expressed by the main figures of the monument is reinforced by the panels on its base, depicting children, the five daughters openly weeping. This is a very different portrayal of children from the simple genealogical rows to be found on earlier monuments. For the tomb of Sir William and Lady Pelham at Brocklesby, Lincolnshire, in 1639, the sculptor, William Wright of Charing Cross, was required to make not just 'exact portraits' of the husband and wife, but also to show all 19 of their children 'as near as may be like them', receiving £100 in payment for this monument.[6] The tombs of the seventeenth century, in the way children are portrayed, suggest a greater depth of feeling between members of the family than was previously the case.

In general these tombs were, in real terms, rather cheaper than the greatest extravaganzas of the Elizabethan age. The new emphasis on the figures, while by no means displacing all architectural decoration, encouraged the use of architectural settings which enhanced rather than dominated the main subjects. As with night funerals, a shift in underlying attitudes caused tombs to become, in general, cheaper; it was not simply a matter of some clear-cut decision to spend less on memorials.

After the Restoration, the heralds' services were even less in demand at aristocratic burials, although casualties in the Dutch Wars kept the members of the College of Arms occupied for a while, organising state funerals. John Gibbon, who was made Bluemantle Herald in 1671, complained that:

> It was my hard hap to become a member of the Heralds' Office, when the ceremony of funerals (as accompanied with Officers of Arms) began to be in the wane ... In eleven years time I have had but five turns.[7]

The heralds no longer campaigned against nocturnal funerals, which were now more a matter of pure fashion than of ideological innovation. Indeed, if requested, members of the College of Arms would officiate at night funerals, as in the case of Margaret, Duchess of Newcastle, buried in Westminster Abbey in 1674, after a torchlight procession through the streets of London.

Some of the considerations which led members of the aristocracy to choose not to adopt the heraldic funeral ritual during this period are revealed in correspondence which passed between various heralds and the Earl of Denbigh, after the death of his wife in 1670. Initially, it was thought that she might be given a heraldic burial, and the earl was advised to contact Garter King of Arms, who would arrange everything. The letter continued:

> The greatest charge will be in blacks . . . Besides yourself and six persons of honour who are to be your assistants (as you are to be the chief mourner) all in close mourning . . . there must be others . . . And for the better state of the proceeding it will be requisite to have as many poor women in coarse black gowns and white kerchiefs as she was years of age at the time of her death.

However, William Dugdale, the writer of this letter, realised that the Earl of Denbigh might decide against full heraldic honours:

> But if your Lordship resolve of a private burial, my opinion is, that it be performed with all possible speed, and in the night time by torches, not divulging the time in regard of concourse of people: for in so doing you will prevent many inconveniences.

Denbigh's reply gave his reasons for choosing a private burial, making plain the grounds of his criticism of the heraldic funeral ritual. The 'horse caparisoned with velvet with all the achievements of her noble ancestors' caused the earl to wonder

> if that ceremony might not be thought more fit for the sons of Mars than for ladies. The custom of white kerchiefs and black gowns is obsolete, it being the custom of my family upon their decease to leave twenty pounds to the poor of the parish. For six of my quality to bear me company in mourning robes, the country will not afford, and for blacks to other families, I never had that respect paid to me.

While the earl was at pains to express his regard for the heralds, ultimately what he wanted was for his wife to have a private funeral that was 'noble and expeditious'. He explained this final decision at some length:

> I have observed in the greatest courts I have been conversant in, that in public ceremonies, and solemnities, such as are used must be real and entire, as the French are wont to say, *tout ou rien*, upon the like occasions, which gave me the resolution of a private funeral when a public one could not be had in the country with that extent of honour due to my wife's birth . . . Finding an impossibility of performing those ceremonies here in the country without a mutilation of what was due to her honour and mine, [it will be performed in] a private way, not without regard had, as the time and place will permit, to the honour of a lady whose memory is so dear to me.

Having totally broken away from the control of the heralds, aristocratic funerals of the eighteenth century lay open to the influence of the spirit of rationalism, which gradually gathered momentum in literate circles during the century. The effects of the new philosophy in superseding the Calvinist doctrines of eternal punishment and predestination have already been examined; in their place was substituted the concept of God as the watchmaker, whose creation, once made, continues to function without his further intervention. This popular image occurs on an epitaph to George Rongleigh, himself a watchmaker, whose 'outside case' was buried at Lydford, Devon. It concludes with the words:

> He departed this life November 14th, 1802,
>   aged 57;

> Wound up
> In hopes of being taken in hand
> by his Maker,
> And of being thoroughly cleaned and repaired,
> And set a going
> In the world to come.

The effects of rationalist philosophy on funeral practices in the eighteenth century are revealing of the whole problem of death in an individualistic society. In many ways, of all the different periods discussed in this book, the mid- to late eighteenth century is closest to our own in its general outlook. It has indeed been suggested, although it is very difficult to prove, that belief in the afterlife was possibly less strongly held during this period; a notable non-believer was David Hume who, by 'persisting in his infidelity, when he was dying', greatly shocked James Boswell. Certainly, as in our own century, the Church's promises of eternal happiness seem not to have brought universal comfort to the dying or to the bereaved — as has been shown in Chapter 2.

A rationalist view of death and burial was succinctly expressed by Lord Chesterfield, in a letter of 1769, when he himself was far from healthy: 'All I desire, for my own burial, is not to be buried alive; but how or where, I think, must be entirely indifferent to every rational creature.' This studied indifference was by no means accepted by all eighteenth-century thinkers; the more traditionally minded Johnson, so Boswell recorded, declared that 'no rational man can die without uneasy apprehension'.

The fear of being buried alive, which even Lord Chesterfield conceded, was still common throughout the eighteenth century; it was noted by la Rochefoucauld, on his visit to England in 1784, who produced the following explanation:

> The reason for this is that apoplexy and long drawn-out lethargy are common in England, and it is alleged that in early days a large number of people were buried alive. Accordingly, to guard against the horror of such a mistake, they choose rather to keep their dead for a longer period — sometimes for as much as a week — before burial.

As an additional precaution, Mrs Elizabeth Thomas of Islington, who died in 1808, directed her doctor to insert a long metal pin into her dead body, so that it pierced her heart, an operation which he duly carried out.[8]

Despite Lord Chesterfield's disclaimer, when it came to funeral practices, the majority of well-born people in the eighteenth century seem to have been far from being 'entirely indifferent'. La Rochefoucauld described with awe the 'magnificent' funerals of English gentlemen; with their carriages 'drawn by six black horses', and the 'thirty or forty outriders on black horses, all of these wear long crape bands, have their hair unpowdered and are in deepest mourning'. The only aspect of the ritual in which indifference was clearly shown was the actual burial service itself, which, in the words of la Rochefoucauld, 'the rector conducts . . . without ceremony'.

One gentleman who rejected the usual paraphernalia, and whose funeral was heavily influenced by classical philosophy, was John Underwood, who was buried in 1733. The peculiarity of his chosen burial ritual was widely reported in the press. Although based on rationalist views it certainly did not reflect the indifference towards burial which Lord Chesterfield expounded. Underwood was interred by night, with the usual rites of the Church of England. However,

> when the grave was filled up, and the turf laid down, the six gentlemen who followed him to the grave sang the last stanza of the Twentieth Ode of the Second Book of Horace. Everything was done according to his desire: no bell was tolled, no one was invited but the six gentlemen; and no relation followed his corpse. The coffin was painted green, according to his direction; and he was laid in it with his clothes on. Under his head was placed a Sanadon's *Horace*; at his feet Bentley's *Milton*; in his right hand a small *Greek Testament* . . . in his left hand a little edition of *Horace* . . . and Bentley's *Horace* was placed under his back.

> After the ceremony was over, they went back to his house, where his sister had provided a very handsome supper. The cloth being taken away, the gentlemen sang the Thirty-First Ode of the First Book of Horace, drank a cheerful glass, and went home about eight.

> He left near six thousand pounds to his sister, upon condition of observing this his will. He ordered her to give each of the gentlemen ten guineas, and desired that they should not come in black clothes . . . The will ends thus: 'I would have them take a cheerful glass, and think no more of John Underwood'.

Most members of the upper classes preferred to confine themselves to traditional rites, continuing the patterns established by their for-bears, with little thought or question. A few aristocrats even kept up the full ritual of heraldic interment, including the ceremonial use of an effigy, during the first decades of the eighteenth century. The last of these was the Duke of Buckingham, buried in 1735. At his funeral, an effigy, dressed in ducal robes, was laid upon the coffin; this wax figure may still be seen among the treasures of Westminster Abbey, lying in the exact posture in which it appeared at his burial.

Even without the heralds, an eighteenth-century nobleman's funeral could be a magnificent affair. When Lord Baltimore was buried in Epsom in 1771, the procession stretched from the church to the far edge of the town. Many aristocrats were buried by night. In 1735, Lord Lansdown was interred in St Clement Danes, London, on the night of 3 February. The bill presented by the church alone came to more than £20 and included, besides the fees of minister, clerk, sexton, bearers and ringers, 10s for lights in the church, 8s for light and charcoal in the vault and a further 10s for late attendance. If the *Gentleman's Magazine* is to be believed, the general disorder arising at the night burials of the aristocracy finally led to the practice being discontinued towards the end of the eighteenth century. The Duchess of Northumberland's funeral in 1776

took place by torchlight at four in the morning, to avoid the mischief of too great a number of persons interrupting the same; which, how-ever, was not the case, as the concourse of people was so numerous . . . that many had their legs and arms broken, and were otherwise much bruised.

It was, of course, greatly in the interests of the professional under-taker to prevent 'indifference' towards burial. In many respects, the undertakers replaced the heralds as the organisers and masters of cere-monies at aristocratic funerals. For example, as at the burial of Lady Diana le Fleming in 1816, reported in a letter by William Wordsworth, a London undertaker would travel to the provinces to perform his duties, just as the herald would have done. However, as Wordsworth made clear, there was an added reason for this particular undertaker's journey:

The funeral of Lady Diana appears to have been conducted with a good deal of pomp. At the head of the attendants came, of course, the master-undertaker; and he brought his lady with him all the way from London, not as an indispensable part of the ceremony but to show her the Lakes. There is something 'bizarre' in this mode of mixing the *utile* with the *dulce*.

The extent to which the undertaker had, by the eighteenth century, usurped the function of the heralds at aristocratic funerals is revealed particularly clearly in the undertakers' bill for the burial of the First Duke of Richmond, the illegitimate son of Charles II, in Westminster Abbey in June 1723. The undertakers, 'Nicholas Strawbridge and the Company of Upholders at Exeter Change', were responsible for hanging the rooms at Goodwood House with black, in the traditional manner, and for transporting the duke's body from Sussex to London, with one night at Guildford where the corpse lay in state in a room 'hung deep in mourning', attended by two watchers. Even more strikingly, the undertakers supplied escutcheons, standards, banners, 'a surcoat of arms' at £2 5s, 'helmet, crest and mantle' at £4, gauntlets and spurs for £1, together with a sword and shield costing £1 15s. The ducal coronet, crimson velvet cap and velvet cushion to lay on the coffin were also provided by the undertakers at a charge of 30s. In short, the undertakers supplied all the accoutrements of a heraldic funeral without the heralds' own participation; at the interment, the 'trophies' were carried by 15 gentlemen in scarves, hatbands and gloves, who were each paid 7s 6d for their services.

The undertakers' bill for the duke's burial came to £656 4s 1d and provides details of the trappings which accompanied an eighteenth-century aristocrat to his grave. In the Jerusalem Chamber, adjoining Westminster Abbey, carpenters constructed 'a large high alcove for the body to lie in, raised on three steps, six fluted pillars, three large arches, and the floor covered'. This was then hung with black velvet, 'and black plumes of ostrich feathers round it'; it was also decorated with streamers, silk escutcheons, crests and ducal stars on pasteboard. The room became so hot while the duke lay in state that the glazier of the Abbey was paid 8s 6d 'to take down the windows of the Jerusalem Chamber and other rooms to cool the rooms, and putting them up again'.

At the funeral itself, 'six conductors in mourning' stood 'at the doors in gowns, with staves dressed with crape, to keep the mob off and walk before the procession', for which they received 7s 6d each. There were 'four managers . . . to fit all the lords and put the whole procession in order', while the undertakers also supplied 'six mutes in mourning to attend by the corpse at 3s 6d', wearing hatbands, gloves and cloaks. Additionally, 58 of the 'choir and others of the Abbey' received 'French topped gloves', while illumination was provided by '150 branch lights of white wax and 150 men in mourning to carry them to light the whole procession in the Abbey', for which the undertakers charged £45. The body was carried by twelve men 'in velvet caps and truncheons': the undertakers' duties even included supplying 'printed tickets on royal paper with the edges japanned to invite the company', at a cost of 10s.

Besides organising the actual funeral, the undertakers were also responsible for putting into mourning both the late duke's country seat, Goodwood, and his London residence. At Goodwood, the mourning remained for twelve months after the duke's death, at a cost of £120. In each principal room, grey curtains were hung, together with grey valences and hangings, while the furniture was re-upholstered in grey. In the bedchamber were 'a fine light grey cloth bed, complete cloth hangings, round the room, two pairs of window curtains with valences and 12 back stools covered short'. Extra was charged for measuring up the rooms and for the cost of sending upholsterers from London to carry out the necessary work. Whereas the heralds' organisational duties were complete after an aristocrat had been laid in his grave, the undertakers managed, by encouraging the hire of mourning furnishings, to extend their influence and profit for a whole year from the time of the aristocrat's death.

Another area in which the eighteenth-century aristocracy appears not to have adopted the rationalists' 'indifference' to things funereal was in the wearing of mourning costume. During the eighteenth century, a far stricter code of mourning dress was established, to be surpassed only by that of the Victorian era in its rigidity and degree of prescription. However, this development was not as antithetical to rationalist thought as might, at first sight, be imagined. As religion lost some of its coercive power, with the perceived dying down of the flames of hell, so the need for strict social rules and regulations became apparent, if society was not to disintegrate into chaos. The mourning code of eighteenth-century England could be interpreted as one small part of this new framework of social organisation.

The two strands of a rationalist attitude towards death, apparent indifference coupled with a concern for social proprieties, are revealed in the letters of Horace Walpole, tinged with his own brand of sardonic humour and snobbery. He wrote: 'As mine is a pretty cheerful kind of philosophy, I think the best way is to think of dying, but to talk and act as if one was not to die; or else one tires other people, and dies before one's time.'

However, Walpole also showed immense concern about the niceties of formal mourning wear, in a letter to the Hon. Henry Conway, who had then just received a substantial legacy of £5,000:

> I am glad you mentioned it: I would not have had you appear without your close mourning for the Duke of Devonshire upon any account. I was once going to tell you of it, knowing your inaccuracy in such matters; but thought it still impossible you should be ignorant how necessary it is. Lord Strafford, who has a legacy of only £200, wrote to consult Lady Suffolk. She told him, for such a sum, which only implies a ring, it was sometimes not done; but yet advised him to mourn. In your case, it is indispensable; nor can you see any of his family without it. Besides, it is much better on such an occasion to over, than under do.

For first mourning, black was worn, silk or bombazine being the materials generally used for ladies' dresses, while the men wore black suits. The length of time for mourning depended on the closeness of the relationship to the deceased; servants too were expected to wear mourning. After a reasonable period had elapsed, second mourning, less sombre in style, would be adopted, until the bereaved finally returned to normal dress. Although still termed mourning, this less austere period could allow considerable licence for the fashion conscious, as this descripton of a trip to the races, written by Lady Elizabeth Noel in 1760, clearly shows:

> We are in mourning, Mamma in her white sprigged lily-of-the-valley negligé, the blond [lace] mourning cap from Tonbridge which was very becoming, treble blond ruffles, a very handsome white spotted satin cloak.[9]

A further area in which 'indifference' was certainly not generally observed in eighteenth-century funerary rituals was the erection of church monuments. A fine example is to be found in Steeple Aston church in Oxfordshire where Sir Francis Page and his wife recline in double-chinned splendour on tasselled cushions, she idly glancing at a book, he proudly surveying the scene, in long wig and robes. Behind the figures is a pyramid, while the pediment which surmounts the whole monument rises as high as the ceiling, supported on two fluted columns. Sir Francis Page's judicial career was characterised by his ambition to hang a hundred men, which he duly achieved, and also by his ghastly jokes in the courtroom, making him a target for Pope's satire. The monument, made by Henry Scheemakers, was commissioned on the death of Page's wife in 1730; Page himself lived on until 1741. Older monuments were destroyed in order that Page's tomb could be erected; the pride which he felt for his memorial is shown by his will in which he left 20s a year to ensure that his tomb would be 'for ever kept and preserved in good, decent and handsome repair, clean and beautiful in all respects', and to pay for 'the locking up and dusting, looking after, keeping and cleaning the same'.[10] It is clear that Page took immense interest in and exercised considerable control over his own memorial, seeing it as an important reflection upon himself. The image he wished to convey to the world was one of immense opulence and solidity, both qualities excellently captured in Scheemakers' sculpture (see Plate 10, p. 130).

This vigorous, if ostentatious, style of tomb sculpture did not last throughout the whole of the eighteenth century. In the second half of the century, changes occurred which themselves reflected one consequence of an increasingly individualistic philosophy, the redefinition of the role and position of the artist. As has been shown, sculptors of the sixteenth, seventeenth and early eighteenth centuries closely followed the dictates of their patrons. In many respects they were simply treated as craftsmen, employed to do a skilled job, rather than as possessors of a particularly superior 'artistic' vision. However, later in the eighteenth century, sculptors and other artists became far more professionalised, as was symbolised by the founding of the Royal Academy in 1768. One result of this was to free them from much of the interference of their patrons in the details of their work.

Together with their improved status came a desire to theorise about the art they practised. Reynolds expounded the doctrine of the 'ideal and the typical', stating that 'the whole beauty and grandeur of art consists, in my opinion, in being able to get above all singular forms, local customs, peculiarities and details of every kind'.[11] Sculptors influenced by these views abandoned representation of contemporary dress in favour of classical draperies, and eschewed the expression of emotion in their work, emulating instead the stillness of Greek art. A not unreasonable parallel could be drawn between sculptors and professional undertakers. The makers of monuments were now a compartmentalised profession whose services took far less account of the clients' own inclinations and whose finished products were less individualised than many earlier memorials. As with the undertakers, the competing effects of individualism led, paradoxically, to a much less personal style in church monuments.

At its best, this new movement produced such works as the famous tomb, carved by Thomas Banks RA, and greatly admired in its time, of Penelope Boothby, who died in 1791. In 1793, when it was put on public display, it caused Queen Charlotte and her daughters to weep. The pathos of this monument is reinforced by the inscription: 'the unfortunate parents ventured their all on this frail bark and the wreck was total'. However, the figure itself, although charming, lacks the realism of earlier monuments, producing a highly idealised image of childhood rather than portraying the girl herself.

One striking element present in some tomb sculpture of the second half of the eighteenth century both recalls an aspect of early seventeenth century — and also of late medieval — funerary practices, and looks towards the Romantic era: the eroticising of death. As in the early seventeenth century, this tendency was not confined to, or even most fully expressed, in tomb sculpture. Both in certain funeral practices themselves, and more strongly in literature, the eroticising of death flourished from the mid-eighteenth century onwards. The literary manifestations began tentatively with Gray's *Elegy Written in a Country Churchyard* and Young's *Night Thoughts*, while gradually developing into the far more explicit genre of the gothic novel, of which Horace Walpole was himself an early exponent. Actual examples of the eroticising of death can be found, as in the case of the well-known agricultural expert, Arthur Young who, in 1797, on the death of his greatly loved 14-year-old daughter, had her buried beneath the family pew, 'fixing the coffin so that when I kneel it will be between her head and her dear heart'.

In tomb sculpture, Roubiliac's monument to Lady Elizabeth Nightingale and her husband, dated 1761, has a certain hint of eroticism about it. The words of an early nineteenth-century writer capture something of the feelings it inspires: a skeleton, 'the grisly King of Terrors . . . in shroudlike habiliments bursting hideous from his darksome cavern', aims a dart at Lady Elizabeth. Her expression is reminiscent of Bernini's St Theresa, while the general composition shows similarities with the tomb of Pope Alexander VII, also by Bernini. Lady Elizabeth's husband vainly attempts to ward off the blow; he 'fondly clasps to his breast the dying female, whose languid helplessness beautifully contrasts with the muscular exertion . . . of her affectionate partner', epitomising, according to Brayley, 'the severe pangs of conjugal affection'.[12] The power of this monument greatly impressed many contemporaries, among them John Wesley.

> I once more took a serious walk through the tombs in Westminster Abbey. What heaps of unmeaning stone and marble! But there was one tomb which showed common sense; that beautiful figure Mr Nightingale endeavouring to screen his lovely wife from Death. Here indeed the marble seems to speak, and the statues appear only [just] not alive.[13]

It is interesting to compare this monument with earlier memorials which use the skeleton as a major part of their composition. Previously, the skeleton acted as a memento mori, emphasising the natural inevitability of death; it actually represented the deceased after decomposition of the flesh (see Plate 9, p. 129). By the latter half of the eighteenth century, such reminders of bodily decay were no longer so accepted or so acceptable. The Nightingale monument, with its personification of death, owed some of its power to the fact that skeletal imagery was not in such common use; it was designed to arouse shock rather than resignation in the face of death. In Roubiliac's work, the lightly clad lady is fought over by her husband and death, emphasising the struggle and heartbreak involved in passing from this world to the next, rather than the natural ease of the transition. The comfort of religion has little part in this eighteenth-century conflict, despite Wesley's admiration.

The eroticising of death is a further testimony to the failure of eighteenth-century rationalism to tackle successfully the problem of death and render it truly a thing of indifference. As is apparent from the experience of the twentieth century, an essentially scientific, rational and materialistic outlook cannot fully compensate for the immensely threatening role of death in a highly individualistic society. In the case of the eighteenth century, this inevitable failure of reason to conquer the dilemma of death was one factor leading to the Romantic and Victorian reversal of the general trend of attitudes towards death, established during the three centuries before the industrial revolution. Thomas Gray, whose famous *Elegy Written in a Country Churchyard* is steeped in melancholy romanticism, touched the heart of the problem:

> The boast of heraldry, the pomp of pow'r,
> And all that beauty, all that wealth e'er gave,

Await alike th' inevitable hour.
The paths of glory lead but to the grave.

Notes

1. The sources for the principal funerals discussed in this chapter are as follows:

Mary, Countess of Northumberland, 1572; Stone, *Crisis of the Aristocracy*, p. 579.
Lucy, Lady Latimer, 1583; London, Public Record Office: PCC Rowe 16.
Robert, Earl of Dorset, 1608; London, Public Record Office: PCC Dorset 23.
Dame Anne Pemberton, 1625; McMurray, *Records of City Parishes*, p. 235.
Sir Richard Deane, 1636; Thiselton Dyer, *Church-Lore Gleanings*, pp. 140-41.
Frances, Duchess of Richmond and Lenox, 1639; 'Will of Frances Stuart', *Archaeologia Cantiana*, xi.
Dame Margaret Verney, 1641; quoted in Cunnington and Lucas, *Costume for Births, Marriages and Deaths*, p. 180.
Frances, Countess of Thanet, 1646; Thiselton Dyer, *Church-Lore Gleanings*, p. 139.
Queen Elizabeth of Bohemia, 1662; Cunnington and Lucas, *Costume for Births, Marriages and Deaths*, p. 237.
Elizabeth, Countess of Denbigh, 1670; Oxford, Bodleian Library: MS. Ashmole 836, fols. 119, 127-139 and 343.
Margaret, Duchess of Newcastle, 1674; Grant, *Margaret the First*, pp. 237-9.
Sir Thomas Bludworth, 1682; McMurray, *Records of City Parishes*, p. 239.
Charles, Duke of Richmond and Lenox, 1723; Steer, 'Funeral Account of Duke of Richmond', *Sussex Archaeological Collections*, XCVIII.
John Underwood, 1733; *Notes and Queries*, 6th series, i, p. 210.
George, Lord Lansdown, 1735; Delany, *Autobiography*, p. 249.
Edmund, Duke of Buckingham, 1735; *Historical Register*, xxi, pp. 70-75.
Frederick, Lord Baltimore, 1771; Delany, *Autobiography*, p. 249.
Elizabeth, Duchess of Northumberland, 1776; Thiselton Dyer, *Church-Lore Gleanings*, p. 140.
Lady Diana le Fleming, 1816; Wordsworth, *Letters of William and Dorothy Wordsworth*, iii, p. 331.

Many further examples of nocturnal burials are to be found in Chamberlain, *Letters*, passim. For the heralds' petition against night funerals, see London, British Library: MS. Harleian 1301, fol. 12.

2. Brown, *Life Against Death*, p. 107.

3. *Journals of the House of Commons*, i, pp. 692-4; London, British Library: Addit. MS. 34,163, fols. 100-101.

4. Wagner, *Heralds of England*, pp. 110 and 238-9.

5. Quoted in Esdaile, *English Church Monuments*. p. 54.

6. Ibid. p. 90.

7. Quoted in Wagner, *Heralds of England*, p. 112.

8. Thiselton Dyer, *Old English Social Life*, pp. 166-7.

9. Quoted in Cunnington and Lucas, *Costume for Births, Marriages and Deaths*, p. 246.

10. Quoted in Brookes, *Steeple Aston*, p. 231.

11. Quoted in Esdaile, *English Church Monuments*, p. 70.
12. Quoted in MacMichael, *Westminster Abbey*, p. 52.
13. Quoted in Esdaile, *Roubiliac*, p. 157.

10 'AND MY LARGE KINGDOM FOR A LITTLE GRAVE': ROYAL AND STATE FUNERALS

The royal funerals of the sixteenth and seventeenth centuries marked the apogee of English burial ceremonies. Primarily, they were visual manifestations of political power, which acted as a counterbalance to the inevitable temporary insecurity arising when one monarch died and another succeeded to the throne. In the eighteenth century, the funerals of monarchs were less magnificent, reflecting more the loss of the private persona, as well as the demise of the public figure. This, in its turn, came about because of the decline in real power wielded by the sovereign under a system of constitutional monarchy. However, a new phenomenon replaced the burial of the sovereign as the funeral ritual of greatest magnificence: the interment of the national hero, a character who, perhaps, best epitomises the philosophy of individualism.[1]

King Henry VIII died at Westminster at midnight on 28 January 1547. First the body was viewed by members of the Privy Council and other nobles to confirm that the King was really dead. Then apothecaries, surgeons and wax chandlers were summoned 'to do their duties in spurging, cleansing, bowelling, searing, embalming, furnishing and dressing with spices the said corpse'. The body was wrapped in fine linen and velvet and tied with silk cords; the plumber and carpenter cased the corpse in lead and placed it in a coffin which was itself covered in blue velvet, decorated with a cross. 'The entrails and bowels were honourably buried in the chapel', and the coffin was set up in the middle of the privy chamber, covered with a pall of cloth of gold and surrounded by lights. 'Masses, obsequies and prayers' were said, and 'continual watch made . . . to the number of thirty persons, besides the chaplains . . . night and day during the time of his abode there, which was five days'. Meanwhile, 'all things ... were continually a doing', to prepare for the dead monarch's funeral.

The 'chambers, galleries, hall [and] chapel' of the palace of Westminster were hung with black cloth decorated with coats of arms. In the chapel a 'goodly formal hearse' was constructed, lit by 80 candles and surrounded by banners. 'In the meantime commandment was given to all manner of estates, as well noblemen and women . . . as to all of them of the King's house, to put apart their several apparels, and put on them every man his mourning weeds.' Henry Grey, Lord Marquis of Dorset, the father of Lady Jane Grey, was appointed as chief mourner, assisted by twelve other peers. 'These noblemen prepared themselves in their mourning habits, as hoods, mantles, gowns and all other apparels according to their degrees; and were in good order and readiness at the court, to give their attendance when they should be called.' Nine bishops prepared to conduct the funeral, led by Stephen Gardiner, the Bishop of Winchester, who was to preach the sermon.

On 2 February, 'betwixt eight and nine of the clock at night, the hearse being lighted', the 'most royal corpse was reverently taken . . . from the chamber, covered with a rich pall . . . and so brought to the chapel', and 'honourably set and placed within the . . . hearse'. The dean of the chapel and the chaplains then 'fell to their orisons and suffrages', remaining with the corpse all night.

The next morning, the mourners, 'with their hoods on their heads', processed two by two to the chapel 'and kneeled about the corpse on either side', with 'the chief mourners at the head'. Then one of the heralds, 'Norroy King of Arms, standing at the choir door, with his face to the people, said with a loud voice, "Of your charity pray for the soul of the high and most mighty Prince, our late sovereign Lord and King Henry VIII".' This was followed by a requiem mass, 'the chapel singing and saying the ceremonies . . . in most solemn and goodly wise'. After the mass had ended, the bishops censed the corpse, while the mourners left the chapel for a 'sumptuous dinner', presided over by the chief mourner 'as if it had been the King's majesty personally present'. In the afternoon, the procession to the chapel and the requiem mass were repeated, in a pattern which continued for the next twelve days.

'In the meantime . . . all other kinds of preparation were doing', especially at Syon and at Windsor, where Henry was to be interred. At Syon, 'the church . . . and the choir, with the house, chambers and lodgings . . . were hung to the ground with black cloth . . . In the midst of the choir there was ordained a royal and stately hearse . . . with a valence fringed with black silk and gold . . . and the floor of the same hearse covered with black cloth to the high altar, which was all covered with black velvet, and preciously adorned with all manner of plate and jewels of the church, silver, gold and precious stones'. At Windsor, more black cloth was hung, decorated with shields, while a third hearse was built, 'of a wonderful state and proportion . . . very gorgeous and valiant'.

'There was also order taken for the cleaning and mending of all the highways between Westminster and Windsor . . . and the noisesome boughs cut down of every side of the way . . . And where the ways were narrow, there were hedges opened on either side, so as the footmen might have free passage'. Doles were distributed to the poor in London, while the clergy of all the parishes through which the funeral procession would pass were given money, torches and escutcheons, to stand along the route, praying and censing the corpse.

On the last day that the corpse lay at Westminster, 'there were sung three solemn masses by bishops . . . the first of our Lady, in white; the second of the Trinity, in blue; the third of requiem, by the right reverend the Bishop of Winchester, in black'.

Early next morning, 14 February, 'the chariot was brought to the court hall door, and the corpse with great reverence brought from the hearse to the same by mitred prelates and other temporal lords.' The chariot — 'sumptuous and valuable' — had four wheels and was 'very long and large, with four pillars overlaid all with cloth of gold at the four corners, bearing a pillow of rich cloth of gold and tissue, fringed with a goodly deep fringe of blue silk and gold . . . the nether part of the . . . chariot was hanged with blue velvet down to the ground between the wheels'. The coffin was 'reverently settled in the bulk of the chariot; over the coffin . . . was cast a pall of rich cloth of gold, and upon that a goodly image like to the king's person in all points, wonderfully richly apparelled, with velvet, gold, and precious stones of all sorts; holding in his right hand a sceptre of gold; in his left hand the ball of the world with a cross. Upon his head a crown imperial of inestimable value, a collar of the Garter about his neck and a garter of gold about his leg'. Two knights travelled in the chariot with the coffin and the effigy, one at the head and the other at the feet. 'So about eight of the clock, the weather being very fair and the people very desirous to see the sight, the nobles mounted their horses and marched forward with the noble corpse.'

The procession, reputedly four miles in length, departed 'in goodly order . . . to the great admiration of them that beheld it'. 'First of all rode two porters of the king's house . . . with two black staves in their hands, to stay, that neither cart, horse nor man should trouble or cumber them in this passage.' Then came the children and priests of the chapel, in surplices, singing, while 'two hundred and fifty poor men in long mourning gowns and hoods, with badges on their left shoulders', walked alongside, bearing torches, accompanied by 'two carts laden with torches, to restore them always as the old wasted'.

Next came an assortment of messengers, ambassadors' servants, chaplains, esquires, 'gentle strangers' and others, kept in order by mounted heralds, and followed by twelve aldermen of London. Then, two by two, came nobles, bishops, and 'ambassadors of divers . . . nations . . . accompanied with such of the lords as best could entertain them and understand their language'. Various heralds were next, bearing the arms, shield, crest and sword of the dead King, followed by knights, bearing banners. The chariot itself was pulled by 'seven great horses wholly trapped in black velvet . . . and upon the seven horses rode seven children of honour all in black . . . Next to the chariot came the chief mourner, alone, his horse trapped all in black velvet. After him followed the other twelve mourners, two and two'. Then came more banners and the yeomen of the guard, walking in threes, dressed in black and bearing halberds with the points downwards. Noblemen's servants, themselves placed according to the rank of their masters, brought up the rear of the procession.

By two o'clock that afternoon they had reached Syon, where the hearse's lights were lit and the coffin placed inside. A requiem mass was conducted, and then the mourners had 'cheer abundantly . . . and great plenty of meat and drink distributed to all that came'. The next church service was at three the following morning, after which the coffin and effigy were returned to the chariot while the mourners had breakfast before setting out again. Church bells rang as the procession passed; at Eton College, 'all the young children scholars . . . in their white surplices, bare-headed, holding in the one hand tapers, and in the other books, saying the seven psalms: and as the corpse came by, kneeled and censed it'.

At one o'clock the chariot passed through the castle gate at Windsor. The coffin and effigy were carried under a canopy to the lighted hearse in the chapel and set inside it. The mourners went to their lodgings in the castle and 'shifted themselves from their riding apparel, and came again in their gowns'. Mass was then celebrated by the Bishop of Winchester. The hearse was surrounded by the banners which had been carried in the procession, while the dead King's hatchments, coat of arms, sword, shield and crest were set upon a second altar draped in black. 'In the Queen's closet above stood the Queen, all the noblemen, ambasssadors, with other notable strangers, to see the divine service and the royal order of the funeral.' For supper, 'they had very liberal and sumptuous fare'.

The next day, 16 February, the interment itself took place. The first of several masses began at four in the morning, with breakfast served at six o'clock. The Bishop of Winchester then conducted mass, at which the chief mourner gave a gold ten-shilling piece for the offertory. The 'two next chief mourners', accompanied by a herald, carried the King's coat of arms and offered it to the bishop, 'with much humility and reverence'; it was then laid upon the altar. The remaining mourners, in twos, offered the shield, sword and other accoutrements of the dead King. A man in complete armour, carrying a poleaxe with the point downwards, rode up to the choir door, dismounted, and was conducted to the bishop, to whom he offered the axe. After he had retired to the vestry to remove his armour, the mourners all offered 'rich palls of cloth of gold'; four were given by the chief mourner, three by each earl and two by barons. The heralds received the palls and laid them at the foot of the effigy. All the ambassadors, nobles and gentlemen present also offered palls, so that a large pile was amassed.

The Bishop of Winchester preached on the text 'blessed are those who die in the name of the Lord'; the bishop 'declared the frailty of man, and community of death to the high and to the low: and showing the pitiful and dolorous loss that all manner [of] men had sustained by the death of so gracious a King'. Then the banners were offered to the bishop, while the Dean of Westminster and his chaplains removed the palls into the vestry and six knights followed with the effigy. The bishops proceeded with the funeral service. The vault was uncovered under the hearse and the coffin winched down into it, 'with the help of sixteen tall yeomen of the guard'. At the words 'dust to dust, ashes to ashes', some 'mould' was thrown on to the coffin. Members of the royal household standing around the grave 'with heavy and dolorous lamentation broke their staves [of office] in shivers upon their heads, and cast them after the corpse within the pit . . . with exceeding sorrow and heaviness, not without grievous sighs and tears, not only of them, but of many others, as well of the meaner sort as of the nobility, very piteous and sorrowful to behold'.

When the grave was covered with planks, the Garter King of Arms 'stood in the midst of the choir, accompanied by all them of his office, in their coats of arms, and with a loud voice proclaimed the King's Majesty still now living in this form: "Almighty God of his infinite goodness give good life and long to the most high and mighty prince, our sovereign Lord, King Edward VI . .. . Vive le noble roi Edward." And the rest of the officers of arms cried the same three several times after him. Then the trumpets sounded with great melody and courage, to the comfort of all them that were there present.'

Most other royal funerals of the sixteenth and seventeenth centuries followed a pattern not dissimilar to that of Henry VIII. The only significant alteration to later royal funerals was the omission of all the masses, which gave the whole proceedings a far more secular air. As the religious element decreased, so the funeral procession took on an even greater significance; for the majority of spectators, of course, the procession was the only part of the funeral they were able to observe for themselves. Queen Elizabeth's funeral procession was recorded in some delightful drawings showing all the mourners walking to Westminster Abbey and the Queen's body with the effigy laid above the coffin, drawn in a hearse surrounded by banners (see Plate 6, p. 126).

The order for the funeral procession of James I lists in minute detail the gradations of society, beginning with the King's own household and then encompassing the nobility and Church. In this procession the King's corpse was placed at the rear with only the chief mourner, Charles I, and his attendants behind it. The fine distinctions of the hierarchy of prestige are therefore fully displayed, with those of highest rank being placed nearest the corpse. The account of the procession runs to several manuscript pages; about 9,000 people were said to have received mourning clothes in order to take part.

It required 50 men 'to make way and keep the streets for the proceedings clear', while a further hundred were employed 'to go up and down on both sides to keep order'. More than 300 poor men walked at the head, followed by the servants of the gentlemen, knights and esquires taking part in the procession. The first members of the royal household to appear were all the children employed in the different departments, as dovekeepers, potscourers, spit-turners and so on. Then came the 'artificers' — arras-makers, potters, basket-makers, purveyors of rushes and several others — followed by the 'grooms to all offices', for example, the boiling house, pitcherhouse, larder, kitchen and many different stables. Among the yeomen were cormorant keepers, spaniel keepers and dog-wagonners, together with those employed about the robes and wardrobes, including picture-drawers, the engineer, actors and comedians. The servants of the nobility had to be placed according to their masters' rank, so that least prestige was given to servants of earls' younger sons, followed by those who served viscounts' eldest sons, then the servants of barons and bishops, followed by those who waited on marquesses' younger sons and so forth. Among the higher members of the royal household came the 'master of the tennis play', the master of the bears, the master of the lions, the clockmaker, the King's printer, jewellers, apothecaries and surgeons. The musicians and members of the Chapel Royal preceded the highest members of the household, the chief clerks of the aviary, spicery and kitchen, the surveyor of the works, chaplains and 'secretaries for the French and Latin', as well as clerks of governmental departments, including the chancery, privy seal and Parliament. Aldermen of London were followed by the masters of the revels, the tents, the wardrobe, jewelhouse, and so on, as well as judges and privy councillors. The nobility of the realm came next, while pride of place was reserved for the Lord Keeper who preached the funeral sermon, the Archbishop of Canterbury, the ambassadors of foreign princes and the Lord Chamberlain.

The organisation of such a procession was no mean feat and, not surprisingly, arguments arose over precedence. Some of these were resolved by following the order established at Queen Elizabeth's funeral, but other disputes must have rankled throughout the proceedings. The effect of such display would have been stunning, underlining most forcefully the power of the monarchy. It also served to reinforce the stability of society at a moment of potential crisis, the death of its ruler, by reaffirming publicly the precise hierarchy of its members.

A significant addition to the funeral procession of Mary II in 1695 was the participation of 'all the parliamentmen [who] had cloaks given them'. Previously, Parliament had automatically dissolved on the death of the sovereign, but because William and Mary were joint sovereigns, on this one occasion only, the death of a monarch did not end the life of that Parliament. Interestingly, female monarchs were originally not subject to the general heraldic rule that the emblems of war were unsuitable for use at a woman's funeral. The full set, including gauntlets, spurs, a horse and battleaxe, appeared at the funeral of Mary I in 1553 and again when Mary Queen of Scots was given a second, more honourable funeral six months after her execution, by the very person who had commanded her death, Elizabeth I. However, at Elizabeth's own funeral, the gauntlets and spurs were omitted. When, at the end of the seventeenth century, Mary II was interred, only her crown and sceptre were displayed, without any military paraphernalia.[2] The decline in the use of these weapons at the burials of queens reflected an increased emphasis on the private rather than the public persona of the monarch, a process facilitated after 1688 by an actual decline in the monarchy's real power.

The need to counteract the possible danger attendant on the death of the monarch also helps to explain the custom, medieval in origin, of using a funeral effigy during the lying in state, procession and actual interment. Some of these figures still survive at Westminster Abbey, although in poor condition; indeed, even by the mid-eighteenth century,

Horace Walpole described them as the 'curious but mangled figures . . . now called the ragged regiment'. The accounts for making them, however, give some idea of their former magnificence. To prepare the effigy of Queen Elizabeth of York, wife of Henry VII, two joiners were employed for 16d to 'frame the body'; seven small sheepskins were puchased at 2s 4d to cover the wooden figure; the hair was hired for 5s; 'laying of the first prime colour' cost 4d; for 'painting of the image', 4s was charged. The 'representation' of Henry, Prince of Wales, the son of James I, who died in 1612, had 'several joints both in the arms, legs and body, to be moved to sundry actions', while the face and hands were 'very curiously wrought'. James I himself had two funeral effigies, and for each one £10 was 'paid to Daniel Parkes for making of one periwig, beard and eyebrows'. Sometimes the clothes for the effigy were specially made and therefore appear in the accounts. For Queen Elizabeth I's effigy, a crimson satin robe was sewn, lined with white fustian, with sabatons and a coif of cloth of gold, while £6 13s 4d was spent on 'the crown, sceptre and ball, being all gilt with fine gold burnished, the crown set with stones'. However, at Anne of Denmark's funeral, her effigy was dressed in one of her own robes and £6 was spent on 'perfuming' it.

The reasons for the use of these effigies were complex and at no time were the 'representations' of dead kings and queens in England vested with the same degree of significance as French royal funeral effigies.[3] However, they had an important role to play as the focus of attention during the inevitable lapse of time between the death of the sovereign and the actual interment, while all the complex arrangements were being made for the funeral. On a political level, the 'representation', lying in gorgeous robes under an enormous black canopy, in a house hung with deepest black, symbolised the undying power of the monarchy. The historian Kantorowicz has argued that the effigy represented the enduring royal dignity of the king. He also suggests that an inversion of the normal order took place after the death of a sovereign, with the effigy representing the body politic of the monarch, which for once became visible, while the normally visible body natural lay concealed in its coffin. However, these effigies, magnificent as they were, do not seem to have been treated in the same manner as the sovereigns themselves, unlike the French tradition; indeed, for James I's funeral, two separate effigies were prepared, one for display at Denmark House and another with joints to be used at the Abbey. No doubt the English fashion for using such effigies reflected a desire not to be outshone by continental rivals, among other considerations.

One further reason for the use of effigies was to rekindle and channel the sorrow felt by the bereaved subjects, which might well have diminished somewhat during the lengthy preparation time before the funeral. Stow's *Chronicle of England* recorded that Queen Elizabeth's effigy had just this effect on the spectators at her funeral procession:

> When they beheld her statue or picture lying upon the coffin, set forth in royal robes, having a crown upon the head thereof, and a ball and sceptre in either hand, there was such a general sighing, groaning and weeping, as the like hath not been seen or known in the memory of man, neither doth any history mention any people, time or state, to make like lamentation for the death of their sovereign.

Whatever the political or legal functions of the royal funeral effigy, it certainly had an intensely dramatic quality. Brilliantly coloured, amid a sea of black-clad mourners, it heightened the impact of an already theatrical event. The use of the royal funeral effigy, first seen at the burial of Edward II in 1327, did not, however, outlive the Restoration. With the change in the political position of the monarch brought about in 1688, the funeral effigy no longer had a part to play in the procession itself, although wax models of sovereigns continued to be made after their deaths: these may still be seen at Westminster Abbey.

The drastic diminution of the religious element in royal funerals, besides increasing the importance of the procession within the ritual, also served to enhance the role of the group of lay people who were principally responsible for organising the whole proceedings: the members of the College of Arms. This alteration in emphasis is, for instance, apparent if one compares the ritual for placing Henry VIII's coffin into the funeral chariot with the same ritual conducted in the case of James I. Henry VIII's corpse, it will be recalled, was preceded by mitred prelates in their robes, giving the event a distinctly ecclesiastical tone:

> The bishops two and two in order, saying their prayers, torches plenty on every side of the corpse, borne by sixteen yeomen of the guard under a rich canopy of blue velvet fringed with silk and gold.

However, when James I's body was transferred from Theobalds, where he died, to Denmark House in London, the royal coffin was laid in the presence chamber

> and after a third warning was given by the trumpets, the officers of
> arms . . . put on their coats of arms and in a reverend manner came
> up towards the body with three obeisances and waited before the
> body while the Gentlemen of the Privy Chamber carried it down to
> the first court. At the hall door it was laid into a carriage.

The perpetuation of lavish ceremony at royal funerals benefited the
heralds financially, as well as in terms of prestige. From the funeral of
Henry VIII onwards, the heralds received £40 to be shared among them
for their attendance at the interment of a monarch. They also received
black cloth for their mourning clothes and shared some of the trappings
of the funeral — in particular the hearse with its rich materials — after
the completion of ceremonies. This perquisite was of considerable
value; after the funeral of James I, the heralds shared out 601 yards of
velvet, a pall made of 68 yards of tissue with its lining, 56¼ yards of
purple satin, 32 black velvet chairs with velvet cushions, 21 stools,
the taffeta which had lined the roof of the hearse and all the innumerable
escutcheons. They also sold additional furniture and cushions and
divided the profits. After Mary II's funeral, the heralds received 461
yards of black velvet from the hearse, which they sold for £175.[4] It was
therefore greatly in the interests of the College of Arms to encourage
extreme luxury at the funerals of royalty. During the sixteenth century
the 'obsequies' of foreign rulers were also celebrated in England,
religious differences notwithstanding, at St Paul's: the heralds received
the same burial fees for officiating at these ceremonies.[5] These rituals
reflect the influence of international considerations on English royal
funeral rites of the period, again underlining the essentially political
role of the ceremony.

However, the heralds did not always receive their various funeral
perquisites unchallenged. Wrangles often broke out between the heralds
and the Dean and Chapter of Westminster, or the Dean of Windsor, as
to who rightfully deserved the trappings of a royal burial. An account of the funeral of Anne of Denmark has a note added by a
herald that 'the hearse of Queen Anne was not taken down before 12th
July and then, after good proof that it belonged to them, was divided at
the Office of Arms amongst us'. In this instance, the heralds' right to
the hearse had been challenged by the Dean of Westminster, but the
Commissioners for the Earl Marshal, with the King's consent, had upheld
their claim. In the eighteenth century, the same argument erupted after

several noble and royal funerals; following the burial of Queen Anne in 1714 the dean actually locked the heralds inside the Abbey until they agreed to leave without taking the furnishings.[6]

These regal extravaganzas, not surprisingly, cost a phenomenal amount of money. At a time when expenditure on the funerals of even the grandest of subjects rarely exceeded £3,000, Queen Elizabeth was buried at a cost of £11,305 1s. During the reign of her successor, James I, expenditure on royal burials reached its zenith. James I took it upon himself to provide monuments to his predecessor, Elizabeth I, and his own mother, Mary Queen of Scots, in Westminster Abbey. Significantly, Elizabeth's tomb, finished in 1606, cost only £765, while that of her Scottish cousin cost, it would appear, in excess of £2,000. The comparison between the two was intentional, with Mary's monument greatly exceeding Elizabeth's in height as well as cost.[7]

When James's wife, Anne of Denmark, died on 2 March 1619, the King directed that £20,000, or more if necessary, should be handed over by the treasury to the Master of the Great Wardrobe, Lionel Cranfield, to pay for the ceremony. However, the money was not that easy to find and the date of the funeral was put back to allow more time, as John Chamberlain recorded on 24 April:

The day of the Queen's funeral is not yet set down, though it be more than time it were done . . . The whole charge spoken of is beyond proportion, above three times more than was bestowed upon Queen Elizabeth, which proceeds not of plenty for they are driven to shifts for money, and talk of melting the Queen's golden plate and putting it into coin.

The accounts for a royal burial, such as that of Anne of Denmark, reveal the extreme complexity, and expense, of mounting the event; indeed, simply to draw up the final bill of all the various charges cost £10, so multifarious were the items.

For the funeral of Anne of Denmark, a vast amount of money was spent on material; thousands of yards were made into hangings and mourning clothes, at a cost in excess of £10,000. Eighteen tailors were employed in this work, for over three weeks, while the King's embroiderer prepared, among other things, 'two pairs of the Queen's arms with the green men her supporters and two great rich crowns all wrought upon cloth of gold, cloth of silver, crimson satin, blue satin with gold and silver twists'. Meanwhile, a quart of ink was consumed in drawing further coats of arms on many reams of fine paper. In the stables, £23 16s 8d was spent on preparing horses' harness, coach reins, feathers and ribbons. In short, all departments of the royal household were involved in a mass of minute and costly preparations.

The funeral of James I was an even more lavish and extravagant affair; John Chamberlain estimated its cost to have been about £50,000, with 9,000 people receiving black mourning garments, to accompany the corpse to the grave. The funeral of James's son, Charles I, was a total contrast as, of course, was the nature of his death, by the executioner's axe. The sum of £400 was deemed sufficient to cover the costs; the number of mourners present was limited to 21, with three servants allowed to each nobleman and no more than two servants for commoners. Charles II, as Evelyn recorded, was also buried quietly 'because of dying in a different religion than that of his people'. Mary II left a written request that there should not be 'any extraordinary expense at her funeral'; unfortunately, the document was not found in time and so £50,000 was spent on the ceremony 'against her desire'. Although the inflation experienced during the seventeenth century made this sum smaller in real terms than the amount expended on James I's burial, it was still an enormous amount of money to spend on a transitory and ephemeral ceremony.

The vast cost of royal funerals begs the question whether they were really worth all the expense. The rationale behind lavish expenditure is clear. The need to assert the power of the monarchy, at the difficult period of transfer of authority from one sovereign to the next, necessitated a public display of strength. There was also, on the international level, a certain rivalry of pomp between rulers of different states and countries. The distribution of black cloth for mourning garments reminded subjects of their subservience to the Crown, and reflected the gratitude due for that, and for other forms of largesse, to the all-providing monarchy. The minute gradations of this distribution, in terms of the length and quality of cloth allowed to each recipient, reasserted and reinforced the social hierarchy, as did the mourners' position in the procession. However, when, as in the case of Anne of Denmark, a mere consort, few of these considerations pertained and yet thousands of pounds were spent, notwithstanding the precarious financial position of the monarchy, it might seem to exceed the limits of reasonable expense. It is also apparent that, on one subject at least, the grand display failed to have its desired impact. John Chamberlain wrote to his friend, Dudley Carleton:

It were to no purpose to make any long description of the funeral which was but a drawling, tedious sight, more remarkable for number than for any other singularity . . . and though the number of lords and ladies were very great, yet me thought altogether they made but a poor show . . . they came laggering all along even tired with the length of the way and weight of their clothes.

Chamberlain also witnessed James I's funeral. Unfortunately, the transportation of the royal corpse from Theobalds to Denmark House was 'marred by foul weather, so that there was nothing to be seen but coaches and torch'. Chamberlain could not fail to be impressed by the actual interment, 'the greatest indeed that ever was known in England', and was especially complimentary about the hearse, designed by Inigo Jones. However, the multitude of participants and the complexity of the whole event seem to have been beyond the organising powers of the usually efficient heralds, and Chamberlain's final verdict on the funeral was that 'in sum all was performed with great magnificence, but the order was very confused and disorderly'.

It was perhaps partly a realisation that the actual ceremony did not always live up to expectation which led to eighteenth-century monarchs being buried 'privately' rather than 'publicly' as their predecessors had been. Another factor accounting for this change in the ritual was the alteration in the political position of the sovereign. As the monarch became more a figurehead, holding less real power, so the problem of the death and succession of sovereigns became less acutely sensitive in political terms. There was no longer such need for the Crown to demonstrate its magnificence or to display the precise hierarchy of society through the distribution of black mourning clothes; at private royal funerals, those invited provided their own garments. This obviously reduced the cost, although the word 'private' does not really describe what actually occurred. Horace Walpole was delighted to have the chance to attend the funeral of George II, as he described in a letter to a friend:

Do you know I had the curiosity to go to the burying t'other night; I had never seen a royal funeral . . . It is absolutely a noble sight . . . The procession, through a line of footguards, every seventh man bearing a torch, the horseguards lining the outside, their officers with drawn sabres and crape sashes on horseback, the drums muffled, the fifes, bells tolling, and minute guns — all this was very solemn. But the charm was the entrance of the abbey, where we were received by the dean and chapter in rich robes, the choir and almsmen bearing torches; the whole abbey so illuminated, that one saw it to greater advantage than by day . . . When we came to the chapel of Henry the Seventh, all solemnity and decorum ceased; no order was observed, people sat or stood where they could or would; the yeomen of the guard were crying out for help, oppressed by the immense weight of the coffin; the bishop read sadly, and blundered in the prayers . . . The real serious part was the figure of the Duke of Cumberland, heightened by a thousand melancholy circumstances. He had . . . a cloak of black cloth, with a train of five yards. Attending the funeral of a father could not be pleasant: his leg extremely bad, yet forced to stand upon it near two hours . . . and placed over the mouth of the vault, into which, in all probability, he must himself so soon descend; think how unpleasant a situation! He bore it all with a firm and unaffected countenance. This grave scene was fully contrasted by the burlesque Duke of Newcastle. He fell into a fit of crying the moment he came into the chapel, and flung himself back in a stall, the archbishop hovering over him with a smelling-bottle; but in two minutes his curiosity got the better of his hypocrisy, and he ran about the chapel with his glass, to spy who was or who was not there, spying with one hand, and mopping his eyes with the other. Then returned the fear of catching cold; and the Duke of Cumberland, who was sinking with heat, felt himself weighed down, and turning round, found it was the Duke of Newcastle standing upon his train, to avoid the chill of the marble.

The political importance of the burial of the ruler was perhaps most clearly demonstrated during the period of the Interregnum. An eminent anthropologist, V. Gordon Childe, has suggested that in periods of political and social instability there is an increase in the grandeur of funeral rituals, reflecting the crucial role of the burial ceremony. This theory, schematic as it may be, seems to be borne out, or at least not contradicted, by the experience of mid-seventeenth-century England. The funeral of Oliver Cromwell, described as 'more than regal', put even James I's obsequies into the shade. The Protector was buried in military style at a cost of £60,000. Even John Evelyn was impressed by the 'archrebel's' burial, as he recorded on 22 November 1658:

Saw the superb funeral of the Protector. He was carried from Somerset House in a velvet bed of state drawn by six horses . . . the pall held up by his new lords; Oliver lying in effigy in royal robes and crowned with a crown, sceptre and globe like a king, the pennons

and guidons were carried by the officers of the army and the imperial banners, achievements, etc. by the heralds in their coats, a rich
caparisoned horse embroidered all over with gold, a knight of
honour armed cap-a-pie, and after all, his guards, soldiers and innumerable mourners.

There were several seemingly anomalous aspects to this magnificent
funeral. The theological grounding of Interregnum burial practices, together with the 'civil respects' mentioned in the *Directory* which acted
as an escape clause, permitting all manner of lavish ceremonials, have
already been discussed in Chapter 2. Perhaps the most striking feature
of Cromwell's funeral was the crowned effigy itself; his actual corpse
had necessarily been buried soon after his death because it 'swelled and
bursted from whence came such filth' that it 'raised . . . a deadly and
noisesome stink'. During the lying in state, the effigy, clothed in purple
velvet trimmed with gold lace and fur, was displayed for several weeks,
with the emblems of royalty.

In the right hand was a sceptre; in the left, a globe. Upon his head
was placed a purple velvet cap, furred with ermines . . . Behind the
head was placed a rich chair of tissued gold, whereon was placed an
imperial crown, which lay high, that the people might behold it.

Later, the effigy was moved to another room 'and now his purple
velvet was changed for a crown'. When, finally, the crowned effigy was
carried to Westminster Abbey as the centrepiece of a 'great funeral . . .
performed with very great majesty', there was nothing to distinguish
the Protector's image from that of an actual sovereign. Having resisted
the offer of coronation during his lifetime, Oliver Cromwell was
crowned at death. The political significance of this move cannot have
been lost on the throng of spectators at the funeral, while it helped to
legitimise the 'succession and installation as Protector' of his son,
Richard Cromwell, a clear instance of the wishes of the deceased being
overriden in favour of the interests of the living.

A further anomaly at this funeral, as indeed at the funerals of other
major figures of the Interregnum, was the role played by the heralds of
the College of Arms. The heralds' fees, particularly those for conducting funerals, had been a source of grievance; Edward Hyde, the future
Earl of Clarendon, complained about the College of Arms in his maiden
speech to the Commons in 1640. However, Parliament discovered that
the heralds were necessary to prevent 'divers abuses' which, according to

an ordinance of 1646 for regulating heraldry, 'may produce great in-
conveniences and debate hereafter if seasonable remedy be not
provided'. Parliament therefore decided that 'the heralds' office door
shall be opened again', and the approved heralds were set to work to
prepare a magnificent funeral for the parliamentary general, Robert,
Earl of Essex, who was buried in Westminster Abbey.[8] Part of the preparations involved the appointment of new Kings of Arms, an extreme
irony, since there was such a rift between Parliament and the actual
King, Charles I. Essex's funeral was performed in October 1646 with
full military honours and set the tone for the other great funerals of
the mid-seventeenth century. The regiments of the trained bands
formed a guard of honour from Essex House to the Abbey, each band
wearing its regimental colours. After the interment had been completed, a signal was given from the top of Westminster Abbey tower to
each of the London forts to fire their guns.

> This being done, the Regiment of Horse, being all drawn up in a
> body in the Abbey church-yard, gave a volley with their pistols,
> which being well and orderly performed, all the nine regiments were
> appointed to fire, from Westminster Abbey to Essex House gate.

The firing of ordnance and pistols took place three times 'and so the
solemnity ended', leaving no doubt of the strength and organisation of
the parliamentary forces. A similar show of military power was displayed at General Ireton's funeral in 1652, the regiments marching at
'a grave pace, drums covered with cloth, soldiers reversing their arms'.
The heralds at Ireton's funeral wore, for the first time, new tabards
embroidered with the arms of the Commonwealth, at a cost of £220.

The military state funerals of the Interregnum, although resulting from
an abnormal political situation, were not the first of their kind to be
seen in England. Sir Philip Sidney, wounded in 1586 at the battle of
Zutphen, was given a splendid funeral, focusing the pride of the nation
on a fallen hero. Thomas Lant, Windsor Herald, made drawings of the
procession; the Lord Mayor and other worthies were on horseback, but
most of the many hundred mourners, including Sir Francis Drake,
walked to the burial. We are similarly fortunate in having a pictorial
record of another great state funeral nearly a century later, that of
General Monk, Duke of Albemarle and prime mover in the restoration
of Charles II, who died in 1670. The splendour of Monk's funeral acted
as a counterbalance to the great funerals of the Interregnum, attempt-

ing to overshadow them in its opulence. Like that of Cromwell, Monk's effigy was carried in the procession, and great care was lavished on its preparation, down to the 'pair of long linen drawers to put under the breeches'. The effigy, clad in armour covered with the ducal robes and coronet, symbolised Monk's two roles as soldier and statesman and cost over £120 to make and dress, of which £35 was paid to John Bushnell for making the head and hands of wax, fixing the wig and modelling a stucco body.

From the beginning of the eighteenth century, as has been indicated, the grandest funerals were no longer those of royalty, but were occasions on which the nation paid tribute to its most eminent men, as for example William Pitt in 1778 or, more spectacularly, Nelson in 1806. It is significant that some of these men, fêted as heroes, were only of relatively humble origins; Nelson came from an unexalted family of Norfolk parsons. The cult of the hero, in which lavish burials played a significant part, was itself another manifestation of the same growing emphasis on individualism with which this book has been centrally concerned. Indeed, during the late eighteenth century there was a plan to institutionalise hero worship by turning St Paul's Cathedral into a national 'Valhalla', a last resting place for Britain's heroes, to be commemorated by neo-classical statues. The hero, the ultimate unique being, typifies the whole individualistic ethos.

When George III heard of Nelson's victory and death at Trafalgar, he ordered that 'the body of the British hero should be buried in St Paul's at the public expense, with military and national honours'. Nelson's corpse was laid in a coffin made from the mast of a ship he had captured at Aboukir. As it was brought up the Thames from Tilbury and Gravesend to Greenwich, guns were fired, while all the ships on the river lowered their flags. The coffin was then displayed in state at the Royal Hospital, Greenwich, where more than 30,000 people came to pay their respects during three days. On the day before the interment, the body was moved again, to Admiralty House, first, by land, to the accompaniment of the 'Dead March' from Handel's oratorio *Saul*, while Captain Hardy walked in front of the coffin. At the riverside, Nelson's body was placed in his own barge, and a host of other barges followed; people lined the banks to watch, and the guns at the Tower were fired at one-minute intervals. In the final funeral procession, ten thousand soldiers

> consisting chiefly of the regiments that . . . had like the deceased Admiral exerted themselves to deliver the world from the tyrannic

ambition of the infidel power of France, preceded the hero to his tomb. The splendid appearance of so gallant a body of men in the funeral procession of a warrior . . . assembled with so much facility and without the smallest bustle, gave no inconsiderable proof to such of our enemies as were present, what the energies of the country could produce.

The streets, lined by twenty thousand volunteers, had been specially covered with a layer of gravel during the night. After the military section of the procession came 48 seamen and marines of HMS *Victory* 'in their usual dress with crape hatbands', together with 48 pensioners of Greenwich Hospital. Next followed the private carriages of commoners and peers and then the royal family, including the Prince of Wales. The flag of the *Victory*, 'torn by the innumerable balls that had passed through it in the fury of the battle', and 'stained with the blood of its intrepid crew', aroused much interest in the procession. At the rear came the naval section, preceded by heralds bearing swords, spurs and other traditional accoutrements. The funeral chariot carrying the body had 'an elevated canopy with plumes, supported by four columns resembling palm trees, and having in its front and back a carved representation of the head and stern of HMS the *Victory*'.

The chief mourners were followed by officers of both navy and army, arranged according to rank. The coffin was carried into the cathedral by officers from the *Victory*:

The procession then moved towards the grave, when the dean pronounced the rites of sepulture, and the last holy dirge to the departed spirit of Nelson was heard throughout the dome; his body is buried in peace, but his name liveth evermore. Thus was the hero buried by the country for which he died.

The attributes which characterise a hero are succinctly expressed by Hamlet, describing the renaissance ideal of manhood, which has dominated the western world ever since: 'how noble in reason, how infinite in faculty, in form, in moving, how express and admirable'. In an individualistic society, each person takes on the importance and uniqueness of a hero within his or her own narrowly restricted and often highly competitive social environment, leaving no place for the wider, more traditional network of social relationships. The greater the celebration of man's individuality, however, the harder it is to accept his death. This paradox is also neatly summed up by Hamlet; while man may indeed be 'the beauty of the world', he still remains merely a 'quintessence of dust'.

Notes

1. The sources for the principal royal funerals discussed in this chapter are as follows:

Henry VIII, 1547; Strype, *Ecclesiastical Memorials*, ii, Appendix A.
Elizabeth I, 1603; Stow, *Chronicle of London*, p. 815. London, British Library: Addit. MSS. 5408 and 35324. Williams, *Elizabeth I*, p. 369.
Anne of Denmark, 1619; Maidstone, Kent Archives Office: U. 269 ON. 6284-528. London, British Library: MS. Harleian 5176, fol. 236. Chamberlain, *Letters*, ii, pp. 232 and 237.
James I, 1625; London, British Library: MS. Lansdowne 885, fols. 115-23. Chamberlain, *Letters*, ii, pp. 609 and 616.
Charles I, 1649; Peck, *Desiderata Curiosa*, ii, p. 412.
Mary II, 1695 (died 1694); Evelyn, *Diary*, p. 560.
George II, 1760; Walpole, *Letters*, pp. 297-8.
Quotations concerning funeral effigies are from Hope, 'Funeral Effigies of Kings and Queens', *Archaeologia*, 1x, pt 2.

Sources for the other principal funerals discussed in this chapter are:

Sir Philip Sidney, 1587; de Bry, *Funeral Procession of Sir Philip Sidney*.
Robert, Earl of Essex, 1646; London, British Library: Thomason Tracts, 699 f. 10/89.
Henry Ireton, 1652; Evelyn, *Letters*, pp. 218-19. Stanford London, 'Heralds Tabards under the Commonwealth', *Notes and Queries*, cxcviii, pp. 226-8.
Oliver Cromwell, 1658; Evelyn, *Letters*, p. 260. Prestwich, *Respublica*, pp. 172-97.
George, Duke of Albemarle, 1670; Sandford, *Funeral of the Duke of Albemarle*.
William Pitt the Elder, 1778; Cunnington and Lucas, *Costume for Births, Marriages and Deaths*, pp. 285-6.
Horatio, Viscount Nelson, 1806; Clarke and MacArthur, *Life of Nelson*, ii, pp. 460-68.

2. Cunnington and Lucas, *Costume for Births, Marriages and Deaths*, pp. 133-4.
3. Giesey, *The Royal Funeral Ceremony in Renaissance France*.
4. Wagner, *Heralds of England*, pp. 113-14.
5. Ibid., p. 109.
6. Ibid., p. 116.
7. MacMichael, *Westminster Abbey*, pp. 67-8 and 75-6.
8. Quoted in Wagner, *Heralds of England*, p. 257.

STATISTICAL APPENDIX

Introduction

The following graph and six tables are constructed from the evidence of the surviving probate accounts for Berkshire, Lincolnshire, Kent and Somerset. For a full description of these documents, the reader should turn to my unpublished thesis, 'Funerals in England, 1580-1640: The Evidence of Probate Accounts', especially Chapters 1 and 2, which give details of their distribution by time periods, inventory sums, social class or occupation of the deceased and by geographical areas. An appraisal is also made of their value to the historian and the possible pitfalls involved in their use. Here it is only possible to raise a few points specific to these particular seven analyses.

Data from all the Berkshire and Somerset probate accounts for the years 1580-1655 were used to construct the graph of funeral costs, together with those Kent accounts with either a detailed breakdown of burial charges or the deceased's social class and a random sample of every tenth account for Lincolnshire. This provided 913 accounts for Berkshire, 385 for Somerset, 1037 for Kent and 761 for Lincolnshire.

The effects of fluctuating inflation during the first half of the seventeenth century were apparent to contemporaries; one Somerset accountant, in 1611, added to her statement of the burial costs the words 'being in the dear year'. To compensate for inflation, thereby allowing a fairer comparison to be made of actual costs, the appropriate amounts have been deflated, using the Phelps Brown and Hopkins Index. This index is calculated from the changing prices of food, drink, crops, fuel and textiles. As some of the main items of funerary expenditure were food and drink, together with cloth for the shroud, it seems relevant to employ this index; the other important costs — fees to the clergy, bell-ringing charges and so on — remained more or less constant throughout the period. All costs have been deflated to a base of the average index figure for the years 1580-90, which is 360. The formula used was:

$$\frac{360 \text{ x Actual Funeral Cost}}{\text{P.B. and H.}} = \text{Deflated funeral cost}$$

The average of the index figures for each five-year period was used to give the divisor. The median funeral charges for each county are shown in the graph, the median being chosen as it is less influenced by freak fluctuations than the arithmetic mean. This analysis reveals no overall decline in the cost of burial during the years 1580-1655.[1]

Of the 1037 Kent probate accounts with detailed funeral costs, or recording the deceased's status, 579 give the social class or occupation of the deceased. To compile Table 1, these have been divided into groups broadly following the classification suggested by D.G. Vaisey in his introduction to *Probate Inventories of Lichfield and District*. Some of the categories are self-explanatory and use the actual designation on the account. 'Civic dignitaries' include mayors, aldermen and jurats, while the military group contains captains of soldiers at Lydd, Deal and New Romney as well as a gunner of Dover Castle. French people living in Canterbury and Dutch residents at Sandwich form the class of foreigners; 'aquatics' include fishermen, boatmen and a 'seafaring man'; the professionals are mainly clergy, but also include a schoolmaster and a physician. Victuallers are all those engaged in the food and drink trades, such as innkeepers; the largest single occupation in the Kent manufacturers group is blacksmith. The 'processors' include a barber and the retailers, various shopkeepers. Table 1 reveals a substantial variation in funeral cost among members of the same social or occupational group.

In Table 2, an attempt has been made to correlate funeral costs with the wealth of the deceased, using the only available indication of financial standing, the inventory sum. The difficulties this raises should not be underestimated and are fully discussed in my thesis. However, as only relative wealth rather than absolute sums are considered here, the problem becomes less severe and in the majority of cases even an incomplete inventory represents roughly the approximate range of a man's possessions, if not the precise value of his goods. This table employs the same probate accounts as the graph. To calculate the figures, the median funeral cost for each inventory group has been expressed as a percentage of the mid-point of each inventory group.[2] It is clear that in all four counties those with the least wealth, in terms of inventory sum, had funerals consuming a greater proportion of their estates than those with larger inventory sums.

Tables 3 to 6 are all compiled from those probate accounts giving a detailed breakdown of funeral costs, mentioning at least two specific items, and usually considerably more. There are 508 such accounts for Berkshire, 337 for Lincolnshire and 764 for Kent. In each of the four analyses, burials in coffins, funeral sermons, burials in churches and funeral doles, the number of accounts mentioning the ritual in a particular time period is expressed as a percentage of the total number of detailed accounts extant for that decade.[3] The total number of accounts which record each ritual is also given as a percentage of the detailed funeral accounts for the three separate counties, to aid overall comparison between the different geographical areas. While both burials in coffins and funeral sermons increased in all three areas during the period, the process was most rapid in Kent; conversely, burials in church and funeral doles, which were decreasing during the period, lingered longest in Lincolnshire.

Notes

1. The Kent probate accounts include people of higher status than the local probate records for other areas, and so the median funeral costs in Kent are higher; for fuller explanation, see Gittings, *Funerals in England*, pp. 48-50.

2. The median funeral costs from which these percentages are derived are to be found in my thesis, Tables 2:5, 2:7, 2:9 and 2:11.

3. The numbers of detailed probate accounts for each time period are as follows:

pre-1581	Berks. 1	Lincs. 19	Kent 31
1581-90	Berks. 11	Lincs. 4	Kent 84
1591-1600	Berks. 87	Lincs. 23	Kent 82
1601-10	Berks. 118	Lincs. 54	Kent 80
1611-20	Berks. 132	Lincs. 87	Kent 161
1621-30	Berks. 99	Lincs. 61	Kent 160
1631-40	Berks. 52	Lincs. 71	Kent 136
1641-50	Berks. 6	Lincs. 17	Kent 30
post-1650	Berks. 2	Lincs. 1	Kent 0

1: The Cost of Funerals in Four English Counties, 1581-1655

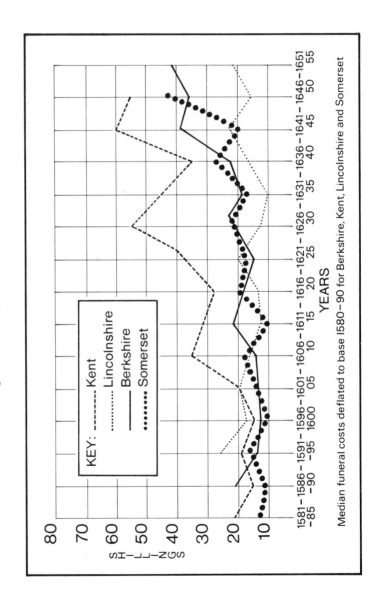

Median funeral costs deflated to base 1580–90 for Berkshire, Kent, Lincolnshire and Somerset

Table 1: Kent Funeral Costs by Social and Occupational Groups

	No.	Median funeral cost			Average lowest 3 funerals			Average highest 3 funerals			Difference between lowest 3 and highest 3 funerals		
		£	s	d	£	s	d	£	s	d	£	s	d
Civic dignitaries	26	19	5	11	2	4	11	87	7	9	85	2	10
Knights/Esquires	25	23	15	0	5	11	5	138	14	11	133	3	6
Gentlemen	121	5	12	6		14	8	148	17	6	148	2	10
Yeomen	101	2	4	8		8	4	24	7	9	23	19	5
Husbandmen	18	1	9	4		8	5	2	14	10	2	6	5
Military	5	5	0	0	2	16	2	15	0	0	12	3	10
Foreign	7	2	0	0	1	0	7	16	16	8	15	16	1
Almsmen	4	2	7	4	1	16	10	3	4	10	1	8	0
Aquatic	13	2	15	0		17	5	6	10	11	5	13	6
Widows	85	2	7	8		4	8	60	13	3	60	8	7
Spinsters	16	4	12	1		12	9	34	2	7	33	9	10
Bachelors	2	3	13	0		—			—			—	
Professional	62	3	7	9		7	7	33	2	0	32	14	5
Victuallers	25	2	0	0		15	2	12	19	5	12	4	3
Manufacturers	24	1	10	0		9	5	7	19	7	7	10	2
Processers	25	1	15	9		10	0	7	12	9	7	2	9
Retailing	20	3	0	0		19	5	20	19	11	20	0	6
	579												

Table 2: Proportion by Percentage of Inventory Sum Spent on Funeral

	Somerset	Berkshire	Lincolnshire (random sample)	Kent
£10 & under	13	18.5	12	19.6
£10-£20	6.8	5.3	4.4	10
£20-£30	4	4	3.4	6
£30-£40	3.6	4	2.8	4.6
£40-£50	4.6	3.3	2.2	5
£50-£65	3.1	2.3	1.5	3.8
£65-£80	2.6	2.3	1.8	2.8
£80-£100	2.2	2	1.6	2.2
£100-£150	2	1.9	1.6	2.2
£150-£200	1	1.7	1.6	1.5
£200-£250)		)	)	2.3
£250-£300)	1.2	) 1.2	) 1.3	1.3
£300-£400	1.3	1	1.6	0.8
£400-£500				0.9
£500-£750				1.6
£750-£1000				1.7
£1000+				1.2

Table 3: Burials in Coffins by Time Periods and Percentage of Detailed Accounts Giving Burial in Coffin

	Berkshire		Lincolnshire		Kent	
	No.	%	No.	%	No.	%
Pre-1581	1	100	2	10.5	7	22.6
1581-90	2	18.2	1	25	28	33.3
1591-1600	20	23	4	17.4	53	64.6
1601-10	43	36.4	8	14.8	64	80
1611-20	69	52.3	15	17.2	134	83.2
1621-30	51	51.5	12	19.7	139	86.9
1631-40	31	59.6	25	35.2	110	80.9
1641-50	6	100	12	70.6	27	90
Post-1650	2	100	–	–	–	–
Total/average	225	44.3	79	23.4	562	73.6

Table 4: Funeral Sermons by Time Periods and Percentage of Detailed Accounts Giving Sermon

	Berkshire		Lincolnshire		Kent	
	No.	%	No.	%	No.	%
Pre-1581	0	0	1	5.3	5	16.1
1581-90	0	0	0	0	11	13.1
1591-1600	9	10.3	3	13	41	50
1601-10	12	10.2	8	14.8	46	57.5
1611-20	37	28	18	20.7	97	60.2
1621-30	29	29.3	19	31.1	106	66.3
1631-40	20	38.5	25	35.2	70	51.5
1641-50	5	83.3	6	35.3	18	60
Post-1650	2	100	–	–	–	–
Total/average	114	22.4	80	23.7	394	51.6

Table 5: Burials in Church by Time Periods and Percentage of Detailed Accounts Giving Burial in Church

	Berkshire		Lincolnshire		Kent	
	No.	%	No.	%	No.	%
Pre-1581	–	–	9	47.4	7	22.6
1581-90	4	36.4	3	75	14	16.7
1591-1600	23	26.4	16	69.6	21	25.6
1601-10	21	17.8	22	40.7	23	28.8
1611-20	48	36.4	28	32.2	22	13.7
1621-30	21	21.2	22	36.1	25	15.6
1631-40	13	25	12	16.9	24	17.6
1641-50	2	33.3	4	23.5	1	3.3
Post-1650	1	50	–	–	–	–
Total/average	133	26.2	116	34.4	137	17.9

Table 6: Funeral Doles by Time Periods and Percentage of Detailed Accounts Giving Dole

	Berkshire		Lincolnshire		Kent	
	No.	%	No.	%	No.	%
Pre-1581	1	100	8	42.1	18	58.1
1581-90	6	54.5	2	50	56	66.7
1591-1600	32	36.8	11	47.8	32	39
1601-10	30	25.4	33	61.1	28	35
1611-20	40	30.3	40	46	22	13.7
1621-30	16	16.2	19	31.1	24	15
1631-40	6	11.5	26	36.6	13	9.6
1641-50	1	16.7	6	35.3	2	6.7
Post-1650	–	–	–	–	–	–
Total/average	132	26	145	43	195	25.5

BIBLIOGRAPHY

Manuscript Sources

Probate Accounts

Chichester, Sussex: West Sussex County Record Office.
    Ep. 1/33, boxes 241-2.
Dorchester, Dorset: Dorset County Record Office.
    Corfe Castle Executors' Accounts.
Lincoln: Lincolnshire County Record Office.
    Ad. Ac. 0-40.
Maidstone, Kent: Kent Archives Office.
    PRC 1/1-8; PRC 2/1-34; PRC 20/1-11; PRC 21/1-16.
Oxford: Bodleian Library.
    MS. Wills Berks, 173-222; MS. Wills Oxon. 160-77;
    Oxford University Archive Executors' Accounts A-W.
Taunton, Somerset: Somerset County Record Office.
    D.D. ct. Adm. Accts. A-W.

Select List. Probate accounts giving particularly extensive funeral details.

Lincoln: Lincolnshire County Record Office.
    William Grave, 1625, Ad. Ac. 19B/98.
    George Heneage, 1632, Ad. Ac. 23/56.
Maidstone, Kent: Kent Archives Office.
    John Dreyton, 1581, PRC 2/2/41.
    Margaret Parker, 1608, PRC 1/1/8.
    Thomas Wilson, 1609, PRC 2/13/436.
    Matthew Mennyce, 1610, PRC 1/1/11.
    Henry Saker, 1614, PRC 20/3/29.
    John Manwaring, 1622, PRC 20/6/316.
    Barbara Mainwaring, 1626, PRC 2/27/106.
    John Marshe, 1628, PRC 2/29/67.
    Susan Omer, 1631, PRC 2/31/53.
    John Haines, 1635, PRC 2/33/55.
    Ethelbert Omer, 1636, PRC 2/33/100.
    George Man, 1637, PRC 2/34/80.
    Isaac Menton, 1638, PRC 2/11/135.
    Anne Undean, 1639, PRC 20/11/490.
Oxford: Bodleian Library.
    John Fleming, 1617, University Archives Exec. Accts. A-H.
    Richard Mocket, 1619, University Archives Exec. Accts. I-W.
    Mary Gardner, 1641, MS. Wills Berks. 192/36.
    Hannibal Baskerville, 1670, MS. Wills Berks. 178/108.

Wills

Maidstone, Kent: Kent Archives Office.
PRC 17/45-70 and PRC 32/35-52.

Select List. Principal manuscript wills quoted.

Chatsworth House, Derbyshire.
Elizabeth, Countess of Shrewsbury, will.
London: British Library.
Joseph Hall, Addit. MS. 5085, fol. 100 (copy).
London: Public Record Office.
Lucy, Lady Latimer, PCC Rowe 16.
Francis Willis, PCC Drake 77.
Robert, Second Earl of Dorset, PCC Dorset 23.
Maidstone, Kent: Kent Archives Office.
Samuel Hurlstone, PRC 32/42/21.
John Brooke, PRC 32/35/19.
Margaret Parker, PRC 17/56/172.
Ellen Love, PRC 17/62/364.
Oxford: Bodleian Library.
James Montague, MS. North b 25, fols. 143-6.

Other Manuscripts

Chatsworth House, Derbyshire.
H/29 (household accounts).
Dorchester, Dorset: Dorset County Museum,
Thomas Hardy Literary Notebook III.
Edinburgh: Register House.
RH9/1/24/2 (child's funeral account); RH91/38.
Lincoln: Lincolnshire County Record Office.
Folkingham/13; Algarkirk/13; Leverton/13 (overseers' of the poor accounts).
London: Lambeth Palace Library.
Arches F.7 (Muniment Book) 1635-62, fols. 169-73.
London: British Library.
MSS. Harleian 1301, 1354, 1368, 3881, 4774 and 5176;
MSS. Lansdowne 23, 25, 50, 79, 82, 88, 109 and 885;
MS. Egerton 2642; Addit. MSS. 5085, 5408, 5805, 34163, 35324 and 45131
(funeral accounts, heraldic documents, etc.).
London: County Hall.
P. 79/JN1/22 (Hackney Churchwardens' accounts).
Maidstone, Kent: Kent Archives Office.
p. 43 12/1, 12/2, p. 99 12/1; p. 152 12/1; p. 233 12/1; p. 241 12/1, 12/2;
p. 400 12/1, 12/2 (overseers' of the poor accounts). U269 (Cranfield)
O.N. 6284-6528 (funeral account, Anne of Denmark).
Oxford: Bodleian Library.
MS. DD Par. St Aldates C. 23 (overseers' of the poor accounts).
MS. Oxford Archdeaconry Paper, Berks. C. 162. MSS. Ashmole 818, 836, 840,
845, 857, 1116; MS. Top. Yorks. d.7; MS. Eng. Hist. c. 480 (heraldic
documents). MSS. North b 12, b 25, c 29 (Montague family papers). MS.
Auct. D.2.6, fol. 176; MS. Univ. Coll. 165. John Johnson Collection; funerals,
box 1 (ephemera).
Reading, Berks.: Berkshire County Record Office.

Bray Churchwardens' accounts; Hurst overseers' of the poor accounts.
West Firle, Sussex: Firle Place.
Drawing with MS. annotations.

Printed Sources

'An Admonition to the Parliament: Second Treatise – A View of Popular Abuses Yet Remaining in the English Church' in *Puritan Manifestoes*, ed. W.H. Frere and C.E. Dogulas (London, 1907), pp. 20-37, esp. p. 28.

Andrews, W., *Burials without Coffins* (Hull, 1899).

—— *Bygone Church Life in Scotland* (London, 1899), esp. pp. 240-53.

Anon., *The True Mannor and Forme of the Proceeding to the Funeral of the Right Honourable Robert Earl of Essex . . .* (London, 1646).

Ariès, P., *Centuries of Childhood: A Social History of Family Life*, trans. R. Baldick (London, 1962).

—— *Western Attitudes towards Death*, trans. P.N. Ranum (London, 1974).

—— *The Hour of Our Death*, trans. H. Weaver (London, 1981).

Aubrey, J., 'Remaines of Gentilisme and Judaisme' in *John Aubrey: Three Prose Works*, ed. J. Buchanan-Brown (Fontwell, 1972), pp. 131-304, passim.

Bacon, F., 'Observations on a Libel' in *The Letters and the Life of Francis Bacon*, ed. J. Spedding, 7 vols. (London, 1861-74), i, pp. 143-208, esp. p. 158.

—— 'Of Death' in *Essays of Francis Bacon*, ed. G. Grigson (Oxford, 1937), pp. 9-11.

Bailey, J.B., ed. *The Diary of a Resurrectionist 1811-12* (London, 1896), esp. p. 139.

Barrow, H., 'A Brief Discovery of the False Church' in *The Writings of Henry Barrow 1587-1590*, ed. L.H. Carlson (London, 1962), pp. 263-672, esp. pp. 460-62.

Becon, T., 'The Sick Man's Salve' in *Prayers and Other Pieces of Thomas Becon*, ed. J. Ayre (Parker Soc., 1844), pp. 92-191, esp. pp. 118-30.

Blauner, R., 'Death and Social Structure', *Psychiatry*, xxix (1966), pp. 378-94.

Blomefield, F., *The History of Thetford* (Fersfield, 1739), Appendix VIII.

Blondel, J., *The Power of Mother's Imagination over the Foetus Examined* (London, 1729), p. 38.

Boaze, T., *Death in the Middle Ages* (London, 1972).

Bolton, R., *Mr Boltons Last and Learned Worke of the Foure Last Things* (London, 1635), esp. pp. 82-3 and 152.

The Book of Common Prayer (London, 1559).

Boswell, J., *The Life of Samuel Johnson*, 2 vols. (Oxford, 1933), ii, esp. pp. 117, 223 and 554-5.

Bourne, H., *Antiquitates Vulgares* (Newcastle, 1725), p. 6.

Brand, J., *Observations on the Popular Antiquities of Great Britain*, 3 vols. (London, 1849), ii, pp. 202-317.

Brookes, C.C., *A History of Steeple Aston and Middle Aston* (Shipston-on-Stour, 1929), pp. 216-34, esp. p. 231.

Brown, N.O., *Life Against Death: The Psychoanalytical Meaning of History* (London, 1970), esp. p. 107.

Browne, Sir T., *Hydriotaphia: Urne Buriall or a Discourse of the Sepulchrall Urnes Lately Found in Norfolk* (London, 1658), esp. pp. 57-8.

Bry, T. de, after T. Lant, *The Funeral Procession of Sir Philip Sidney* (London, 1587).

Burgess, F., *English Churchyard Memorials* (London, 1963).

Burn, R., *Ecclesiastical Law*, 4 vols. (London, 1781), iv, p. 289.

Burne, C.S., *Shropshire Folk-Lore* (London, 1974).

Calendar of State Papers, Domestic Series 1619-23, ed. M.A. Everett Green (London, 1858), p. 431.

Calendar of State Papers, Domestic Series 1623-25, ed. M.A. Everett Green (London, 1859).

Calendar of State Papers, Domestic Series 1637-8, ed. J. Bruce (London, 1869), p. 169.

Camp, A.J., *Wills and Their Whereabouts* (London, 1963).

Canne, J., *A Necessity of Separation from the Church of England*, ed. C. Stovel (London, 1849), esp. p. 113.

Cartwright, T., see Hooker, R., *Of the Laws of Ecclesiastical Polity*.

Chamberlain, J., *The Letters of John Chamberlain*, ed. N.E.M. McClure, 2 vols. (Philadelphia, 1939), passim.

Childe, V.G., 'Directional Changes in Funerary Practices during 50,000 Years', *Man*, xlv (1945), pp. 13-19.

The Christian Reformer, xxxiv, 1848, p. 495.

Clarke, J.S. and MacArthur, J., *The Life of Admiral Lord Nelson*, 2 vols. (London, 1809), ii, pp. 460-68.

Clarkson, L., *Death, Disease and Famine in Pre-Industrial England* (Dublin, 1975).

Cleland, J., 'The Pompous Funerals, of the Gracious Prince Lodovick, Duke of Richmond and Lenox' in *A Monument of Mortalitie, upon the Death and Funerals, of the gracious Prince, Lodovick, late Duke of Richmond and Lenox . . .* (London, 1624), pp. 35-54.

Coles, W., *The Art of Simpling. An Introduction to the Knowledge and Gathering of Plants* (London, 1656), p. 65.

Collins, A., *Peerage of England*, 9 vols. (London, 1812), iii, pp. 72-8.

Collinson, P., ' "A Magazine of Religious Patterns". An Erasmian Topic Transposed in English Protestantism' in D. Baker, ed., *Renaissance and Renewal in Christian History* (Studies in Church History, xiv, 1977), pp. 223-49.

Colquhoun, P., *Treatise on Indigence* (London, 1806), pp. 111-14.

Cooper, C.H., *Annals of Cambridge*, 5 vols. (Cambridge, 1842), ii, p. 542 and v, pp. 342-3.

Cox, J.C., *The Parish Registers of England* (London, 1910), passim.

——*Churchwardens' Accounts* (London, 1913), esp. pp. 170-73.

Cunnington, P. and Lucas, C., *Costume for Births, Marriages and Deaths* (London, 1972), pp. 123-293.

The Curates' Conference: Or, a Discourse betwixt Two Scholars; both of them Relating their Hard Condition, and Consulting which Way to Mend it' in *The Harleian Miscellany. A Collection of . . . Pamphlets and Tracts . . . from the Library of Edward Harley, second Earl of Oxford*, ed. W. Oldys, revised T. Park, 2nd edn., 10 vols. (Londn, 1808-13), i, pp. 495-500.

Curl, J.S., *The Victorian Celebration of Death* (Newton Abbot, 1972).

Dekker, T., *The Wonderful Year*, ed. E.D. Pendry (London, 1967), p. 55.

Delany, M., *The Autobiography and Correspondence of Mary Granville, Mrs. Delany*, 3 vols. (London, 1861), i, pp. 249 and 526.

Dictionary of National Biography, ed. L. Stephen and S. Lee, 63 vols. (London, 1885-1900).

A Directory for the Publique Worship of God Throughout the Three Kingdoms of England, Scotland and Ireland (London, 1644).

Donne, J., 'Sermon V at St Pauls, Christmas Day, 1627' in *The Works of John Donne*, ed. H. Alford, 6 vols. (London, 1839), i, pp. 79-105, esp. p. 90.

—— 'Devotions upon Emergent Occasions' in *The Oxford Book of English Prose*, ed. A. Quiller-Couch (Oxford, 1925), pp. 169-72.

——— 'A nocturnall upon St Lucies day, Being the shortest day' and 'The Funerall' in *The Poems of John Donne*, ed. H.J.C. Grierson (London, 1937), pp. 39-41 and 52-3.

Dube, C.S., *Indian Village* (London, 1955).

Eden, F.M., *Observations on Friendly Societies* (London, 1801), p. 15.

Emmison, F.G., *Elizabethan Life: Morals and the Church Courts* (Chelmsford, 1973), esp. pp. 173-4.

Esdaile, K.A., *English Church Monuments 1510-1840* (London, 1946).

——— *The Life and Works of Louis François Roubiliac* (London, 1928), pp. 156-7.

Evelyn, J., *Memoirs Illustrative of the Life and Writings of John Evelyn*, ed. W. Bray (London, 1871), passim.

Featley, D., *Clavis Mystica, A Key Opening Divers and Difficult Texts of Holy Scripture Handled in Seventy Sermons . . .* (London, 1636), esp. pp. 575-6.

Firth, R., *Human Types: An Introduction to Social Anthropology* (London, 1956), esp. p. 183.

Folklore, xlvii (1935), p. 230.

Folklore, lxix-lxv (1954-5).

Foster, C.W., ed., *Lincoln Wills* (Lincoln Record Soc., v, x and xxiv, 1914, 1918 and 1930), passim.

Frere, W.H. and Kennedy, W.M., ed. *Visitation Articles and Injunctions of the Period of the Reformation* (Alcuin Club Collections, xiv-xvi, 1910), passim.

Furer-Haimendorf, C. von, *The Sherpas of Nepal. Buddhist Highlanders* (London, 1964).

Furnivall, F.J., ed., *The Fifty Earliest English Wills in the Court of Probate, London* (Early English Texts Society, 1882), esp. p. xii and passim.

Gemmelli, F., *Viaggi per Europa* (1701), vol. i, p. 328 quoted in Italian in L. Radzinowicz, *A History of English Criminal Law and Its Administration from 1750* (London, 1945), i, p. 182.

Gennep, A. van. *The Rites of Passage*, trans. M.B. Vizedom and G.L. Caffee (London, 1960), esp. pp. 147 and 164-5.

George, M.D., *London Life in the Eighteenth Century* (London, 1930), esp. pp. 303, 353 and 398-9.

Giesey, R.E., *The Royal Funeral Ceremony in Renaissance France* (Geneva, 1960).

Gittings, C., *Brasses and Brass Rubbing* (London, 1970), p. 67.

——— 'Funerals in England, 1580-1640: The Evidence of Probate Accounts', unpublished M. Litt. thesis, University of Oxford, 1978.

Glyde, J., *Folklore and Customs of Norfolk being Extracts from 'The Norfolk Garland'*, ed. M.D.C. Watkins (Wakefield, 1973), p. 29.

Godfrey, E., *Home Life Under the Stuarts 1603-1649* (London, 1903), esp. p. 270-71.

Godolphin, J., *The Orphan's Legacy or a Testamentary Abridgement*, 4th edn. (London, 1701), pp. 222-6.

Goody, J., *Death, Property and the Ancestors* (London, 1962).

Gorer, G., *Death, Grief, and Mourning in Contemporary Britain* (London, 1965), esp. pp. 172-3.

Grant, D., *Margaret the First* (London, 1957), pp. 237-9.

Gray, T., *An Elegy Written in a Country Churchyard* (London, 1751).

Greenhill, T., *The Art of Embalming* (London, 1705), esp. pp. 107-20.

Grigson, G., ed., *The Faber Book of Epigrams and Epitaphs* (London, 1977), p. 170.

Grindal, E., *The Remains of Edmund Grindal*, ed. W. Nicholson (Parker Soc., 1843) esp. pp.325-6.

Gutch, H., *County Folk-lore. Printed extracts, No. IV, Examples of printed folk-lore concerning the North Riding of Yorkshire, York and Ainsty . . .* (London,

1899), esp. p. 308.

—— and Peacock, M.G.W., *County Folklore. Printed Extracts, No. VII, Examples of Printed Folklore Concerning Lincolnshire* (London, 1908).

Hair, P.E.H., 'Accidental Death and Suicide in Shropshire 1780-1809', *Transactions of the Shropshire Archaeological Society*, lix (1969-70), Part I, pp. 63-75.

Hall, J., *A Common Apologie of the Church of England against the Unjust Challenges of the Over-just Sect commonly called Brownists* (London, 1610), esp. pp. 104-7.

Hardy, C.F., ed., *The Benenden Letters, London, Country and Abroad 1753-1821* (London, 1901), pp. 222-4.

Hardy, T., *Far From the Madding Crowd* (London, 1914), esp. Chapter 43, 'Fanny's Revenge', pp. 342-53.

—— 'The Withered Arm' in *Wessex Tales* (London, 1920), pp. 63-104, esp. pp. 89-90.

Hartland, E.S., *County Folklore. Printed Extracts, No. I, Gloucestershire . . .* (London, 1895), esp. p. 51.

Herbert, G., 'Mortification' in *The Works of George Herbert*, ed. F.E. Hutchinson (Oxford, 1941), p. 98.

Hertz, R., 'The Collective Representation of Death' in *Death and the Right Hand*, trans. R. and C. Needham (Aberdeen, 1960), pp. 27-113, esp. pp. 50-51.

Hill, J.E.C., *Economic Problems of the Church. From Archbishop Whitgift to the Long Parliament* (Oxford, 1956).

Hindley, C., ed., *The Roxburghe Ballads*, 2 vols. (London, 1873-4), i, p. 246.

Hinton, J., *Dying* (Harmondsworth, 1967).

Historical Manuscripts Commission. Salisbury, Hatfield House, vol. i (London, 1883), p. 415; vol. vii (London, 1899), p. 117.

Historical Manuscripts Commission. Buccleuch and Queensberry, Montague House, Whitehall (London, 1899), vol. i, p. 253.

Historical Manuscripts Commission. Hastings, Ashby-de-la-Zouch (London, 1930), vol. ii, p. 45.

Historical Register, vol. xxi, No. 81 (1736), pp. 70-75.

Hooker, R., *Of the Laws of Ecclestiastical Polity*, Everyman edn., 2 vols. (London, 1907), ii, esp. pp. 401-6.

Hope, W.H. St. J., 'On the Funeral Effigies of the Kings and Queens of England with special reference to those in the Abbey Church of Westminster', *Archaeologia*, vol. lx, pt. 2 (1907), pp. 511-64.

Huizinga, J., *The Waning of the Middle Ages* (Harmondsworth, 1972).

Huntington, R., and Metcalf P., ed., *Celebrations of Death: The Anthropology of Mortuary Ritual* (Cambridge, 1979).

Huxley, A., *Brave New World*, Penguin Modern Classics (Harmondsworth, 1969), esp. pp. 131-2 and 157-64.

Illich, I., *Limits to Medicine Medical Nemesis: The Expropriation of Health* (London, 1976), esp. p. 204.

Ives, G., *A History of Penal Methods: Criminals, Witches, Lunatics* (London, 1914), p. 289.

Jacob, G., *A New Law Dictionary*, 2nd edn. (London, 1732), p. 4.

James, M.E., 'Two Tudor Funerals', *Transactions of the Cumberland and Westmorland Antiquarian and Archaeological Society*, new series, lxxi (1966), pp. 165-78.

Jones, W., *The Diary of the Reverend William Jones 1777-1821*, ed. O.F. Christie (London, 1929), esp. pp. 210, 228, 241 and 255.

Jones-Baker, D., *The Folklore of Hertfordshire* (London, 1977), pp. 82 and 164.

Jordan, W.K., *Philanthropy in England 1480-1660* (London, 1959), esp.

pp. 146-7, 169, 187 and 202.

The Journals of the House of Commons from November 8 1547 . . . to March 2 1628 (vol. i), esp. pp. 692-4.

The Journals of the House of Commons from April 13 1640 . . . to March 14 1642 (vol. ii).

The Journals of the House of Commons from October 17 1745 . . . to November 22 1750 (vol. xxv), p. 274.

Kantorowicz, E.H., *The King's Two Bodies* (Princeton, 1957), esp. p. 421.

King, T.W. and Raines, F.R., ed. *Lancashire Funeral Certificates* (Chetham Soc., old series, 1xxv, 1869).

Larkin, J.F. and Hughes, P.L., ed., *Stuart Royal Proclamations*, vol. 1 (Oxford, 1973), i, No. 229.

Latimer, H., *Sermons by Hugh Latimer*, ed. G.E. Corrie (Parker Soc., 1844), esp. p. 305.

Leather, E.M., *The Folklore of Herefordshire* (London, 1912), esp. p. 229.

Lebrun, F., *Les Hommes et La Mort en Anjou aux 17e et 18e Siècles* (Paris, 1971).

Linebaugh, P., 'The Tyburn Riot against the Surgeons' in Hay, D. *et al.*, ed., *Albion's Fatal Tree: Crime and Society in Eighteenth-Century England* (London, 1975), pp. 65-117, esp. pp. 81-3.

London Magazine, July 1752, p. 333.

Londons Lamentation or a Fit Admonition by E P for John Wright Junior (London, 1641), Thomason Tracts E. 166.10, esp. title page.

Ludwig, A.I., *Graven Images: New England Stonecarving and Its Symbols, 1650-1815* (Middletown, Connecticut, 1966).

Macfarlane, A., *The Origins of English Individualism* (Oxford, 1978).

McFarlane, K.B., *Lancastrian Kings and Lollard Knights* (Oxford, 1972), pp. 207-20.

Machyn, H., *The Diary of Henry Machyn*, ed. J.G. Nichols (Camden Soc., x1ii, 1847), passim.

McManners, J., *Death and the Enlightenment: Changing Attitudes towards Death among Christians and Unbelievers in Eighteenth Century France* (Oxford, 1981).

Macmichael N.H., ed., *Westminster Abbey Official Guide* (London, 1977).

McMurray, W., *The Records of Two City Parishes* (London, 1925), pp. 235 and 239.

Malinowski, B., *Magic, Science and Religion* (London, 1926), esp. pp. 47-50.

Mandelbaum, D.G., 'Social Uses of Funeral Rites' in H. Feifel, ed., *The Meaning of Death* (London, 1959), pp. 189-217.

Mandeville, B. de, *An Enquiry into the Causes of the Frequent Executions at Tyburn* (London, 1725), p. 26.

Mauss, M., *The Gift*, trans. I. Cunnison (London, 1954), esp. pp. 10-11, 15-16 and 37-41.

Meister, J.H., *Letters Written during a Residence in England* (London, 1799), p. 62.

Misson, M., *Memoirs and Observations of His Travels over England*, trans. J. Ozell (London, 1719), esp. pp. 88-93 and 214-15.

Mitford, J., *The American Way of Death* (New York, 1963).

Moore, J., *A Mappe of Man's Mortalitie* (London, 1617), esp. p. 156.

Morley, J., *Death, Heaven and the Victorians* (London, 1971).

Morris, C., *The Discovery of the Individual 1050-1200* (London, 1972), esp. pp. 146-8.

Muret, P., *Rites of Funeral Ancient and Modern in Use throughout the Known World*, trans. P. Lorrain (London, 1683), esp. pp. 224-5.

Nadel, S.F., *Nupe Religion* (London, 1954).

Nashe, T., *Martins Months Minde* (London, 1589), unpaginated.

Newman, J., *The Buildings of England: North East and East Kent* (Harmonds-worth, 1969), p. 325.

Nicolas, N.H., ed., *Testamenta Vetusta . . . Illustrations from Wills . . .* 2 vols. (London, 1826), passim.

Noble, M., *A History of the College of Arms* (London, 1804), esp. p. 257.

Notes and Queries, VI Series, vol. i (1880), p. 210.

Overbury, Sir Thomas, 'A Fair and Happy Milkmaid' in *Character Writings of the Seventeenth Century*, ed. H. Morley (London, 1891), pp. 69-70.

The Paston family, *Selections from the Paston Letters*, ed. A.D. Greenwood (London, 1920), esp. p. 23.

Peck, F., ed. *Desiderata Curiosa*, 2 vols. (London, 1779), ii, pp. 246-7, 252-6 and 412.

Penny, N., *Church Monuments in Romantic England* (London, 1977).

Pepys, S., *The Diary of Samuel Pepys*, ed. R. Braybrooke, 5 vols. (London, 1848), passim.

Person, D., *Varieties: Or A Surveigh of Rare and Excellent Matters* (London, 1635), esp. pp. 164-5.

Peyton, S.A., ed., *The Churchwardens' Presentments in the Oxfordshire Peculiars of Dorchester, Thame and Banbury* (Oxfordshire Record Soc., x, 1928).

Phelps Brown, E.H. and Hopkins, S.U., 'Seven Centuries of the Price of Consum-ables Compared with Builders' Wage Rates', *Economica*, new series, xxiii, No. 92 (1956), pp. 296-314.

Phythian Adams, C., *Local History and Folklore: A New Framework* (London, 1975).

Picton, J.A., ed., *The City of Liverpool. Selections from the Municipal Archives and Records from the 13th to the 17th Century Inclusive*, 2 vols. (Liverpool, 1883), i, p. 234.

Pilkington, J., *The Works of James Pilkington,* ed. J. Scholefield (Parker Soc., 1842), esp. p. 317.

Pope, A., 'Moral Essays', in *The Poetical Works of Alexander Pope*, ed. A.W. Ward (London, 1927), p. 235.

Porter, B., *Cambridgeshire Customs and Folklore* (London, 1969), esp. pp. 26-7 and 34.

Prestwich, J., *Respublica; or a Display of the Honours, Ceremonies and Ensigns of the Commonwealth* (London, 1787), pp. 172-97.

Proctor, F. and Frere, W.H., *A New History of the Book of Common Prayer* (London, 1901).

Puckle, B.S., *Funeral Customs Their Origin and Development* (London, 1926).

Pullan, L., *The History of the Book of Common Prayer* (London, 1900), esp. pp. 237-45.

Quarles, F., *Emblemes* (London, 1635).

Raine, J., ed., *Testamenta Eboracensia, a Selection of Wills from the Registry of York* (Surtees Soc., vols. iv, xxx, xlv, liii, lxxi, cvi, 1836-1902), esp. vol. iv, passim.

Ravenshaw, T., *Antiente Epitaphes from AD 1250-AD 1800* (London, 1878), passim.

Registers of All Hallows, Honey Lane, London, ed. W.B. Bannerman (Harleian Soc., Registers, xliv, 1914), pp. 262-77.

Registers of St Botolph, Bishopsgate, London, ed. A.W.C. Hallen, 3 vols. (London, 1889-95), i, p. 437.

Register of St Peter, Cornhill, ed., G.W.G. Leveson Gower (Harleian Soc.,

Registers, i, 1877), p. 169.

Register of Burials at the Temple Church 1628-1853, ed. H.G. Woods (London, 1905), pp. 4-5.

Report of the Ritual Commission, Parliamentary Papers xxxviii (London, 1868), Appendix E, pp. 401-682, passim.

Robinson, H. ed., *The Zurich Letters 1558-1579* (Parker Soc., 1842), pp. 259-60.

Rochefoucauld, F. de la, *A Frenchman in England 1784*, ed. J. Marchand, trans. S.C. Roberts (Cambridge, 1933), pp. 93-4.

Royal Commission on Historical Monuments: England. An Inventory of the Historical Monuments in the City of Oxford (London, 1939), p. 45 and plate 30.

Rylands, J.P., ed., *Cheshire and Lancashire Funeral Certificates* (Lancashire Record Soc., vi, 1882).

Salter, B.H., ed., *Oxford Council Acts 1583-1626* (Oxford History Soc., 1xxxvii, 1928), p. 77.

Samwaies, P., *The Wise and Faithful Steward* (London, 1657), pp. 27-8.

Sandford, F., *The Order and Ceremonies Used for and at the Solemn Interment of . . . George Duke of Albemarle . . .* (London, 1670).

Sandys, E., *Sermons and Miscellaneous Pieces by Archbishop Sandys*, ed., J. J. Ayre (Parker Soc., 1841), esp. p. 162.

'The Second Maiden's Tragedy' in *A Select Collection of Old English Plays Originally Published by Robert Dodsley in the Year 1744*, ed. W.C. Hazlitt, 4th edn., 16 vols. (London, 1875), x, pp. 381-468, esp. Act III, Scene 3 and Act V, Scene 2.

Smith, J., *The Berkeley Manuscripts: The Lives of the Berkeleys*, ed. J. Maclean, 3 vols. (Gloucester 1883-5), ii, pp. 388-91.

South, J.F., *Memorials of John Flint South*, ed. C.L. Feltoe (London, 1884), pp. 80-101.

Spelman, H., 'De Sepultura' in *The English Works of Sir Henry Spelman . . .* , 2nd edn. (London, 1727), pp. 173-90.

Stanford London, H., 'The Heralds' Tabards under the Commonwealth', *Notes and Queries*, vol. cxcviii, 1953, pp. 276-8.

Stanhope, P.D., *Letters of Lord Chesterfield*, ed. P. Jones (London, 1929), p. 365.

Stannard, D., *The Puritan Way of Death: A Study in Religion, Culture and Social Change* (Oxford, 1977), esp. pp. 68-70, 73, 101, 128 and 149.

The State Civil and Ecclesiastical of the County of Lancaster about the year 1590, ed. F.R. Raines in *Chetham Miscellanies*, vol. v (Chetham Soc., vol. xcvi, 1875), pp. 1-13.

State Trials of Norton, Owen and Stayley in *A Complete Collection of State Trials*, ed. T.B. Howell, 21 vols. (London, 1816-31), i, cols. 1084-6; ii, cols. 879-84; and vi, cols. 1501-12.

Steele, R.R., ed., *A Bibliography of Royal Proclamations of the Tudor and Stuart Sovereigns . . . 1485-1714*, 2 vols. (London. 1910), i. No. 1225.

Steer, F.W., 'The Funeral Account of the First Duke of Richmond and Lennox', *Sussex Archaeological Collections*, vol. xcviii (1960), pp. 156-64.

Stephenson, M., *A List of Monumental Brasses in the British Isles* (London, 1926), pp. 229 and 417.

Stone, L., *Sculpture in Britain in the Middle Ages* (London, 1956).

—— *The Crisis of the Aristocracy* (Oxford, 1965), esp. pp. 572-81 and 784-6.

—— *The Family, Sex and Marriage in England 1500-1800* (London, 1977).

Stow, J., *The Annales, or Generall Chronicle of England begun first by Maister John Stow and after him continued . . . by Edmond Howes* (London, 1615), p. 815.

Strange, N., 'To the Reader' in B. Carier, *A Missive to his Majesty of Great Britain by Dr. Carier, conteining the Motives of his Conversion to the Catholike Religion* (Paris, 1649), pp. 1-28.

Strype, J., *Ecclesiastical Memorials relating chiefly to Religion and the Reformation of it*, 3 vols. (London, 1721), ii, Appendix A, passim.

Stubbes, P., *A Motive to Good Workes . . .* (London, 1593), p. 122.

Tate, F., 'Of the Antiquity, Variety and Ceremonies of Funerals in England' in T. Hearne, *A Collection of Curious Discourses by Eminent Antiquarians upon several Heads in our English Antiquities*, 2 vols. (London, 1771), i, pp. 215-21.

Taylor, J., *The Rule and Exercises of Holy Dying*, 4th edn. (London, 1658), pp. 319-36, esp. pp.326-8.

Thiselton Dyer, T.F., *Church-Lore Gleanings* (London, 1891), pp. 128-52.

——*Old English Social Life as Told by Parish Registers* (London, 1898), esp. pp. 166-8.

Thomas, K.V., *Religion and the Decline of Magic* (London, 1971), esp. pp. 591 and 603-5.

Thompson, E.P., *Whigs and Hunters: The Origin of the Black Act* (Harmondsworth, 1977).

Turner, V.W., *The Ritual Process: Structure and Antistructure* (London, 1969).

Tymms, S., ed., *Wills and Inventories from the Registers of Bury St Edmunds and the Archdeaconry of Sudbury* (Camden Soc., xlix, 1850), passim.

Vaisey, D.G., 'Introduction' to *Probate Inventories of Lichfield and District* (Staffordshire Historical Collections, 4th series, v, 1969), pp. 1-38.

Veron, J., *The Huntynge of Purgatorye to Death, Made Dialoge-wyse* (London, 1561), esp. fols. 33 and 48.

Villette, J., *The Annals of Newgate; or, Malefactors Register*, 4 vols. (London, 1776), i, p. 373.

Vovelle, G. and M., *La Vision de la Mort et de L'Au-delà en Provence après les Autels des Ames du Purgatoire XVe – XXe Siècles* (Paris, 1970).

Wagner, Sir A., *Heralds of England* (London, 1967).

Walker, D.P., *The Decline of Hell: Seventeenth-Century Discussions of Eternal Torment* (London, 1964), esp. p. 3.

Walpole, H., *Letters of Horace Walpole*, ed., C.B. Lucas (London, 1904), esp. pp. 297-8, 366, 399 and 578.

——*The Castle of Otranto* in *Three Gothic Novels*, ed. P. Fairclough (Harmondsworth, 1972), pp. 37-148.

Walton, I., *The Life of Dr John Donne* in *The Compleat Angler and the Lives of Donne, Wotton, Hooker, Herbert and Sanderson*, ed. A.W. Pollard (London, 1901), pp.187-243, esp. pp. 234-5.

Warner, R., *A Second Walk through Wales* (Bath, 1800), pp. 302-3.

Waugh, E., *The Loved One* (Boston, 1948).

Weaver, F., ed., *Somerset Medieval Wills 1383-1500* (Somerset Record Soc., xvi, 1901), passim.

Webster, J., *The Duchess of Malfi*, in G.B. Harrison, ed., *Plays of Webster and Ford*, Everyman edn. (London, 1933), esp. pp. 95-184, Act IV, Scene 2, p. 157.

Weever, J., *Ancient Funerall Monuments within the United Monarchie of Great Britaine, Ireland and the Islands adiacent* (London, 1631), esp. 'To the Reader', unpaginated, and pp. 9-12, 17-18, 22 and 32.

Westermarch, E., *The Origin and Development of Moral Ideas*, 2 vols. (London, 1906), esp, ii, pp. 524, 545, 548 and 559.

Whaley, J., ed., *Mirrors of Mortality: Studies in the Social History of Death* (London, 1981).

Whinney, M., *Sculpture in Britain 1530 to 1830* (Harmondsworth, 1964).

Whitgift, J., *The Defence of the Answer to the Admonition* in *The Works of John Whitgift D.D.*, ed. J. Ayre, 3 vols. (Parker Soc., 1853), iii, pp. 1-564, esp. pp. 361-80.

'Will of John Hopkins' in *Notes and Queries for Somerset and Dorset*, xxix (1968-73), p. 223.

'Will of Sir John Millicent' in *The Proceedings of the Cambridge Antiquarian Society*, xvi (1912), pp. 147-8.

'Will of Frances Stuart, Countess of Richmond and Lenox' in *Archaeologia Cantiana*, xi (1877), pp. 232-50.

Williams, N., *Elizabeth I, Queen of England* (London, 1971), p. 369.

Williams, W., *A West Country Village: Ashworthy* (London, 1963).

Wilson, A., and Levy, H., *Industrial Assurance: An Historical and Critical Study* (Oxford, 1937).

—— *Burial Reform and Funeral Costs* (London, 1938), esp. pp. vi, 13, 65-6, 92 and 102-3.

Wood, A., à, *The Life and Times of Anthony Wood, Antiquary, of Oxford 1632-1695*, ed. A. Clark, 5 vols. (Oxford Historical Soc., vols. xix, xxi, xxvi, xxx, xl, 1891-5), *passim*.

Woodforde, J., *The Diary of a Country Parson 1758-1802*, ed. J. Beresford (London, 1935), esp. pp. 241 and 528.

Wordsworth, D., in *Dorothy Wordsworth: A Biography*, by E. de Selincourt (Oxford, 1933), pp. 122-3 and 230.

Wordsworth, W., *The Letters of William and Dorothy Wordsworth vol. iii, The Middle Years. Part 2, 1812-1820*. ed. E. de Selincourt, 2nd edn., M. Moorman and A.G. Hill (Oxford, 1970), No. 417, p. 331.

Wortley Montagu, M., *Letters and Works of Lady Mary Wortley Montagu*, ed. Lord Wharncliffe and W.M. Thomas, 2 vols. (London 1887), ii, p. 186.

Wright, E.M., *Rustic Speech and Folk-Lore* (Oxford, 1914), esp. p. 281.

Wyrley, W., *The True Use of Armorie* (London, 1592), esp. pp. 21-5.

Young, A., *The Autobiography of Arthur Young*, ed. M. Betham-Edwards (London, 1898), pp. 263-311, esp. pp. 278, 281 and 284.

Young, E., *Love of Fame, the Universal Passion* (London, 1728).

—— *The Complaint: or, Night Thoughts on Life, Death and Immortality* (London, 1750).

INDEX OF PEOPLE AND PLACES

Aristocrats appear under their titles and are then listed by date. English places are indexed alphabetically under their respective counties; there is a separate entry for London. (Index of people and places compiled by Maureen Street.)

INDEX OF SUBJECTS

DATE DUE